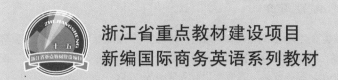

浙江省重点教材建设项目
新编国际商务英语系列教材

新编商务英语函电教程
Business English Correspondence

（修订本）

主　编　管春林　章汝雯
副主编　阮绩智　李　乐
　　　　曹　霞　沈永年

文泉云盘
防盗码

刮开涂层，扫描二维码，可获取配套电子资源

清华大学出版社
北京交通大学出版社
·北京·

内 容 简 介

全书共16章，大致可分为两部分，第1、2章为商务函电写作的基本知识，其余14章围绕对外贸易的各主要环节组织内容，分别包括建立业务关系、询盘与答复、报盘与还盘、推销、订单及履行订单、支付、包装及唛头、交货及售后服务、装船、货物保险、代理、投诉与处理、服务贸易、其他常用商务信函等内容。

本书选材范围广，内容丰富，语言规范，条理清晰，重点突出，并配有明晰的概括和总结。

本书可供高等院校英语专业、经贸专业、商务英语专业、工商管理专业、金融专业的学生作为外贸英语写作教材使用，也可用作涉外经贸人员的案头工具书，同时对于国际商务人员和具有一定英语基础并有志于国际商务工作的人员也是一本颇具实用性的参考书。

本书封面贴有清华大学出版社防伪标签，无标签者不得销售。
版权所有，侵权必究。侵权举报电话：010-62782989　13501256678　13801310933

图书在版编目（CIP）数据

新编商务英语函电教程／管春林，章汝雯主编. —修订本. —北京：北京交通大学出版社：清华大学出版社，2013.9（2022.8重印）
（新编国际商务英语系列教材）
ISBN 978-7-5121-1641-2

Ⅰ.①新…　Ⅱ.①管…　②章…　Ⅲ.①国际商务-英语-电报信函-写作-高等学校-教材　Ⅳ.①H315

中国版本图书馆CIP数据核字（2013）第215157号

新编商务英语函电教程
XINBIAN SHANGWU YINGYU HANDIAN JIAOCHENG

责任编辑：张利军　　特邀编辑：易　娜
出版发行：清 华 大 学 出 版 社　邮编：100084　电话：010-62776969　http://www.tup.com.cn
　　　　　北京交通大学出版社　邮编：100044　电话：010-51686414　http://www.bjtup.com.cn
印 刷 者：艺堂印刷（天津）有限公司
经　　销：全国新华书店
开　　本：203×280　印张：14　字数：550千字
版 印 次：2020年1月第1版第1次修订　2022年8月第3次印刷
印　　数：4 001～5 000册　定价：39.00元

本书如有质量问题，请向北京交通大学出版社质监组反映。对您的意见和批评，我们表示欢迎和感谢。
投诉电话：010-51686043，51686008；传真：010-62225406；E-mail：press@bjtu.edu.cn。

前　言

近几年来，有关商务英语的教材出版得越来越多。在各种商务英语教材中，商务函电教材可谓是品种繁多。这说明，商务函电在商务英语的课程体系中占据着重要的位置。事实上，在国际商务人员必须具备的诸多技能中，商务函电写作可以说是最重要的一项技能，因为随着当今信息传输技术的飞速发展，书面信息的传递已显得越来越重要。此外，善于进行书面沟通不仅有利于公司业务的增长，而且对于树立企业形象也具有重要的意义。

《新编商务英语函电教程》就是为顺应这一形势发展的需要，同时也为满足高校英语、外贸、商务英语、金融等专业学生的学习需求而精心编写的。本书从当前外贸业务的实际需求出发，按照外贸业务的各个环节编写而成。与国内同类教材相比，本书主要具有以下几方面的特点。

(1) 选材广泛，内容丰富。为适应当前国际商务发展的需要，本书在选择样板信件时，既考虑到了英国商务函电的风格，同时也考虑到了美国商务函电的特点，同时也适当照顾到目前商务函电出现的新变化，因此本书所选择的样板信件无论是内容、风格、结构、措辞等均具有广泛的代表性。本书的内容除包括外贸流程的主要环节外，还加上了大多教材不做重点讨论的包装、唛头、交货、售后服务等方面的内容，并增加了服务贸易方面的信件及求职简历等内容，以提高学生多方面的商务写作能力。

(2) 重视写作能力与英语水平的共同提高。为了加深学生对商务英语写作的了解和熟练掌握，本书不仅介绍了商务英语写作所要遵循的一般原则及技巧，还对每一类具体商务信函的组织结构及写作技巧作了详细的阐述。另外，本书的主要内容全部用英文编写，这主要是考虑到两个方面：一是目前的大学生大多在入学前已有多年的英语学习经历，英语水平普遍较高；二是希望通过这样的安排培养学生直接用英语进行思维的习惯，提高他们对英语的实际应用能力。

(3) 重视读与写的结合。我们认为，要学会书写成功的商务信函，首先要学会欣赏成功的商务信函，因此我们在每章的"Model Letters"前首先提出问题，这些问题大多启发和引导学习者去寻找信中的成功之处；同时，在每章的"Sample Letters"前，我们则给出简单的点评，以帮助学生领会这些信件的优点和长处，从而使学生尽快掌握写作的技巧。

(4) 结构清晰，使用方便。全书共16章，去期期中期末复习，每周可以安排一章。本书除第1、2章外，其余各章的内容安排完全相同，这给教师的教和学生的学提供了方便。本书的第3～16章，每一章提供专题简介、经典信件分析、信函组织原则、写作技巧、难点解释、实用句型、写作小贴士、练习等，使学生对需要掌握的学习内容一目了然。

(5) 把样板信件分为两个层次，便于教学。样板信中的"Model Letters"一般是被认为比较标准的信件，在该章的同类信件中具有代表性，因此需要教师做详细的分析，而"Sample Letters"则是相对不标准的信件，即是与该体裁的常规结构有一定出入的信件。这样编排的目的是要让学习者首先认识这一体裁的常规结构和内容安排，然后再认识这一体裁的变体，从而达到循序渐进学好该类信件的目的。

(6) 增加了有关国际服务贸易的内容。在当今时代，服务贸易在整个国际贸易中的重要性日益突出，围绕服务贸易的信函也在不断增加，了解和学习服务贸易领域中外贸函电的写作也变得日益重要，因此本书编入这方面的内容，以期引起必要的重视。但由于服务贸易涉及面相当广泛，然而限于篇幅，本书在这方面的内容还显单薄。

在信件体例的安排上，本书正文中的样板信件采用目前普遍使用的齐头式（Block Style），而练习中的信函采用传统的缩进式（Indented Style），这样做的目的是要让学生对这两种信件的体例做重点掌握。

本书由管春林、章汝雯担任主编，阮绩智、李乐、曹霞、沈永年担任副主编。在本书的编写过程中，沈惠佳、王晨、吕丽盼、彭怀兰编写了部分内容，并参与了书稿的打印工作，陆娟红、朱荣荣、田希波做了部分校对工作。

本书可供高等院校英语、外贸、商务英语、工商管理、金融等专业的学生作为商务英语写作教材使用，也可供涉外经贸人员用作案头工具书，同时也可供国际商务人员和具有一定英语基础并有志于从事国际商务活动的人员用作自学参考书，还可作为各外贸公司的培训用书。

在编写过程中，编者参考了大量国内外有关的书籍和资料，在此谨向有关作者表示衷心的感谢。由于时间仓促和编者水平有限等原因，书中难免存在不妥之处，敬请广大读者批评指正。

编　者

2013 年 9 月

Contents
目 录

Chapter 1　The Basics of Business Letter Writing　(1)

Chapter 2　Components of a Business Letter　(14)

Chapter 3　Initiating Business Relationships　(28)

Chapter 4　Enquiries and Replies　(41)

Chapter 5　Quotations and Offers　(54)

Chapter 6　Sales Promotion　(68)

Chapter 7　Orders and Execution　(81)

Chapter 8　Terms of Payment　(95)

Chapter 9　Packing and Marking　(112)

Chapter 10　Delivery and After-sale Service　(126)

Chapter 11　Shipment　(139)

Chapter 12　Cargo Insurance　(152)

Chapter 13　Agency　(163)

Chapter 14　Complaints and Adjustments　(175)

Chapter 15　International Trade in Services　(189)

Chapter 16　Other Business-related Letters　(204)

References　(218)

Chapter 1

The Basics of Business Letter Writing

Your goals for this chapter are to understand:
- ☑ why we need to learn business letter writing;
- ☑ what changes are taking place in business letters;
- ☑ what are the essential qualities of a good business letter;
- ☑ how to improve a business letter.

1.1 Lead-in

Before you begin your learning of this chapter, please discuss with your partner(s) about the following questions.

(1) Why is it particularly important for an international trader to learn the skill of writing effective business letters?

(2) Have you got any experience in reading or writing a Chinese business letter?

1.2 Why Is Business Letter Writing So Important?

The Internet, e-mail, express delivery, teleconferencing, and e-commerce have shrunk the world into a global village. Accordingly, it is no longer feasible to think of business in exclusively regional or even national terms. Many companies are multinational corporations with offices throughout the world. So communications among companies are getting increasingly important. There can't be any business activities taking place without messages being exchanged. But there are several ways in which a businessman can communicate with his business partners, for example, he can exchange messages on the telephone or in a face-to-face talk with them, why is the skill of business letter writing still essential in the modern world?

First, a business letter is a formal communication tool which you can adopt to meet many specific purposes. It provides a direct and effective means of communication on a wide range of topics and can help you to establish and maintain relationships with your customers, suppliers, partners etc.

Second, business letters can be filed and kept as formal and legal documents for later check or reference. What was earlier transmitted over the phone is now done by writing because messages exchanged on a telephone can not be retrieved easily.

Third, improvements in communication technology have also led to increases in writing. Nowadays, businessmen are prone to travel from place to place, they usually use laptops to send and receive e-mails.

Besides, there are some other factors which merit the importance of business letter writing. Written communications are cheaper than telephone calls and may sometimes be more effective, especially when they are delivered by e-mail or fax or express mail service. What's more, time zones make talking by phone difficult.

Therefore, effective writing has become central to success of a business and writing letters in English has become an important part of business professionals' daily work in companies of foreign concerns. If you want to have a successful business career, you have to be able to write business letters effectively because writing keeps business moving.

1.3 Changes in Business Letters

The business world has been increasing its pace of development. Companies, in order to keep pace with the quickly-changing business world and to seize the market opportunities, have to adapt their messaging systems. Traditional letters which are distributed by postmen, are now giving way to electronic or digital messages. Thus developments in communication technology have resulted in changes in the style of written business communications.

Business communications, in terms of the means for conveying the message, can be divided into traditional business letter (TBL), telephone, telex, telegraph, fax, e-mail etc. Now telexes and telegraphs are almost extinct. So this book will mainly deal with the writing of TBL, e-mail and fax, which are the three main means for written information exchange among businesses.

Computers and fax machines, which provide for us more convenient and more prompt communication channels, have not only changed our ways of communication, but also altered the styles of business letters, so we often say that changes are taking place in written business communications.

1.3.1 About Faxes

Fax originates from the word "facsimile", which means an exact copy of reproduction. So a fax is a duplicate of a message transmitted quickly and accurately on a fax machine. In comparison with letters and e-mails, a fax is more efficient, dependable and timesaving.

Sample Fax

Kee & Jee Co., Ltd

34 Regent Street, London, ND6 7BK, UK
Tel: 44(0)20 9865 8888   Fax: 44(0)20 9865 8866

To: TIANJIN ELECTRIC CRANES IMPORT & EXPORT CORPORATION
Attn: MR Wills ZHANG
Fax No: 0086-22-8666 6666
From: Jonathan Wilson
Date: 16 July, 2011
Subject: Inquiry about your XP-2012A
No. of Pages: 1

Dear Sir,

We are an importer of electric cranes. We learned from Mr. Hutchinson that your new Model XP-2012A is much more efficient than XP-2012B, and their prices are the same.

We wish to place a trial order for five sets of XP-2012A, so please send us the necessary information such as the specifications, prices etc. If your quotation is competitive and delivery date reasonable, large orders will follow. Right now, there is a heavy demand for this type of cranes.

We expect your early reply.

Yours sincerely,

Jonathan Wilson
Jonathan Wilson

There is no unified format for faxes. It depends mainly on a company's preference or the software used to generate the faxes. However, there are still certain practical considerations which may affect some aspects of the layout, such as the need to know how many pages are being sent and the need to specify the sender's and the recipient's fax numbers in case of failed transmission. The format of a fax tends to be clear and simple and the style of the language used in a fax may be comparatively free. It can be formal, informal or neutral depending on the subject and the relationship between the sender and the recipient. In faxes, many highlighting devices such as underlining, bold typing, italicizing can be identified. Some use a combination of these various devices so that the reader won't miss any important points.

Fax also has its disadvantages like poor security and inconvenience in editing. Its recipient frequently has to turn the hardcopy fax back into electronic form for editting purpose. Faxes are also expensive compared with e-mails and are not quick enough when the line is busy.

1.3.2 About E-mails

E-mail is the short form for "electronic mail". It is a modern means of telecommunication depending on the service provided by the Internet. E-mail is relatively low in cost, and does not require a trained operator. It is also fast, relatively reliable, and messages can be sent or picked up anywhere in the world and anytime in a day. It can be kept permanently in the mailbox. This can be particularly advantageous for users who are communicating across international time zones. So e-mail is now the most popular way of written communication and is taking the place of faxes and TBLs gradually.

Sample E-mail

From: Cathrine
To: Susie Huang
Cc: jessie.long@ligumark.com
Sent: Thursday, June 06, 2011 12:29 PM
Subject: Fabric export business

Dear Susie,

I hv reviewed yr swatches, found you are missing cotton mesh fabric. Pls note the mesh fabric is not the one you mentioned, it should be 100% cotton mesh, with small holes on the fabrics, you should know that. Pls adv when you can send to me, thks.

Best Rgds,
Cathrine

The style of language used in e-mail is usually natural and less formal, or rather, conversational. Some abbreviations may appear in some e-mails. The following are some commonly-used abbreviations and their full forms.

Abbreviations	Full forms
AAMOF	as a matter of fact
AFAIK	as far as I know
brb:	I'll be right back.
btw:	by the way
CUL	See you later
cu2morrow:	See you tomorrow.

continued

Abbreviations	Full forms
duwnt2goout2nite:	Do you want to go out tonight?
fanx4urelp:	Thanks for your help.
FYI	for your information
gr8	great
IAC	in any case
IKWUM	I know what you mean.
imho	in my humble opinion
lol	laughing out loud
mte	my thoughts exactly
oic	Oh, I see.
OTOH	on the other hand
TIA	thanks in advance
2L8	too late

There may be many possible explanations for the informality of e-mails. First, most traditional business letters are written by secretaries who have received professional training in business letter writing while e-mails are mostly written by the senders themselves. Secondly, the time taken to create an e-mail message is typically considerably less than writing a business letter. What most e-mail writers concern about is the meaning they convey but not the form in which they are conveyed, so they don't have much time to plan and revise their writing. The last possible explanation for this phenomenon may be that some speech-like sentences have the advantages of making the letter more personal, practical and effective.

E-mail also has some perceived deficiencies like no service level guarantees and the lack of a robust, practical and universally-agreed security framework. Another deficiency of e-mail is that it may transmit viruses.

1.3.3 A Comparison among TBL, Fax and E-mail

With the availability of more medium choices for delivering messages, we need to be aware of the appropriateness for each of them. In order to have a clearer idea about the advantages and disadvantages of TBLs, faxes and e-mails, let's make a comparison among these three types of written communications.

	TBL	Fax	E-mail
Letter head	Printed letter-head with address, Tel No. etc.	Usually with a letter head	No letter head needed
Receiver's address and Tel No.	Usually printed on left-hand side, against the margin	Usually without receiver's address	E-mail address appear at the top, on left-hand side
Date	Date printed on right hand side	Generated automatically by the fax machine	Generated automatically by the computer
Tel/Fax No.	Tel/Fax No. printed	Tel/Fax No. printed	Usually none

continued

	TBL	Fax	E-mail
Ref No.	Ref. No. included, sometimes receiver's Ref. No. quoted	Ref. No. included, sometimes receiver's Ref. No. quoted	Usually no Ref. No. included
Subject	Usually having a subject	Usually having a subject	Always having a subject
Salutation	Formal salutation	Salutation needed, but not as formal as in TBL	Personal greetings may be used
Confidentiality	Confidentiality/non-confidentiality shown on envelope or letter	Less confidential than TBL, but more than e-mail	Not open to all, password needed
Language	More formal	Between TBL and e-mail	More oral and personal
Complimentary Close	Exquisitely used	Exquisitely used	Usual ending, casually used
PS/Note	PS/Note may be included	PS/Note may be included	PS/Note may be included
Signature	Formal signature	Formal signature	Usually no signature, or scanned signature included
Job Status of Writer	Sometimes stated	Usually stated	Previously formatted

As can be seen from the above table, each method of communication has both its advantages and disadvantages. Letters are seen to be formal and e-mails informal, with faxes somewhere in between. So most companies may use them selectively. First contacts are usually made through more formal postal letters or faxes, whereas e-mails are used for follow-up contacts. But there are also some exceptions. The proportion of fax and e-mail varies depending on the size of a company, requirements of customers and the importance of documents. Besides, the choice of medium depends on other underlying reasons. They can be time limit, convenience or communicative purposes. Under pressure of time, faxes and e-mails can be the right choices.

1.3.4 Why Do We Still Need to Learn TBL Writing?

Business correspondence has undergone significant changes in form and style with the rapid development of communication technology, then is it still necessary for us to learn how to compose TBLs?

The answer is positive for the following reasons: First, the main principles for the composition of a TBL are still applicable in the writing of an e-mail or a fax. Some basic rules relevant to TBLs such as good grammar, clarity and brevity are also the basic requirements for the writing of e-mails and faxes. So we can still adopt some basic rules relevant to TBLs in our teaching of e-mail and fax writing.

Secondly, as far as the communicative purposes are concerned, letters are appropriate for confidential messages, whereas faxes and e-mails are suitable for ordinary messages, such as making requests and supplying information. Furthermore, since the appearance of courier services, postal service has regained its momentum in delivering samples, greeting cards, advertisements, invoices, documents and invitations for meetings etc.

Thirdly, every business, whether large or small, has to appeal to diverse international markets to be competitive. These international readers will have varying degrees of proficiency in English and different preference for transmission media. So you will have to adapt your writing to respect their language needs and communication protocols.

Fourth, e-mails and faxes may display some informality, but we EFL teachers are still charged with the responsibilities to teach widely acceptable English to our learners.

Fifth, business e-mails and faxes have their disadvantages such as no service level guarantees and the lack of confidentiality. That's why we sometimes still need to send a message via a TBL although they are getting less commonly-used in our present business life.

1.4 The Essential Qualities of a Good Business Letter

A business letter can be seen as an advert for a company. If the letter is clear and concise, the firm seems well-organized and competent, so a good message can portray a professional outfit, while a bad message can result in unwanted publicity and customer dissatisfaction, which can ultimately lead to lost business.

Different book-writers suggest different criteria for a good business letter, for example, some set forth the "ABC" principle, which stands for Accurate, Brief and Clear. There are also some others who put forward the seven "Cs", i.e. completeness, concreteness, clarity, conciseness, courteousness, considerateness and correctness. These writing principles are now widely accepted for a good business letter.

1.4.1 Completeness

Completeness means that the letter ought to provide all the necessary information for a specific issue to help the reader to understand the purpose of the letter. If any necessary piece of information is lacking, the reader will have to ask you for clarification, which means that you will have to write another letter. It will not only waste time, energy and money, but also damage the image of your company. So whenever you have finished a letter, check it to see whether all the necessary information has been included.

1.4.2 Concreteness

Concreteness means being specific, definite and vivid rather than vague, general and abstract. To achieve such a purpose, you should try to use specific facts, figures, time and active verbs to stress concreteness.

In the following two examples, the earlier message leaves something unstated and indefinite while the second gives all the necessary details.

Poor: The goods you ordered will be arriving soon.

Better: The goods under your order No.0890 for silk pajamas were shipped this morning and will reach you in about 25 days.

1.4.3 Clarity

Clarity means that the letter is written in such a clear and plain way that it cannot be misunderstood. If your letter is ambiguous and confusing, it might bring trouble to yourself as well as your reader. So it is quite important for the writer to use accurate words and simple sentences where appropriate. It is advised not to use such words as *instant* (this month), *ultimo* (last month) or *proximo* (next month).

Please compare the following sentences. In the following example, because the word "bimonthly" has two meanings, one of which being "twice a month" and the other of which being "once every two months", the use of this word may make the letter confusing.

Poor: As to the steamer sailing from Ningbo to New York, we have bimonthly direct services.

Better: We have a direct sailing from Ningbo to New York every two months.

Better: We have two direct sailings every month from Ningbo to New York.

Besides, clarity also means that while presenting an idea, you need to follow a clear logic. A casual layout of the information may also turn your letter into a confusing and unsuccessful one.

1.4.4　Conciseness

Conciseness means to express a message in the fewest possible words without sacrificing completeness and courtesy. To achieve this end, you should avoid wordy expressions and redundancies, use short sentences instead of long ones, and compose your message carefully. Let's compare the following sentences to see what conciseness exactly means.

Poor: In compliance with your request, we immediately contacted our head office in London and now wish to inform you of the result as follows.

Better: As requested we immediately contacted our head office in London with the following result.

The first sentence is a failure because it is much lengthier but it conveys no more information than the second one.

1.4.5　Courteousness

Courteousness not only means using some polite words but also shows the writer's enthusiasm, consideration and friendliness. While writing business letters, you should bear in mind the effect of your words and actions upon the receiver. If you put yourself in the reader's shoes, consider their needs, problems and emotions, your letter would most probably be courteous.

Poor: You are requested to ship the goods we ordered on July 7 without any delay.

Better: Your prompt shipment of the goods we ordered on July 7 will be highly appreciated.

Besides the above points, courteousness also means punctuality. In business correspondence, punctuality is usually stressed as an important aspect of courtesy. A prompt letter is always more valued than a delayed one.

1.4.6　Considerateness

Considerateness means you should be considerate of your reader. It emphasizes "you-attitude" rather than "we-attitude". When writing a letter, you should keep in mind the reader's requests, needs, desires, as well as their feelings. If you cannot meet your customers' needs or requests, you should show your interest in and concern for their requests, use positive sentences instead of using negative ones, and stress what you can do, but don't stress what you cannot do. Look at the following examples to see how you can show your considerateness.

Poor: Your order will be delayed for three weeks.

Better: Your order will be shipped in three weeks.

They convey the same information, but the latter sentence does it from a positive perspective, so it is more considerate.

1.4.7 Correctness

Correctness means that the writer must make every effort to ensure that the letter is correct in style, language and typing.

Firstly, a business letter should be linguistically correct. Correct grammar, punctuation and spelling will give your letter a good appearance. Secondly, when you are giving information regarding date, specification, price, quantity, discount, commission etc., you should be particularly careful. A minor mistake in these respects sometimes may mean a big loss. Thirdly, the letter should be written in an appropriate style and format.

To sum up, in a business letter, your aim should be to ensure a high standard in all important areas: layout, medium-related protocols and structural frames, grammar, spelling, and punctuation. Attention and care given to these details will help you create and enhance the goodwill towards yourself and the company you represent.

1.5 How to Make Your Business Letter Work?

1.5.1 Choice of Words

When we are clear about how a good business letter should be like, the next thing we should consider is how to improve our writing to make it close or up to the standard. To make our letter work, we must select words carefully to convey a clear message.

First, please always remember to use clear words to avoid ambiguity. Ambiguity means using words having more than one meaning and may be misunderstood. Secondly, you should also try to avoid cliché, colloquialism, slang and commercial jargon. Constant use of cliché may produce staleness in writing and speech. Colloquialism, which is proper in speech, is not suitable in formal writing like business letters because it may give the impression of informality, laziness and slackness. Slang is used in some special sense by a class or a special trade or profession. The use of slang may weaken the language. Commercial jargons are technical words or expressions familiar only to those working in the commercial field.

Jargons and Clichés	Ordinary Expressions
a draft in the amount of 500 USD	a draft for 500 USD
as per, in accordance with	according to
at this time	now
at your earliest convenience	as soon as possible
awaiting the favor of your early response	looking forward to hearing from you
cheque to cover 50 pounds	cheque for 50 pounds
in advance of, prior to	before
I would like to take this opportunity to	(delete it)

Jargons and Clichés	Ordinary Expressions
make an inquiry regarding	inquire
pursuant to your request	as you requested in your letter
please be good enough to advise us ...	please advise us
under separate cover	separately
we beg to thank you	thank you
we wish to acknowledge receipt of	we have received ...

Thirdly, always remember to use positive words instead of negative words. For example:

Poor: Your negligence in this matter caused the damage to the shipment.

Better: If you had taken proper care of the shipment, there would have been no damage.

Fourth, you should select small and short words instead of big and long-winded words for your letter to avoid redundancy, as redundancy is against the principle of brevity. A comparison of the pairs of words in the following table shows clearly that the brief expressions are better and much easier to understand.

Wordy Expressions	Brief Expressions
at a later date	later
at the present time	now
avail oneself of/utilize	use
in a manner similar to	like
inasmuch as	as
inform me of the reason	tell me why
in the course of	during
are of the opinion that	believe that
arrive at the conclusion	conclude
an the event that	if
duplicate	copy
finalize	finish
Would you be so kind	Please
I would like to take this opportunity to ...	Don't use this at all. Start with your sentence like "Thank you for ..."
acknowledge receipt of	Thank you for
enclosed please find	enclosed, here
be in receipt of	have received
kindly	please

1.5.2 Choose Simple and Clear Sentences

While selecting sentences for your letter, remember to follow the following points.

(1) Try not to use out-of-date sentences like "Would you be so kind as to ...", "Under separate cover please find ..." and "I am looking forward to hearing from you". These old sentences may show that you are old fashioned.

(2) Never push your recipient to do something. Sentences like "I am looking forward to your favorable reply" are pushy and should not be used.

(3) Use direct questions to give your letter more impact. In the following two examples, the latter is clearer and more direct than the first one.

Poor: We'll appreciate your advising us if you want to continue this account or transfer it.
Better: Do you want to continue your account or transfer it?

(4) Always prefer the active to the passive voice and use personal references to personalize the letter. Compare the following two sentences, and you will see that the second one is more natural.

Poor: Your contact information has been changed in our records.
Better: We have changed your contact information in our records.

1.6 Writing Tips

In this section, you can find some rules applicable in business letter writing. They are introduced in some books about business writing. Discuss with your partner and try to add some more rules to the list.

(1) Give your letter a heading if it can help to attract the reader's attention.

(2) Decide what you are going to say before you start to write or dictate a letter. In other words, you should always plan before you settle down to writing.

(3) You should answer all the questions relevant to your audience: Who? What? When? Where? Why? How? Use the "5W+H" formula to try to anticipate any questions your readers might ask.

(4) Always use short, simple sentences and short words that everyone can understand.

(5) Adopt a plain writing style. In writing, plainness is beautiful. It will save your time, the reader's time, and your company's money.

(6) Put each separate idea in a separate paragraph. Number each of the paragraphs if it will help the reader to understand better.

(7) Think about your reader. Your reader can understand better if your letter is clear, complete, concise, courteous, and correct.

(8) Pay special attention to names, titles, and genders. If you're not positive about the spelling of someone's name, their job title, or their gender, you can check with someone who does know.

(9) Write once, check twice. Proofread immediately after you have finished writing. Remember that mistakes in business are costly because people may judge you from those mistakes.

Exercises

1. Compare the following pairs of sentences to see why Sentence B is better.

(1) **A:** If you will remit to us your canceled check, we will be in a position to determine how the aforementioned remittance was applied.
   B: If you will send us your canceled check, we will be able to find out how we applied your payment.

(2) **A:** In order that shipment can be made without delay, furnish the L/C in advance of December 14th.
   B: In order that we can make the shipment immediately, may we have the L/C before December 14th?

(3) **A:** Our Guangzhou branch brought this fact to my attention.
   B: Our Guangzhou branch told me about this.

(4) **A:** There are changes in the organization to be expected by us.
   B: We expect some changes in the organization.

(5) **A:** Referring to your communication of recent date, we wish to take this opportunity to state that mobile phones about which you inquired were shipped as per your instructions on January 9th.
   B: According to your instructions, we shipped the mobile phones on January 9th.

(6) **A:** In the event that this does not meet with your approval, please notify this writer as to your wishes.
   B: Please tell me if you approve or not.

(7) **A:** We have been endeavoring to ascertain the answer to the question as to whether or not Mr. Allen will pay us a visit next month.
   B: We've been trying to find out if Mr. Allen will visit us next month.

(8) **A:** Due to the above-stated reasons, effectuation of a decision in your favor will have to be delayed by me.
   B: Therefore, I must delay a favorable decision.

2. Rewrite the following sentences to make them clearer and simpler.

(1) This is to inquire at what address we can reach you.
(2) We are awaiting the favor of your early response.
(3) Please send us your latest price-list at once and by return mail.
(4) By this letter we would ask you to consider our proposal.
(5) Whenever there is any way in which we can be of any assistance to you, please don't hesitate to contact us.
(6) I would like to express my sincere gratitude for your kind help.
(7) To avoid the loss of your credit rating, please remit the payment within a week.
(8) Enclosed is a brochure outlining this company's goods available for export.
(9) We wish to inform you that we specialize in the export of Chinese textiles and shall be glad to build a business relationship with you.
(10) Please send us your specific enquiry if you take interest in any of the items in the catalogue.

3. The following letter is a letter of rejection. The meaning of the letter is clearly expressed but the way to present the bad news may irritate the reader. Rearrange the letter to make it more acceptable. You may change some of the expressions if necessary.

> Gentlemen,
>
> It is a pity that we have to point out the unreasonableness of your price. The price for your paint is too high for us to work on. Although we are keen to trade with you, we regret that we can by no means accept your offer. Therefore, it is impossible for us to place an order with you at such a high price.
>
> I think anyone who has some common sense will know that prices for furniture paint have been declining in recent years. An American company, which also specializes in the production of furniture paint, has quoted us a price approximately 20% lower than that of yours. Although the quality of their products does not measure up to that of yours, we still think that the price gap between yours and theirs is too wide for us.
>
> So sorry again for our rejection. We wish you can sell your high-priced paint to other importers successfully.
>
> Yours faithfully,

4. Correct the mistakes in spelling, grammar, punctuation, or capitalization in the following sentences.

(1) Our company is one of the major importer of handkerchieves in Canada.
(2) It give me much pleasure to notify you of that your application has been approved.
(3) We are looking for some electric heaters from suppliers experienced exporting to European markets.
(4) Should your price be found competitive and delivery date is acceptable, we intend to place a trial order to you.
(5) I have enclosed our recent catalogs illustrated many of our popular items.
(6) Perhaps you could let us know your terms of business and the time requiring for delivery after you receive the order.
(7) We learned from Smith & Company that you manufacture a range high-fashion handbags in a variety of leathers.
(8) In reply, we would like to make the following offer, is subject to our final confirmation.
(9) As you are aware that China is a very big market with a huge potential for industrial raw materials, in which we are already so well established.
(10) There is a steady demand here for high quality brocade handbags, we would like you to send us your illustrated catalogues.

Chapter 2

Components of a Business Letter

Your goals for this chapter are to understand:
☑ the basic components of a business letter;
☑ the placement of these components in a business letter;
☑ how to address an envelope;
☑ the different formats of business letters.

2.1 Lead-in

Before you begin your learning of this chapter, please discuss with your partner(s) about the following questions.

(1) How many components does an ordinary Chinese letter usually consist of?
(2) What do you usually write at the beginning of a Chinese letter?
(3) Where do you usually place the most important part of your letter, at the beginning, at the end, or neither?

2.2 The Components of a Business Letter

2.2.1 The Common Components of a Business Letter

The components of an ordinary business letter can be roughly classified into two main parts: the essential part and the optional part.

1. The Essential Parts

The essential part of a letter includes six elements detailed as follows: the letterhead, the inside name and address, the salutation, the body of the letter, the complimentary close and the signature.

1) The letterhead

A business letterhead, which is usually printed, aims to give some information about the writer's company. It contains all or some of the essential particulars about the writer such as the company's name, street address (and mailing address, if different), post code, telephone number, fax number, e-mail address, website, the addresses of branches or a logo of the company etc. For example:

CHIATAI QINGCHUNBAO PHARMACEUTICAL CO., LTD.
No. 551, Xixi Road, Hangzhou, China, Post Code: 310023
Tel: 0086-571-85121024; Fax: 0086-571-85152635
E-mail: master@cnqcb.com

Among these particulars listed above, the following parts are the most important: the company name, the address of the sender, the contact information and the date.

In some books, the date is regarded as a part of the letterhead while in some others it is seen as an independent element. When you begin your letter writing, you must add the date a few lines below the last line of the letterhead. The date is vital because it plays a role of evidence of an arrangement or contract in case of any disputes in law courts. The date line consists of month, day and year, and it is normally typed in a month-day-year sequence. The month should not be abbreviated or represented by figures. The date, then, should be expressed as "August 6 2011", not "Aug. 6, 2011" or "8/6/11". A comma should be used to separate the day from the year.

Some businesses are, however, adopting a date system that has long been followed in military correspondence. This is the date-month-year sequence. No punctuation is used in this sequence, so this sequence saves one keystroke. It is a system that is widely used in Europe, and so it is suitable to use in international correspondence. For example:

January 12, 2011 (Business Style)

12 January 2011 (Military Style)

Because of the development of communication technology, the date and address are not as important as before because the fax machine or computer may generate the fax number or e-mail address automatically.

2) The inside name and address

This part, which occupies 3–5 lines, usually includes the full name, the title and the address of the recipient. The usual sequence of display of the inside address in a business letter is: name of the person addressed, title of the person addressed, name of organization, street number and name, city, state/province and postal code, country of destination.

In this part, the writer may use a courtesy title (e.g. Miss, Mr.) or an academic title (e.g. Dr. or Prof.). The title of a person's position within an organization may be included and typed either on the same line as the person's name or on the line below the receiver's name. For example:

Miss Ellis Chapman, President

Samuel Goodier Company

1347 Tufnel Ave.

Minneapolis, MN 55106

USA

Or:

Miss Jane Smith

Chief Executive Officer

The Richardson & Jenkins Corporation

898 Pendwin Drive

New York 10205, N.Y.

USA

When the receiver's name is unknown, we can use the examples listed as follows:

Hitachi Ltd.

The Hitachi Atago Building

No.15-12, 2-Chome, Nishi-Shinbashi

Minatoku, Tokyo 105

Japan

3) The salutation

A salutation is the word or phrase of greeting which conventionally comes immediately before the body of a letter. Here are some points which the writer should pay special attention to.

(1) "Madam" and "Sir" should not be followed by a name.

(2) Miss/Mr./Mrs./Ms. should always be followed by a person's surname.

(3) "Gentlemen" should always be in its plural form.

(4) If you don't know a reader's gender, use a nonsexist salutation, such as "Dear Sir/Madam". It is also acceptable to use the full name in a salutation if you cannot determine gender.

(5) After the salutation, a comma or a colon may be used.

Inclusion of a salutation should never be neglected because it has the following two benefits.

(1) It acts as a double check to the recipient that the message is indeed intended for him.

(2) It clarifies the context in which the message has been sent to the recipient.

4) The body of the letter

The body of the letter is the most important part because it is this part that fulfills the task of conveying the main message, so it deserves our special attention.

The arrangement of the paragraphs depends on which letter format you have chosen. It is advisable to arrange the message in at least two paragraphs. Single spacing is usually used, but if the message is very short, double spacing can be applied. If the letter is too long to fit into one page, the message can be continued onto a second page, which should carry at least two lines. On each continuation page, the name of the addressee, the page number and the date should be typed in either of the ways specified below.

(1) Mr. Wilson   2   January 30, 2011

(2) Mr. Wilson

　　Page 2

　　January 30, 2011

5) The complimentary close

The complimentary close is an expression used to close the letter in a polite way. The expression must be suitable for the occasion and should reflect the writer's relationship with the addressee.

In a traditional letter, if the salutation used is "Dear Sir" or "Dear Madam", it is better to use "Yours faithfully" or "Faithfully yours" to close the letter. If the letter begins with "Dear Mr. Kolin" or other exact names, then"Yours sincerely" or 'Sincerely yours" would be a better choice for a complimentary close. If the letter is written to a close friend or a colleague, "Best wishes" or "Best regards" may be used to end the letter. But such rules are obviously no longer applicable for an e-mail because they are too formal for e-mails. The comma after the complimentary close can be either used or omitted.

The most commonly used sets of salutation and complimentary close are shown in the following table.

Relationship	Salutation	Complimentary Close
If you know the recipient's name	Dear Sir/Madam (Br) Dear Sirs/Madams (Br) Ladies and Gentlemen (Am) Dear Sales Director (Am)	Yours faithfully (Br) Faithfully yours Yours truly (Br) Truly yours
If you know the recipient's name	Dear Mr/Mrs Kolin (Br) Dear Mr./Mrs/Ms. Kolin (Am)	Yours sincerely (Br) Sincerely yours (Am)
If you don't know the recipient's gender	Dear Berit Virtanen Dear B. Virtanen	Yours sincerely (Br) Sincerely yours (Am)
If the recipient is your close friend or your colleague	Dear David/David Dear Mary/Mary	Best wishes Best regards Yours

6) The signature

Letters should be individually signed unless it concerns a bulk mailing. In the signature no courtesy titles should be put before the writer's name except his academic degree or title such as "Doctor" or "Professor". If professional titles should be included, they are usually typed after the typewritten name. If the signer is a lady, "Miss" or "Mrs." is often typed in the parenthesis before her handwritten signature.

Usually four spaces are reserved for handwritten signature, followed by the typewritten name. If the company name is added, it should be capitalized and placed immediately below the complimentary close, but before the signature. It can also be positioned below the name and title of the writer.

2. The Optional Parts

Besides the parts discussed above, when appropriate, any of the following additional parts can be included: the reference line, the attention line, the subject heading, the enclosure notation, the C.C. line, the identification initials, the N. B. and the P. S. notations.

1) The reference line

Some letters may have a reference line, the purpose of which is for convenient reply, filing and classification. It may include a file number, departmental code or the initials of the signer or the typist. For example:

Your ref: CNN-002/018
Our Ref: 008A/GZD/ssy

2) The attention line

If the letter is directed to a specific person or department, it is necessary to include an attention line in the letter. This line means that the specified person or department should give attention to this letter. The attention line may take any of the following forms:

Attention: Marketing Department

Attention of Mr. Zhu Wei

For the attention of Miss Shen Shiyi

Attention Sales Manager

3) The subject heading

The subject heading functions as a title of the letter, which can tell the reader immediately what the letter is about and whether it is worth reading. When more than one topic is dealt with, you can give a subject heading for the more important topic or simply omit the heading. The following examples may give us some ideas about how a subject line is arranged.

Subject: Letter of Credit No. 9867

Re: Letter of Credit No. 2468

Letter of Credit No. 9631

SUBJECT: LETTER OF CREDIT NO 9538

Because you only have a few seconds to capture a prospective customer's attention, you should always remember to provide your letter with an attractive heading.

4) The enclosure notation

If the writer needs to enclose a contract or a price-list with the letter, he should type an enclosure notation on the line below the reference initials. Its purpose is to tell the recipient how many other pieces of paper are enclosed. For example:

Enclosures: (1) A catalogue
           (2) Invoice No. 5980

Enl: 4 pages

5) The C.C. line

If the writer wants the addressee to know that he is sending a copy of the letter to somebody else, he should type a copy notation — the C.C. line at the end of the letter. C.C. stands for "Carbon Copies". This line usually prefaces the names of people who have received a copy of the letter and may be indicated in one of the following ways:

Copy to Alan Smith

cc: Miss Shen Shiyi

cc Nathan Jackson

c/c: Mr. R. Leung

If there are several persons who receive the copy of the letter, their names should be listed in alphabetical order. For example:

Copies to Alan Smith
        Zhu Wei

6) The identification initials

This part is made up of the initials of the signer's or the typist's name. They are used for administrative purposes in the office where the letter originated. Different typing styles are accepted. The most common style is like this: GZD/ssy or GZD:ssy. The former are the initials of the signer in all uppercase characters and the latter are the typist's. If the person who writes the letter is not the person who signs it, all three persons' initials — the signer's, the dictator's and the typist's — will all appear in this way: GZD/ybz/ssy.

7) The N.B. and P.S. notations

N.B. is short for a Latin word "Nota Bene", which means "to observe carefully". It is used to call the reader's special attention to some points. For example:

N.B.: We have decided to entrust you with the sole agency for our products.

If the writer makes an addition to the letter after it is typed, he can use a P.S. line for the addition. P.S. is short for "postscript", meaning an extra message added at the end. If the writer wants to add a second postscript, "PPS" can be used. For example:

P.S.: Wish to meet you at the Canton Fair on April 18th, 2011.

PPS: Our manager will arrive at Heathrow at 4:45

The meeting may be postponed because of the delayed flight.

In formal business writings, use of a postscript should be avoided because it may suggest that the writer had planned his letter poorly before he wrote it.

3. The Placement of the Components

The following is a table which may help you to better remember the ways to place the above components properly.

	The components	Placement
The essential parts	The letterhead	The name of the firm is usually centered at the top or on the right-hand side. If the writer must print on blank paper, he must remember to print on the right corner. The date should be written on the right-hand side, double space below the last line of the letterhead.
	The inside name and address	Kept flush with the left margin, four lines below the date line.
	The salutation	Placed three typing spaces below the last line of the inside address and kept flush with the left margin.
	The body	Usually positioned two lines below the salutation.
	The complimentary close	Placed double space below the body, preferably aligning with the date line or conforming to the style of the letter.
	The signature	Placed double space below the complimentary close.
The additional parts	The reference line	Placed against the left-hand margin, in line with the date.
	The attention line	On the second line between the inside address and salutation, with a single space above and below, usually kept flush with the left margin.
	The subject heading	Often centered, between the salutation and the body with a double space above and below.

	The components	Placement
The additional parts	The enclosure notation	Usually placed against the left-hand margin, below the identification initials.
	The C.C. and B.C. line	Positioned against the left-hand margin, below the enclosure notation.
	The identification initials	At the left-hand margin above the enclosure notation, but below the signature.
	The N.B. and P.S. notations	At the left-hand margin, following the C.C. and B.C. line.

2.3 Learning to Write

2.3.1 What Is the Effective Way to Write a Business Letter?

It is widely accepted that we can use models for imitation to raise a learner's awareness of the accepted forms and wording of good business letters, so many business writing programmes provide examples and models for learners to follow without attempting to develop learners' language awareness. But no matter how many sample letters a course book provides, it is impossible for the book to include samples which may meet various contexts. So imitation is not the best way to teach business letter writing, although imitation may prove to be necessary at times.

The theory we've adopted for the compiling of this book is genre analysis because the notion of genre is very useful in the analysis of business discourse. We believe that analysis of the business letter conventions and linguistic features can help to raise learners' awareness of English business letter conventions and help them in writing business communications in a way which meets the expectations of the discourse community. Through analysis of some model letters, learners may become armed with such knowledge and become more capable of producing genres required in their profession. Thus it can assist learners in producing the patterns of language required in diverse business contexts.

In this book, learners are first required to study closely the given model letters, from which they can gain some basic ideas on the common structures of the different genres discussed in the chapter. Because learners obtain the information from their own observation, they may have a deep impression about the structure and style of business letters. Then armed with the writing guidelines summarized from the model letters, they will go on to the analysis of more variants and learn how to adjust the arrangement of different moves to achieve different communicative purposes.

2.3.2 Steps of Business Letter Writing

A general business letter usually consists of three parts: an introductory paragraph, a body and a conclusion paragraph. The introductory paragraph usually gives the main message, the purpose of the letter or the reasons for writing. This part aims to get favorable attention, to set a friendly tone, or to establish a link with previous correspondence. The body gives the main message, so it is the most important part. The conclusion paragraph is used to express expectations, requests for action or recommendations.

Then what steps should you follow to fulfill the task of writing a letter? First, before you write, you should be clear about the following questions.
- Who will read your letter?
- Why are you writing this letter?

Secondly, you must assemble all the relevant information and documents: copies of previous correspondence, reports, figures etc. Select the necessary points centering around the following question.
- What should you include in your letter?

Thirdly, when all points are ready, you should think about the next question.
- How can you best communicate, that is, in what style and/or tone can you convey the message?

At this stage, you need to consider how to arrange the points in order of importance. Decide which points are irrelevant and can be left out. Make rough notes, then you can write an outline in note form.

Fourth, you can develop the outline and try to turn it into a draft, leaving plenty of space for changes and revisions.

Fifth, you should revise your first draft by considering these questions.
- Does the letter cover all the essential points?
- Is the information relevant, correct and complete?
- Are the grammar, spelling and punctuation correct?
- Does it look attractive?
- Does it sound natural and sincere?
- Is it clear, concise and courteous?
- Will it give the reader the right impression?

Finally, you can write or type your final version, sign it and then deliver it. But before you deliver your letter, remember to take the reader's position and read it again to see whether the message is clear. Never let a letter go without being satisfied with it.

2.4 The Layout of a Business Letter

The layout or format is the visual organization of a business letter and it makes the first and important impression on the reader. There are four common layouts of business letters. They are:
(1) the indented style;
(2) the block style;
(3) the modified block style;
(4) the simplified style.

Of the four layouts, the indented style is the most formal while the simplified style is the least formal of the four types.

1. The Indented Style

This is a traditional British style. It looks attractive but is not convenient to type. The main characteristics in this style are that the inside name and address are in block form and should be indented 2-3 spaces, and the first lines of each paragraph are all indented 3-8 spaces to show the separation of paragraphs clearly.

```
                              Letterhead

  Inside Address

                                                      September 1, 2011

  Dear Sir or Madam,
  _____
  _____
  _____
  _____
  _____
  _____

                                                      Yours Sincerely,
                                                      Signature
```

2. The Full Block Style

The full block style is an American style. It came into being because typewriters and computers began to be widely used since the upper half of last century. Its striking feature is that all letter elements are flush with the left margin; it is business-like and easy to prepare; it is unbalanced and less social. It is the commonest style among the four, and is used in more than 80% of all business letters.

```
                    Letterhead (including writer's address)

  September 1, 2011
  Inside Address
  Dear Sir or Madam,
  _____
  _____
  _____
  _____
  _____
  ……

  Yours sincerely,
  Signature
  J. Roland
```

3. The Modified Block Style

To avoid the disadvantages of the block style, some writers began to modify it in the 1970s because they wanted to cater for the older readers' taste for the composition of a business letter. The modified block style has the following characteristics: all elements are against the left-hand margin except the date, subject heading and the signature block; it appears more balanced and more gracious, more social and more persuasive; its demerit is that it is somewhat more difficult to use than the block style. The person keying in the letter must locate the horizontal center of the page for the date and signature block.

```
                          Letterhead
                                              September 1, 2011
Inside Address

Dear Sir or Madam,
                       Subject Heading
_____
_____
_____
……
_____
_____
                                              Sincerely yours,
                                              Signature
```

4. The Simplified Style

Some professionals believe that neither the salutation nor the complimentary close are read, and therefore, neither should be included. This has produced the "simplified style". The simplified style is used in less than 10% of all business letters. It emphasizes content over more personal or complimentary aspects of the letter. It has the following characteristics: the salutation and complimentary close are omitted and the subject heading is capitalized.

```
                          Letterhead
September 1, 2011
Inside Address
SUBJECT HEADING
_____
_____
_____
……
_____
_____
                                                    Signature
```

2.5 Addressing an Envelope

Although envelopes are no longer as frequently used as they were in the past, it is still necessary to learn how to address them in a proper way. The following are some points which deserve your attention in writing an envelope.

(1) No punctuation is used at line end.

(2) Use single space within the block.

(3) The recipient's address should be the same with the inside address and be centered on the front side of the envelope.

(4) The return address should be in the upper left corner, on the second line from the top of the envelope and three spaces from the left edge of the envelope.

(5) If the envelope is not big enough for both addresses, you can write the sender's address on the back of the envelope.

1. Blocked Form of Address

Wahaha Group Co., Ltd.
160 Qing Tai Street, 310009
Hangzhou, Zhejiang Prov, China

      Miss A Haracre
      32 Glenhurst Avenue
      London NW5 7A

2. Indented Form of Address

      Miss A Haracre
      32 Glenhurst Avenue
      London NW5 7A

In addressing an envelope, please always keep in mind the following three requirements: accuracy, clearness and good appearance.

2.6 Writing Tips

Mavor, in his book *English for Business* (1988), has suggested some rules for good business letters.

(1) Use the concrete word, not the abstract.

(2) Prefer the short word to the long word.
(3) Do not use more words than necessary.
(4) Prefer the familiar and clearly-written word, avoid long-winded words.
(5) Cultivate the transitive verb.
(6) Guard against the over-use of adjectives.
(7) Prefer the active to the passive voice.

Please discuss with your partner about whether they are reasonable. Try to add some more points to the above list.

Exercises

1. Correct the mistakes in the following sentences.

(1) A traditional business letter usually is consisted of six components.
(2) Presenting requirement should be stressed as the most important movement in an inquiry letter.
(3) You should arrange the points in order to importance and decide which points can be left out.
(4) When you finish a letter, take the reader's position and read it again to see whether the message is clear and concise.
(5) You will need to adopt your message to fit your audience.
(6) The reader's needs and your communicative goal can help you formulating your purpose.
(7) With your purpose clearly identifying, you are on the right track.
(8) A good e-mail marketing strategy can be very effective to find new customers.
(9) You should not put several e-mail addresses together and send one message to all of them once.
(10) The word "introduce" should not be used when trying to sell your products.

2. Compare the following two letters to see which is better and find out what strategies have been applied in the revised version.

Original Version:

Dear Sirs,

　　We are the largest dealer in art & craft products in this district where Chinese hand-made art and craft items are especially popular. We have recently received many inquiries from our retailing shops about art and craft products. Please send us a copy of your catalogue and your current price list.

　　Messrs J. Harvey Co., who has been our regular customers for many years, told us your name and address. We know that you are one of the leading producers of handmade art and craft products in your country. We want to enter into business relations with you.

　　We are sure there might be brisk demands on our side. If the quality of your products is satisfactory and your prices are acceptable, we will place regular orders with you for considerably large numbers.

　　Give us your reply as soon as possible.

Yours faithfully,

Revised Version:

Dear Mr. Zhang,

Your name was given to us by Messrs J. Harvey Co., who has been our regular customers for many years. We know that you are one of the leading producers of handmade art and craft products in your country, and we are now writing to express our wish of entering into business relations with you.

We are a major dealer in art & craft products in this district, where Chinese hand-made art and craft items are especially popular. We have recently received many inquiries from our retailing shops about the said items. We want to import some handmade bracelets from you, so will you please send us a copy of your catalogue and current price list for your newly-designed bracelets?

We are sure there will be brisk demands on our side. If we find the quality of your products satisfactory and the prices acceptable, we will place regular orders with you for considerably large numbers.

We are looking forward to hearing from you in the near future.

Yours faithfully,

3. There are some mistakes in the placement of the components in the following letter. Please point out these mistakes and correct them.

VOGEL ENERGY COMPANY LIMITED
Tel: 86-571-78965432
Fax: 86-571-89087650
788 Canton Road
Kowloon, Hong Kong, SAR

February 7th, 2012

Our Ref: VJ008-12

Mr. Macabin Bearry
2782 Harvard Boulevard
Los Angeles, CA 90007

Attn: Mr. Bearry

Subject: Our Latest Catalogue

Dear Mr. Bearry,

Thank you for your enquiry of January 4th, 2012, asking for the latest edition of our catalogue. We are pleased to enclose our latest brochure which explains the aims of our organization.

If you have interest in our work, please fill in the form attached to the enclosed leaflet.

An annual subscription of HK$100 brings full membership, all issues of our journal and any other occasional publications.

If you require any further information, please let me know.

We look forward to welcoming you as our customer.

Yours faithfully,
Jenny Liu (Miss)
(Signature)
JL/xw

Encl: 4 leaflets
PS: We shall meet you in Hong Kong next week.
CC: Mr Johnson

---

4. The following is an informal letter. Use more formal language to make it better.

From: richard0303@163.com
To: snakegreen@163.com
Subject: Goods shipped

Hi, Chen,

Ur L/C (No. 234-A-01) rved. We are writing you the goods (200 Bamboo Beds, 500 Bamboo Chairs and 100 Bamboo Benches) shipped today. We believe you'll be satisfied with them. All items been examined individually before packed. We hope you can unpack and examine them ASAP after delivery, and if there is any breakage or damage to them, tell us soonest.

Best wishes,
R. Jackinson

Chapter 3 Initiating Business Relationships

> *Your goals for this chapter are to understand:*
> ☑ the importance of establishing business relationships;
> ☑ the channels from which you can find an international business partner;
> ☑ how to structure a letter for initiating business relationships;
> ☑ some patterns commonly used in such types of letters.

3.1 Lead-in

Before you begin your learning of this chapter, please discuss with your partner(s) about the following questions.

(1) Suppose you are now working as an international businessman, how can you find some business partners?
(2) Can you list some sources from which a company can find some business partners?
(3) How do you usually begin a letter which aims to initiate a new interpersonal relationship?

3.2 Basic Information

Just as a factory requires a complete set of machinery to proceed with its production, any firm engaged in international trade needs extensive business connections to maintain or expand its business activities. Therefore, initiating a business relationship is of vital importance to any corporation. A business must not only do what it can to cement its established relations but also develop and revitalize its trade by looking for new trading partners. For a newly established firm, to seek prospective clients is of even greater importance because it may have a bearing on how far it can go.

In the field of international trade, the information you have obtained about your customers through various channels makes it possible for you to communicate, esp. in writing, with the new counterparts in the hope of establishing business relations. If an exporter or importer wishes to open up a market to sell or buy something in a foreign country, he or she may approach his prospective clients abroad through the following channels.

(1) writing to potential clients directly.
(2) attending all kinds of commodities fairs or exhibitions.
(3) searching in trade directories of various countries or regions.
(4) sending trade groups and delegations abroad for business talks.
(5) opening branches or sales agents abroad.
(6) placing advertisements in foreign media.
(7) contacting some commercial institutions such as the chambers of commerce, the commercial counselor's offices etc. both at home and abroad for help.
(8) asking old clients or friends to make recommendations.
(9) surfing the internet.

Of all these channels, the Internet merits special attention because it has become a powerful tool for reaching consumers. Therefore, any business, especially business starters should make the most of the World Wide Web, and search for potential customers.

3.3 Analysis of Model Letters

Read and analyze the following letters. While reading, please try to find answers to the following questions.
(1) Why is Model Letter 3-1 written in such a detail?
(2) In Model Letter 3-2, which is the most important paragraph?
(3) Do you think the writer of Model Letter 3-3 is impolite because he has declined a request? Why or why not?

Model Letter 3-1: Exporter expressing a desire to establish a business relationship

Dear Sir or Madam,

We learned your company and address from the *Promotion of International Trade*, from which we know that you are in the market for Telecontrol Racing Cars produced in China. Now, we are writing you to express our desire to trade with you.

Our company was founded in 1948, specializing in the research and manufacture of toys and handicrafts, and has now become one of the biggest toy producers in China. We have been engaged in exporting toys and handicrafts for over 30 years. Our Telecontrol Racing Car is our new product, and it is very popular all over the world.

Our products hold very high reputation by worldwide clients with their high quality and favorable prices.

To acquaint you with our products, we are airmailing you under separate cover our latest catalogue covering the main items suppliable at present.

Our bankers are the Bank of Tokyo, Japan. They can provide you with the information about our credit standing.

Please let us know immediately if you are interested in any of our products. We await your favorable reply in the nearest future.

Yours faithfully,
(Signature)

Model Letter 3-2: A positive reply to an inquiry for establishing a business relationship

Dear Sirs,

Thank you very much for your fax dated 13th of this month. We also have heard of you for a long time and we are willing to build a business relationship with you.

Will you please send us some detailed information about your products together with the prices and the terms of payment? We should find it most helpful if you would also send us some samples.

We are looking forward to your early reply.

Yours sincerely,
Luna Wang

Model Letter 3-3: Importer declining exporter's request

Dear Mr. Wright,

We are in receipt of your letter of March 23rd, 2011 and we thank you very much for your interest in co-operating with us.

In reply to your letter regarding establishment of a business relationship with us, we regretfully have to say that we are unable to do so because we have recently made the decision to import nutritious food since we are no longer in the market for pharmaceutical chemicals.

If you have any newly developed nutritious foods, however, please let us know as we are always open to new opportunities.

Sincerely yours,
Magret Taylor

3.4 Writing Guidelines

In the above letters, Model Letter 3-1 aims at starting a business relationship with the recipient. In a letters of this type, you usually need to include the following parts.

(1) Giving the source of information, e.g. how you got to know your recipient's name and address.

(2) Making a self-introduction, e.g. the nature of your company's business and your business scope etc. if your company is unknown.

(3) Stating the purpose of the letter, i.e. starting a business relationship.

(4) Giving references as to your firm's financial position or integrity etc.

(5) Expressing expectations or hopes to co-operate smoothly in the future.

Model Letter 3-2 and Model Letter 3-3 are both responses to letters expressing the desire to begin a business relationship. The response may be negative or positive. A careful examination of the two model letters shows that they, in general, consist of the following parts.

(1) Acknowledging receipt of the initiating letter.

(2) Giving your opinions about the request mentioned in the letter received. Here you should state clearly whether you want to meet his desire or have to reject it.

(3) Making a counter-request or giving some explanations. If you agree to your counterpart's request, you may ask for some information like catalogues or pricelists. If you can't accept it, give your explanations here.

(4) Ending your letter by expressing an expectation, e.g. a wish for successful co-operation or other opportunities to trade with each other.

3.5 More Sample Letters

The following letters comply basically with the above writing guidelines, but they are different from the above models in one way or another. Read them to see how each letter is structured and worded to achieve its respective communicative purpose.

Sample Letter 3-1: Exporter desiring to establish business relations

Instead of giving references for credit standing or financial standing, the writer of the following letter tells his reader how he can guarantee the quality and quantity of his commodities.

> Dear Sir/Madam,
>
> We owe your name and address to the Commercial Counselor's Office of the Japanese Embassy in Beijing. We wish to inform you that we specialize in the export of silk clothes, and shall be pleased to build up a business relationship with you.
>
> In order to give you some idea about our products, we are enclosing an illustrated catalogue showing various products being handled by our corporation with detailed specifications and means of packing.

Quotations and samples may be dispatched to you upon receipt of your specific enquiries.

Business between us will be concluded on the basis of shipping quality while testing and inspection will be made by the Shanghai Commodity Inspection Bureau prior to shipment. Necessary certificates in regard to the quality and quantity of the shipment will be provided.

We would be obliged if you would reply at an early date.

Yours faithfully,
Peter Zhang
Sales Manager

Sample Letter 3-2: An exporter asking an intermediary to introduce new customers

The most important content of the letter is the question in the middle, which expresses its request directly and clearly. Before that are the reasons for the request. The letter is simple, but the necessary points are all covered in it.

Dear Sirs,

We have been a major exporter of cotton piece goods for over 20 years, and are planning to extend our business activities to our neighboring countries. That's why we are writing to you in the hope of starting business relations with some importers in your locality.

Would you please introduce us to some of the most reliable importers of the same lines?

As to our financial standing, we are permitted to mention the CITIC Industrial Bank, China as a reference.

We are looking forward to your favorable and prompt reply.

Yours faithfully,

Sample Letter 3-3: Exporter approaching a new customer via a go-between

This letter begins with a question. When the reader's interest is aroused, more details about the "favor" then follow.

Dear Steve,

I wonder if you could do me a favor? I am going to be in Yorkshire on Monday, October 16, and would like to meet Tom Hopkins at Hoppers. Could you give him a call to introduce me?

Chapter 3 Initiating Business Relationships

I think Tom may be interested in the new range of cotton blankets we are producing and I would welcome the opportunity to show these to him. I am sure that an introduction by you would increase my chances of visiting him.

If you could call him in the next week or so, I would be extremely grateful as this will enable me to set up a meeting in time for Wednesday, 18 October. Many thanks indeed.

All good wishes to you.

Your Sincerely,
Ross Camery

Sample Letter 3-4: Importer's voluntary request for relationship establishment

This is a very informal letter transmitted in the form of e-mail. Many abbreviations are found and some informal words are used in it. The letter is very short and simple, but the main messages are clearly conveyed.

From: Mikel9821@126.com
To: KarterJ@163.com
Cc: rossymay@ligumark.com
Sent: Thursday, July 09, 2011, 15:31 PM
Subject: gsm accessories

Goodday,

i have seen some of ur products such as desktop charger in the internet n i want to know if u can be our supplier of gsm accessories n if u have any in stock? i want u to plz send the name n prices if there is any.

Thanx.
(Signature)

Sample Letter 3-5: Importer agreeing to exporter's request

This is a positive reply to a letter aiming at establishing a business relationship. As this letter conveys a pleasing message, no more comments on the acceptance are needed.

Dear Mr. Zhang,

Thank you very much for your fax dated 20th of this month.

After reading through your enclosed catalogue, we find that most of your products fall into our business scope, so we also take pleasure in entering into business relations with you.

Should we wish to place an order, we shall send you specific inquiries by fax.

Yours sincerely,

Sample Letter 3-6: Recommending a new customer to the recipient

In the following letter, the writer does not accept his counterpart's request for establishing a business relationship. But it is still a friendly letter because the writer recommends a new supplier of finished clothes to the reader and closes the letter in a very friendly way.

Dear Sirs,

Thank you for your interest in establishing business relations with us. We regret to say that we do not manufacture finished clothes. Our factory produces only silk cloth which we sell to textile merchants and clothing manufacturers.

We can, however, recommend to you a factory here that produces high-quality silk clothes and would be able to manufacture clothing to your own design to the highest European standards:

Binjiang Clothing Corporation, The Industrial Development Zone, Xiasha District, 310018, Hangzhou, Zhejiang, P. R. China

We supply the factory with all the silk materials they need. I enclose a swatch of our stock materials for your examination. Should you need any of these samples of finished products, we can ask the Binjiang factory to send them to you directly.

We hope that this will be of some help to you and wish you every success in your business dealings.

Yours faithfully,

3.6 More Useful Sentences

1. Sources of Information
- We have seen your advertisement in *The New York Times* and should be glad to ...
- Your name was recommended to us by the P.R.C consul in your city as a large exporter of textiles.

- On the recommendation of Johnson & Co., Ltd. in your city, we are given to understand that you are in the market for electric appliances.
- Through the courtesy of Mr. Zhang, we have got to know your name and contact information.
- We have been informed by the Bank of China, Beijing that you are one of the leading importers of textiles in Britain.
- We are indebted for your name and address to Mr. John Smith, Canadian Ambassador in Beijing.

2. Self-introduction
- May we introduce ourselves as an exporter of Chemical Products having a considerable amount of experience in foreign trade?
- We have the pleasure of introducing ourselves as an experienced exporting company dealing primarily in computers.
- We have been engaged in exporting clothing for 30 years and are closely connected with large manufacturers in our country.
- This is to introduce ourselves as confectioners and bakers having many years' experience in this particular line of business.
- We are a state-operated company, handling the export of animal byproducts and we desire to establish trade relations with your firm.
- As an exclusive export representative of food in Shanghai, we are sure we are fully capable of satisfying your requirements.

3. Stating Purpose of the Letter
- Having been deeply interested in the quality of your products, we are desirous of doing business with you.
- Specializing in the export of Chinese foodstuffs, we wish to express our desire to trade with you in this line.
- We avail ourselves of this opportunity to write to you and see if we can build up business relations with you.
- We take the liberty of writing to you with a view to establishing business relations with you.
- We are now writing to you for the purpose of exploring the possibilities of developing trade with you.

4. Offering References
- Our bankers are the Industrial Bank of China, Shanghai Branch.
- The Bank of China in your city will give you any information concerning our credit standing.
- As to our credit standing, please refer to the Industrial and Commercial Bank of China, Zhejiang Branch.
- For any information as to our financial standing, please refer to The Standard Chartered Bank, Shanghai, who, we feel, will be glad to furnish you with any information you require.

5. Expressing Expectations
- We await your favorable reply in the near future.
- We look forward to pleasant business relations with you.

- We thank you in advance for your kind attention and hope to hear from you soon.
- Your prompt reply will be highly appreciated.

6. Giving Responses
- This is in reply to your letter of December 18th.
- We really appreciate your interest in co-operating with us.
- We are appreciative of your favorable reply.
- Your desire to establish direct business relations with us coincides with ours.
- As this item falls within the scope of our business activities, we shall be pleased to enter into direct business relations with you at an early date.
- We find your proposal attractive and would like to proceed with discussions on this matter.
- We are willing to enter into business relations with your firm on the basis of equality and mutual benefit and exchanging what one has for what one needs.
- In reply to your letter regarding establishment of business relations, we regretfully have to say that we are unable to co-operate with you as ...

3.7 Writing Tips

Some English majors have proposed the following points to note in writing letters for establishing business relationships. Read the following list quickly and then discuss with your partner to see whether they are appropriate. Please try to add some more ideas to the list.

In writing a letter for initiating a business relationship, you should keep the following points in mind.

(1) Try to introduce your firm or your products in broad terms in order to attract the widest possible interest. You should not make your introduction too specific, otherwise, some recipients may conclude quickly whether your letter is interesting to them and thus some potential customers may be excluded.

(2) If you are the recipient of such a letter, you ought to answer it in full without the least delay and with courtesy so as to create goodwill and leave a good impression on your counterpart.

(3) There is no standardized way of writing such a letter. As long as the letter can help you achieve your purpose, you can arrange the different items of your letter in any way you like.

(4) A letter declining a request for establishing a business relationship may be disappointing to your reader, so while writing these letters, always remember to give adequate explanations or recommendations.

Notes and Explanations

1. have a bearing on 与……有关系，对……有影响
2. establish business relations with sb. 与……建立业务关系
   We are glad to learn your desire to establish direct business relations with us.
   我方很高兴获悉，贵方想与我方建立直接的贸易关系。
   常见的表达式还有：open up (build up/enter into/establish) business relations (contacts/connections) with sb., commence business with sb.等。
3. a commodities fair 商品交易会

4. chambers of commerce　商会
5. commercial counselor　商务参赞
6. to merit special attention　值得特别注意

   Their improvements in packing method merits our special attention.
   他们在包装方式上的改进值得引起我们的特别关注。
7. be in the market for　想要购买

   One of our customers is in the market for Chinese Black Tea.
   我方有一位客户想要购买中国红茶。
8. under separate cover　另函，另外单独邮寄
9. credit standing　资信状况，信誉（也可以说成 credit status，即"信用评价"）

   As to our credit standing, we are permitted to mention the Bank of England, London, as a reference.
   关于我方的信誉情况，我们已征得伦敦英格兰银行的许可，他们愿意提供咨询信息。
   有关"财务状况"的表达方法有：financial standing（财务情况），finances［财源，资金情况（常用复数）］，financial position（财务状况）。
10. trade with　与……做生意
11. owe your name and address to sb.　多亏了某人的介绍（推荐等）才得以了解你们的名号和地址
12. specialize in　专营，专门从事

    We specialize in the import and export of arts and crafts.
    我们专门从事工艺美术品的进出口业务。
    表示"经营（某类商品）"的说法很多，常见的有：deal with，handle，deal in，trade in，be in the line for 等。
13. to conclude a business transaction　达成贸易交易

    to conclude sth. with sb.　达成，缔结（条约等）
    Once the price had been agreed upon, a deal was quickly concluded.
    价格一经商定，交易很快就达成了。
14. importers of the same line　同类商品的进口商，进口同类商品的商人
15. on the recommendation of　由于某人的推荐

    a recommendation letter　推荐信
    speak in recommendation of sb./sth.　口头推荐某人/某事
16. through the courtesy of sb.　承蒙某人的介绍

    (by) courtesy of　承蒙某人的允许，承蒙某人的好意
    This program comes by courtesy of a local company.
    本节目由当地的一家公司提供赞助。
17. to avail oneself of an opportunity to do sth.　利用一个机会去做某件事

    You must avail yourself of every opportunity to speak English.
    你应该利用一切机会说英语。
    avail 既可以用作动词，也可以用作名词。例如：
    avail oneself of sth.　利用某事物（如优势、机会等）
    of little/no avail　没有一点儿帮助、用处或效果
    to little/no avail　没有什么成果
18. on the basis of equality and mutual benefit and exchanging what one has for what one needs　在平等互利、互通有无的基础上

1. Multiple choices.

(1) We have been _____ contact with that firm for nearly two years.
   A. on   B. in   C. with   D. for

(2) We believe that some of these items in the list will be _____ interest to you.
   A. at   B. in   C. on   D. of

(3) We have learned that you specialize _____ the export of sowing machines.
   A. in   B. with   C. under   D. beyond

(4) As to our credit rating, you can refer _____ the Bank of China in New York.
   A. over   B. at   C. to   D. with

(5) We are one of the most important exporters of a wide range of Electric Goods _____ Canada.
   A. with   B. over   C. from   D. of

(6) We are expecting your inquiries for all types of electric goods, _____ which we will send you our quotation.
   A. from   B. for   C. with   D. against

(7) Could you please let us have some names and addresses of likely importers _____ good standing from your customers?
   A. of   B. at   C. in   D. for

(8) The signing of the Trade Agreement will be _____ far-reaching significance in the development of our bilateral trade.
   A. for   B. at   C. in   D. of

(9) Your letter of November 8 addressed to our Head Office has been forwarded to us _____ attention and reply.
   A. with   B. in   C. for   D. to

(10) We were very interested to hear that you are looking for a Brazilian distributor _____ your teaching aids.
   A. in   B. for   C. with   D. from

2. Translate the following English sentences into Chinese.

(1) We hope you can kindly provide us with all possible information on your market.

(2) We have pleasure in acknowledging receipt of your sample of the 8th June.

(3) We take the liberty of writing to you with a view to establishing business relations with you.

(4) We notify you with pleasure that we have commenced a business as a commission agent for British goods.

(5) Should you desire, we would be pleased to send you catalogs together with export prices and estimated shipping costs for these items.

(6) We have obtained your name and address from the Korean Chamber of Commerce, who have informed us that you wish to import electric goods manufactured in China.

(7) We were pleased to learn your interest in our products and enclose our conditions of sale and terms of payment.

(8) We have gone into the matter and are prepared to make you a reasonable compensation, but not the amount you claimed.

(9) Should it be necessary, we shall be pleased to take the matter up on your behalf with the shipping company concerned.

(10) We are looking for a manufacturer who could supply us with a wide range of sweater for the teenage market.

3. Fill in the blanks with proper words to make the letter complete.

| specialize | produce | current | establish | hold | favor |
| especially | make | handle | popular | obtain | succeed |

Dear Sir/Madam,

    We _____ your name and address from the Internet. We have learnt that you are interested in wrist watches _____ in China. Now, we are writing you to express our desire to _____ business relations with you.

    Our company was founded in 1952, _____ in the manufacturing of wrist watches. It has now become one of the most _____ watch producers in our country. Model 11-07A is our new product, and it is very _____ all over the world.

    Our product _____ high reputation by the clients in the world wide with the high quality and _____ price.

    In order to acquaint you with various kinds of the product that we are _____, we are airmailing you under separate cover our _____ catalogue for your reference. Please let us know immediately if you are interested in any of them.

    We look forward to your soonest reply.

                                                              Yours faithfully,

4. Read the following letter and answer the questions.

Dear Mr. Sandella,

    After watching your company's demonstration in your website, we find your products have very strong effectiveness and are also human and environmental friendly. Therefore, we are now writing to enquire whether you are willing to establish business relations with us.

    Our company — Hong-yue Chemical Co., Ltd. — has been in the field of making aerosol cans and doing contract filling for nearly 20 years in China. Hong-yue has also been focusing on Original Equipment Manufacturing (OEM) business, manufacturing and developing products such as automobile care product, personal care product, household chemical series, special industrial product, etc. And we can fill the products in your formulation or ours if you need. We have taken the lead in obtaining ISO 9001 certification in China.

Though Hong-yue only focuses on manufacturing and OEM business, we have business partners who focus on marketing and consumer sales networks. We are always looking for new technologies and products to strengthen our product ranges.

I am writing you to get some samples for further applications and trials. Besides, I want to discuss how we can co-operate to introduce your products into the Chinese market. We believe that with your high technologies and our local marketing advantages, we should be the very good business partner to enhance both your and our business.

For your convenience, you may contact us by e-mail: sales@hongyuechemical.com.cn. We look forward to your early reply.

Yours sincerely,

(Signature)

(1) What is the main purpose of this letter?
(2) Why does the writer introduce his own company in details in the second paragraph?
(3) Why is it necessary for the writer to introduce his partners in his own country?
(4) Why does the writer say these encouraging words at the end of the fourth paragraph?
(5) Is it really necessary to give the e-mail address at the end? Why or why not?

Chapter 4

Enquiries and Replies

Your goals for this chapter are to understand:
- ☑ the definitions and classifications of enquiries;
- ☑ the structure of an enquiry letter;
- ☑ how to write a reply to an enquiry;
- ☑ some useful sentence patterns used in enquiries and replies.

4.1 Lead-in

Before you begin your learning of this chapter, please discuss with your partner(s) about the following questions.

(1) When do you usually make an enquiry in your life?

(2) If you want to write an enquiry letter to a firm, what do you usually include in your letter besides your request for information?

(3) Suppose you were asked to write a reply to an inquiry, could you suggest some advice for writing such a letter?

4.2 Basic Information

Enquiries play a very important role in import and export negotiations in international trade because without enquiry, you cannot obtain the information you need and business cannot move smoothly.

An inquiry is a request for some information about a product or service the writer is interested in, such as the quality, the name, the specifications, the packing, the time of shipping, the terms of payment etc. Enquiries can be made either by the exporter or by the importer, however, the importer makes most of the enquiries in practice.

Generally speaking, there are two kinds of enquiries: general enquiry and specific enquiry. A general inquiry is usually made after the establishment of business relations but before a specific inquiry. A specific enquiry is usually made when the writer has a particular product in mind and wants the seller to provide more detailed information or make an offer for this product in question.

When making the enquiry, the buyer should state clearly, concisely and politely the exact requirements, inclusive of prices, product specifications, packing, delivery, terms of payment and so on. Because an enquiry means potential business, it should be treated with caution and care although it has no legal binding effect at this stage yet.

A reply to an enquiry is the response to the enquirer's requirements for some information about a certain product. In such a letter, the writer should give answers to the questions posed in the enquirer's letter, or some additional information which may stimulate the enquirer's desire to place an order. If the requests cannot be met, a detailed explanation or alternative solution should be provided in such a reply.

4.3 Analysis of Model Letters

Read and analyze the following letters. While reading, please try to find answers to the following questions.

(1) In Model Letter 4-1, the writer makes several requests. How does he make these different requests?

(2) Why does the writer of Model Letter 4-2 introduce his client in the third paragraph?

(3) Some say that the third paragraph in Model Letter 4-3 is unnecessary. Do you think so?

(4) As a reply to a specific enquiry, Model Letter 4-4 seems to be too simple. Does this letter provide enough information?

Model Letter 4-1: Making a general enquiry after reading an advertisement

Dear Sirs,

We have read your advertisement in the fifth issue of *Business Weekly* and are glad to know that you are an exporter of silk blouses in China.

We are taking the liberty to ask you to send us some samples of the advertised products. We would also be glad to know some details of your various types, including sizes and colors. Also please send us the quotation based on FOB Ningbo and CIF Athens, as well as the rest of the terms of cooperation with your company. Besides, could you include the discounts you would allow on purchases on over 5000 items?

If terms and delivery date are satisfactory, we would expect to place regular orders with you.

We look forward to hearing from you soon.

Yours sincerely,
Tony Smith

Model Letter 4-2: Making a specific enquiry after a visit

Dear Mr. Lee,

It was very nice to meet you at the Benz Show in Shanghai last November and to visit your factory afterwards.

We have now contacted our clients and are requested to provide a sample and price for your product No. DKL9T. Please quote us your best possible price on an FOB basis at the earliest date and supply all other necessary information for the product.

Our client is a regular buyer of this particular product. They are eager to find a long-term supplier who can provide the best quality at the best possible price.

We look forward to your prompt reply.

Yours faithfully,
Tom Johns

Model Letter 4-3: A reply to a general enquiry

Dear Mr. Green,

We welcome your enquiry of 28th April and thank you for your interest in our commodities.

We are enclosing our illustrated catalogue and a price list with the details you asked for, together with the sample book you want under separate cover. If you need any further information, please let us know.

You will agree that our products and prices could appeal to the most critical buyer. And we also allow a proper discount according to the quantity ordered.

Thank you again for your interest in our products. We are looking forward to the pleasure of receiving an order from you.

Yours sincerely,
Edward Zhou
Export Manager

Model Letter 4-4: A reply to a specific enquiry

Dear Mr. Yap,

Many thanks for your enquiry of September 20 and your interest in our product (Item No.24-7869).

The details for this product are as follows:
(1) FOB Los Angeles;
(2) Price: USD10.80/pc;
(3) Minimum Order: 2,000 pcs;
(4) Packing: Packed in kraft paper and water-proof paper, 10 pcs in a cardboard box;
(5) Delivery Time: 30 days after the receipt of your L/C.

We are a professional bamboo products manufacturer with 14 years' experience in China, offering over 1,500 various kinds of bamboo products, with monthly output up to 5 millions pcs. We are the best manufacturer that you can trust in China. The item you are enquiring about sells very well in North America and European markets. We believe it will also become a best seller in your country too.

If you need any other information not mentioned therein, please let us know.

We look forward to receiving your orders.

Yours sincerely,
Peter Jones

4.4 Writing Guidelines

Model Letter 4-1 and 4-2 are enquiries, while 4-3 and 4-4 are replies. By analyzing the enquiries, we can see that an enquiry letter, whether general or specific, usually consists of the following parts.

(1) Mentioning how you obtained your potential supplier's name and address, or referring to a meeting or an exchange of information before.

(2) Introducing your company briefly and showing your market conditions if this is your first time to contact the recipient of your letter.

(3) Giving causes for the enquiry e.g. being interested in the addressee's products, service, or programs, etc.

(4) Stating clearly your requirements. If it is a general enquiry, ask for a catalogue or price list etc. If it is a specific enquiry, you should require some concrete information like prices, discounts, delivery time and other concerns.

(5) Asking for a quick and favourable reply in the end.

When giving responses to enquiries, you should remember to include the following points.

(1) Acknowledging receipt of the enquiry and expressing thankfulness for the enquirer's interest in your products.

(2) Giving replies to the requirements. If the answer is a negative one, you should tell the reason clearly for your disappointing answer.

(3) Introducing your own products to the enquirer correctly, stressing the characteristics and advantages of your commodities.

(4) Including all the necessary information which the enquirer asks for, especially the price list, catalogue and samples etc..

(5) Expressing your hope that an order may be placed or more enquiries may follow.

4.5 More Sample Letters

The following samples may differ from the above models in one way or another. Read them to see how each letter is structured and worded to achieve its respective communicative purpose.

Sample Letter 4-1: Importer's informal enquiry about tape-recorder

In the following letter, the use of a list of questions makes the enquiry clear and simple. It can also help the receiver of this letter to give a comprehensive reply.

Dear Sir,

I learned about your products through the Advertisement in *China Daily*. We are interested in your portable tape-recorder. Please answer the following questions:
1. How much would it cost for 800 units?
2. How long does the guarantee last?
3. How soon could you deliver?
4. Could you give us a discount? If so, how much?
5. What colors are available?
6. Could you give me your e-mail address?

We are waiting for your earliest reply.

Sincerely yours,

Sample Letter 4-2: A simple specific enquiry

This is an enquiry which initiates a business relationship, that's why source of information, cause for the enquiry are provided. The letter is neat and to the point.

Dear Mr. Green,

We learned from the Commercial Counselor's Office of the Embassy in the UK that you are a leading manufacturer of printers.

We are interested in your printers, particularly Type E-315, for use in offices and shall be glad if you will send us a copy of your illustrated catalogue and current price list.

Yours sincerely,
Michel Lee

Sample Letter 4-3: Giving a definite reply to an enquiry

This letter begins with an emphatic and definite "Yes, we can", which leaves a deep impression on the reader. It is a detailed reply because, besides the messages in the letter, more information can be found in the enclosure.

Dear Jones,

Subject: Activated Carbon for Vapor Application

Yes, we can. We do supply pelleted and granular activated carbon suitable for vapor phase applications.

We are one of the largest manufacturers of activated carbon in China. We are making a great variety of activated carbon, ranging from vapor phase applications to water phase applications. Enclosed is a catalogue showing all our standard products. However, we also design and manufacture goods to the specifications of our customers.

We believe one of our products may particularly suit your application and have enclosed a technical data sheet for your evaluation. We can send a sample for testing.

We look forward to a close cooperation with you.

Yours sincerely,

Enclosure: Two copies of catalogue
           Technical data sheet

Sample Letter 4-4: Giving a reply with further promotion

    The writer of this letter avails himself of this enquiry received to make a sales promotion of a new product after giving the expected answer.

Dear Sirs,

We thank you for your enquiry of 18th June, and have pleasure in enclosing the requested details of our nylon-coated metal garden furniture.

We should like to draw your attention to the separate brochure on our recently launched range of reproduction Victorian garden furniture in cast aluminum alloy. This range is on a special introductory offer, the terms of which are set out at the end of the brochure.

If you wish to take advantage of this offer, please use the enclosed order form. We look forward to hearing from you and to receiving your orders.

Yours faithfully,

Encl: An order form

Sample Letter 4-5: Offering a substitute

    The writer of this letter, unable to provide the mountain bicycle asked for, recommends a new model so that this opportunity can be seized.

Dear Mrs. Brown,

Thank you for asking about our Silver Streak mountain bicycles. We regret to tell you that this model is temporarily out of stock because of the Christmas rush, but we could deliver one to you by the end of May.

We also have other models that could be delivered immediately. The ZX-05 model, for instance, is becoming one of our most popular bicycles because it is light in weight (only 20 pounds) but very strong. The cost is a little more than the Silver Streak, but if you would like to receive Christmas delivery of this or any other bicycle in the enclosed brochure, please inform us immediately.

In the meantime, we send you our best wishes for a happy Christmas! Looking forward to your prompt reply.

Sincerely yours,
Redding Scanlon

4.6 More Useful Sentences

1. Acknowledging Receipt of an Enquiry
- Your letter enquiring for our furniture was brought to our attention.
- We thank you for your letter of May 20 and are pleased to inform you that …
- We take pleasure in acknowledging your letter of October 8, enquiring for …
- We welcome your enquiry of May 26 and thank you for your interest in our products.
- Thank you for your fax dated March 8th requesting information about our prices for …

2. Giving Reasons for Enquiries
- We have received a number of enquiries for portable electronic games, which we think will have great demand here.
- We are interested in your men's shirts displayed in your showroom.
- Your products are of great interest to one of our clients in Tianjin, who wishes to have your quotations for the items specified below.
- We are a large dealer in textiles and believe there is a promising market in our area for moderately-priced goods of this kind.
- Having been in this line for more than 40 years, we have a high reputation in this area and have an edge in marketing these products in our country.
- Your advertisement in this month's issue of *China Foreign Trade* interests us, and we should like to receive full details of your commodities.

3. Making Enquiries or Requests
- We would be much obliged if you could send us a complete set of leaflets so as to give us a general idea of the export items you handle.
- Please advise if you are able to offer this product and include lead time, packaging and price FOB China port and CIF Chicago.
- It would be quite helpful if you could supply us with your newly-developed products.
- We would like to have a booklet which includes your latest designs for building up the equipment.
- We are thinking of getting a supply of quilts. Please send us your best offer by fax indicating origin and packing.
- We have pleasure in enclosing our enquiry No. 0086, against which you are requested to make us an offer on FOB basis.
- We should appreciate further information with regard to the infant suits advertised by you in *Beijing Weekly*.

4. Giving Replies
- We are appreciative of your effort to put our new products on your market and hope the information enclosed herewith will be of great help to you.
- In compliance with the request in your letter, we inform you that we have long-term established relations with major dealers in the line of printing.

- We are now sending you a quotation sheet for your consideration. Please be informed that, on account of the fluctuations of foreign exchange, the quotation is subject to change without previous notice.
- Should your prices be found competitive and delivery date acceptable, we intend to place a large order with you.
- We are sorry that we have run out of raw material for the product and cannot supply until early next year.
- Unfortunately we are not in a position to make delivery within 2 months from receipt of your order, owing to a heavy demand for the article from Canada.
- We regret to inform you that we are not in a position to cover your need for the said goods. Once our supplies are replenished, we shall be only too pleased to revert to this matter.
- As the goods of your specifications are in short supply, we intend to furnish you with our T-315 as a substitute, which is of good quality and very close to your specifications but will be offered at a more favorable price.

5. Expressing Expectations and Friendly Close
- We look forward to concluding the deal with you.
- Please get back to us at your earliest convenience.
- May we expect a trial order from you while prices are greatly in your favor.
- We are ready to provide any further information or samples as requested and look forward to your favorable reply.
- Thank you for your cooperation in this matter.
- I should like to express my appreciation for your assistance.
- Please feel free to contact us if you have any questions.

4.7 Writing Tips

Here are some tips suggested by an expert in Business English. Discuss with your partner(s) to see whether they are all reasonable. If you find any of them improper, pick it/them out and give your reasons.

(1) Before settling down to writing an enquiry, you should be clear what you want to achieve with this letter. It is advisable to make a list of information you want to ask for.

(2) In order to obtain the needed information, enquiries should be tailored to enable the receiver to answer the questions completely, clearly and concisely. Any material which does not serve this purpose should be excluded.

(3) Remember to make your enquiry reasonable. In an enquiry letter, you should avoid asking questions that pertain to confidential matters. If asking for free materials or information, you should use good judgment in the amount you request.

(4) Sometimes the justifications for your enquiry should be given so that your partner will be glad to give you a prompt reply.

While giving replies, you should take care of the following points.

(1) Give your reply to the enquiry promptly. An enquiry means a golden opportunity to the

recipient's company. In order to seize the opportunity, the writer should give the reply, if possible, within 48 hours.

(2) A reply should be polite. In order to create goodwill so that a long-term business relationship may be established and sustained, the replier ought to give the answers courteously.

(3) A reply should also be complete. No important information should be missed, otherwise, the receiver may be disappointed so as to fail to make prompt and appropriate decision.

(4) No matter whether the enquiry is from a regular customer or a new one, the writer should express how much he appreciates it and expects a long-lasting and friendly business relationship.

(5) Sometimes after giving the required answer, you may avail yourself of the opportunity to offer some more information which may be interesting to your recipient so that another transaction may be expected.

Notes and Explanations

1. in practice   实际上，事实上
2. have no legal binding effect   没有法律上的约束力
3. take the liberty to do sth.   冒昧地做某事

   I have to take the liberty to write to you to ask for a short leave of two days.
   我不得不写信给您，要求请假两天。
   类似的说法还有: take the liberty of doing sth.（冒昧地做某事）。
   I took the liberty of borrowing your dictionary while you were absent.
   你不在时我冒昧借用了你的词典。

4. best price   最低价

   表示"最低价"的词组还有 the lowest price, the most favorable price, the most competitive price, the bottom price, the lowest price, the rock-bottom price, the minimum price 等。

5. to appeal to the most critical buyer   对最挑剔的买家都具有吸引力

   appeal to 的意思很丰富，除表示"对……有吸引力"外，还可以表示以下意义。

   (1) 求助于，诉诸于
   They appealed to arms to settle the disturbance in the city.
   他们诉诸武力来解决这个城市的动乱。

   (2) 向……提出恳求
   The prisoner appealed to the judge for mercy.
   罪犯向法官恳求宽大处理。

   (3) 上诉
   He appealed to the Supreme Court.
   他向最高法院提出上诉。

6. minimum order   最少起订量，最低起订量
7. a best seller   畅销货
8. pelleted and granular activated carbon   颗粒状的活性炭
9. to manufacture goods to the specifications of our customers   按照我们客户所要求的规格制造产品
10. out of stock   已脱销，已没有现货

    in stock   有存货，有现货

to supply from stock 现货供应

11. be in this line 从事这一行业
    If you are not in this line, please transfer our letter to any company working in this field.
    假如你们不从事这一行业，请将我们的信件转交给从事该行业的任何一家公司。

12. to have an edge in marketing 在营销方面有优势
    edge 在这里的意思是"优势"，例如：
    A has the edge over/on B. 甲比乙略胜一筹。

13. lead time 产品设计与实际生产之间相隔的时间，订货至交货之间的时间间隔

14. against
    在商务英语中，against 的用法比较复杂，必须根据语境做出判断。如在"you are requested to make an offer against our enquiry"中，against 的意思是"针对"，即"要求你们针对我们的询盘给出报价"。

15. in compliance with 听从，依从，按照
    She gave up the idea in compliance with her parents' desire.
    她依从父母的愿望放弃了自己的想法。
    in full compliance with 完全按照

16. be subject to change without previous notice 在事先没有通知的情况下随时做出改变

17. be in a position to do 能够做某事，有能力做某事
    We are sorry to say we are not in a position to meet your requirements.
    很抱歉，我们不能满足你们的要求。

Exercises

1. Fill in the blanks with appropriate prepositions.

(1) We are very interested _____ working _____ you on this project.
(2) We would be interested in receiving your enquiry _____ all types of electric goods.
(3) We will notify you _____ our areas of interest.
(4) Enclosed _____ your interest is our new catalogue and price-list.
(5) We were pleased to receive your enquiry _____ 15th May, in which you asked us to send details of our line of men's shoes.
(6) We feel that we have the expertise to supply you _____ products _____ which you will certainly receive recognition.
(7) From the price list you will see that the prices we quote _____ FOB Tokyo basis are competitive _____ similar recorders from other sources.
(8) The lines you showed _____ teenagers, the "Fairy" dresses & trouser suits, would be most suitable _____ our market.
(9) We would appreciate it if you could forward us the samples and price-list _____ your newly-developed camera.
(10) We are a large chain of retailers and are looking for a manufacturer who could supply us with a wide range of sweater _____ the teenage market.

2. The following two letters have similar communicative purposes. Compare them to see which is better, and then tell the reasons.

Mr. Smith,

We have seen your advertisement for Men's coat and synthetic fiber goods in the latest issue of *American Trade Directory*. In reply we are writing you for some additional information.

We want to know your terms of payments and discounts. It is best if you can send us a sample for each category, with the lowest quotations, together with an illustrated catalogue.

If the information we receive is favorable to our needs, we will inspect the property.

Give us your soonest reply.

Sincerely yours,
Jones Smith

Dear Mr. Smith,

We are very interested in the coats advertised in the latest issue of *American Trade Directory*, so will you kindly send us as soon as possible your terms of payment and discounts. We would appreciate it very much if you could send us your current price list for Men's coat, with the lowest quotations, together with an illustrated catalogue.

If we feel that your information is satisfactory, we may place a trial order.

Your early reply will be appreciated.

Yours faithfully,
Jones Smith

3. Complete the following sentence according to the Chinese given.

(1) _____ （承蒙中国商会的关照）, we have learned that you specialize in the export of sowing machines.

(2) We will _____ （给你们特殊的折扣）on orders over US$100, 000 net value.

(3) If terms and delivery date are satisfactory, we would expect to _____ _____ （向你们尝试订货）.

(4) We have been trying to find suppliers of tax disc holders in China but _____ （毫无结果）.

(5) From these you will see that we can offer a wide range of carefully designed high-quality stereo equipment, _____ （用上等配件制成）.

(6) It would be kind of you to send us a copy of brochure, _____ （外加销售条件）, prior to October 20.

(7) We are a large dealer in toys and wish to _____ （扩大我们的业务范围）with more fashionable plush toys.

(8) Please quote us for the supply of the items listed on the estimate sheet enclosed, giving you the _____ （尽可能最优惠的上海离岸价）.

(9) We believe there is a _____ （有前景的市场）in our area for moderately priced goods of the kind mentioned.

(10) We may now prefer to buy from your company because we understand that you are able to supply larger quantities _____ （以更加诱人的价格）.

4. Write a reply to the following enquiry letter.

Dear Mr. Zhao,

　　Thank you for your latest catalogue, which we received yesterday.

　　We are interested in your ABD series, especially ABD-0002, ABD-0098 and ABD-0158. We would be obliged if you could send us a quotation per kilogram on FOB Shanghai basis, all including a 3% commission. It would also be appreciated if you would forward us your price-list.

　　Meanwhile, we would like to have some samples of the above items for our customers to test before we could place a trial order. If the lab tests go well, and your prices are competitive, we would certainly be pleased to place a substantial order.

　　We look forward to hearing from you soon.

　　　　　　　　　　　　　　　　　　　　　　　　　　　　　　　　　　Yours truly,
　　　　　　　　　　　　　　　　　　　　　　　　　　　　　　　　　　Jack Brown

Chapter 5

Quotations and Offers

Your goals for this chapter are to understand:
☑ the basic knowledge about quotations and offers;
☑ how to write quotation letters and offer letters;
☑ some tips for writing counter-offer letters;
☑ some useful expressions used in quotation letters and offer letters.

5.1 Lead-in

Before you begin your learning of this chapter, please discuss with your partner(s) about the following questions.
(1) Have you got any experiences in bargaining with a seller or a buyer?
(2) How do you usually bargain with the seller before you decide to buy something?
(3) What strategies do you usually apply when you are dissatisfied with a quotation or reply received?

5.2 Basic Information

A quotation is a promise to supply goods or service on the terms stated. A quotation letter is a response to an inquiry about prices, range and availability of goods. In a quotation letter, the description of the goods, prices, terms of payment and delivery terms should be clearly stated. Discounts should be included if applicable. If there is a limiting period, it should be indicated.

An offer is made when a seller promises to sell goods at a stated price within a stated period of time. It is usually a reply made by a seller to the enquiry by a buyer. It not only quotes the prices for products the exporter wants to sell, but also makes clear all the necessary terms of sales for the buyer's consideration and acceptance. An offer is unchangeable if the offeree accepts it.

Though used interchangeably, quotations and offers are not the same. A quotation is not an offer in the legal sense, because the seller can withdraw it. When an importer asks for a quotation, he or she is under no obligation to buy the goods under quotation. When a supplier quotes, the quote becomes a firm offer subject to the prospective buyer's acceptance.

A firm offer is also called an offer with engagement. It is usually made when the exporter promises to sell goods at a stated price within a stated period of time known as validity period. Once a firm offer is made, it cannot be withdrawn within the valid period. A firm offer must satisfy the following requisite conditions.

(1) It must be sent to one or more than one offeree.
(2) It expresses the wish to sign a contract.
(3) Its contents must be definite, complete, clear and final.
(4) It takes effect only after the offer reaches the offeree.

A non-firm offer is sometimes called offer without engagement, which is usually indicated by means of sending catalogues, price-lists, proforma invoices and quotation. It has no binding force upon the offeror or offeree. In other words, the company withholds the right to revise or withdraw the offer at any time.

In the course of business negotiation, the buyer may find some terms or conditions in the offer unacceptable, and then he will state his or her own opinion to renew the received offer. This opinion is called a counter-offer. A counter-offer is virtually a partial rejection of the original offer and also a counter-proposal by the buyer who may amend the price, payment or shipment when they are not acceptable. Such amendments, no matter how slight, signify that the deal is negotiable on the renewed basis. There are often several rounds of counter-counter offers before both parties come to terms.

Acceptance is the absolutely necessary step for successful business conclusion and contract. It indicates that the offeree absolutely accepts all points offered by the offerer within the validity time when receiving the offer or counter-offer. It is an intention of agreement by the offeree to place an order or sign a contract with the offerer.

5.3 Analysis of Model Letters

Read the following letters. While reading, please try to find answers to the following questions.
(1) Model Letter 5-1 aims to ask for information, why does the writer begin the letter with an introduction about their enlargement of their car spares department?
(2) What is the advantage of listing the quotations with numbers?
(3) What strategies have been applied in Model Letter 5-3?
(4) Why is the acceptance letter so simple?

Model Letter 5-1: An enquiry for a quotation

Dear Mr. Brown,

We are glad to inform you that we have now enlarged our car spares department and are considering the addition of new lines to our stock.

Your tyres are solid and would fit in well. Would you please send a complete range of catalogues and samples which are in production? We wish to know the full details of your products, prices and other terms and would like to know whether you can supply from stock.

We look forward to your early reply.

Yours sincerely,

Model Letter 5-2: Making a firm offer

Dear Mr. Brown,

Subject: Forever Brand Bicycles

Thank you for your letter of 12 December, 2011, inquiring about our Forever Brand Bicycles.

We are exporting bicycles of many makes, among which the Forever Brand is the most famous. Our products are in great demand and enjoy high sales due to their light weight, good quality and reasonable price.

As requested, we are quoting as below:

(1) 40″ Men's Style	@	USD27/unit	
(2) 40″ Women's Style	@	USD29/unit	
(3) 45″ Men's Style	@	USD35/unit	
(4) 45″ Women's Style	@	USD36/unit	
Payment		confirmed, irrevocable sight L/C	
Shipment		within two weeks of receiving the L/C	

The above prices are understood to be on CIF Karachi basis net. Please note that we do not allow any commission, but a discount of 3% will be granted if the quantity for each specification is more than 1,000 units.

The above offer is firm, subject to your reply reaching us by 20 December, 2011.

We look forward to receiving your order.

Yours sincerely,
Wang Hao
Sales Manager

Model Letter 5-3: Making a counter-offer

Dear Sirs,

Thank you for your letter of 11th October, 2011 and the samples of cotton underwear you very kindly sent us.

We appreciate the good quality of these garments, but unfortunately your prices appear to be on the high side even for garments of this quality. To accept the prices you've quoted would leave us with only a small profit on our sales since this is an area in which the principal demand is for articles in the medium price range. We like the quality of your goods and also the way in which you have handled our enquiry and would welcome the opportunity to do business with you.

May we suggest that you could perhaps make some allowance, say, 5%, on your quoted prices, which would help us to introduce your goods to our customers? If you cannot do so, then we have regretfully to decline your offer.

Waiting for your favourable reply.

Yours faithfully,

Model Letter 5-4: Importer accepting an offer

Dear Sirs,

With reference to your letter of May 10, 2011, we are pleased to accept your offer of 1,000 pcs of Rattan Table as per your Offer Sheet No. B70/02.

Please go ahead and apply for your Export License. As soon as we are informed of the number of the Export License we will establish the L/C immediately.

Best wishes for good co-operation.

Sincerely yours,

5.4 Writing Guidelines

The first model letter is actually an enquiry, so it has the common features which enquiry letters have.

The second model letter is a reply, in which the writer gives the expected information. An offer or quotation letter usually includes the following parts.

(1) Acknowledging the related enquiry or cause for the quotation or offer.

(2) Giving the quotation or offer, in which the name of commodities, quality, quantity, and specifications, prices, terms of payment etc. are introduced. If it is a non-firm offer, the validity of the offer may be mentioned here.

(3) Providing further information to encourage an early order. This part is optional but most of the time it is included.

(4) Expressing an expectation for acceptance or making a friendly close.

Generally speaking, a counter-offer is more difficult to write because the writer must try to keep a balance between making a rejection and maintaining a friendly relationship. A counter-offer letter should include the following essential parts.

(1) Thanking the seller for the offer received.

(2) Expressing regret at inability to accept the offer and stating convincing reasons.

(3) Putting forward new proposals or a counter-offer if appropriate in the circumstances.

(4) Expressing hopes for mutually beneficial business cooperation, or wishing the reader to accept writer's counter-offer, or urging the reader to accept early.

5.5 More Sample Letters

The following letters comply basically with the above writing guidelines, but they are different from the models in 5.3 in one way or another. Read them to see how each letter is structured and worded to achieve its respective communicative purpose.

Sample Letter 5-1: Exporter giving a quotation

Besides giving the required information, i.e. the catalogue and quotation sheet, the writer of the following letter gives some additional introductions about his products — the popularity of their products in some countries and their extensive connections with some leading suppliers for the purpose of sales promotion.

Dear Sirs,

We are in receipt of your letter of August 5, 2011, and we are willing to enter into direct business relations with you on the basis of equality and mutual benefit.

As requested, we are enclosing our latest illustrated catalogue and quotation sheet covering all our products available for export, subject to our final confirmation.

Having specialized in spices business for about 20 years, we are well connected with the leading suppliers in China and our commodities are very marketable in America, Canada, Japan, Korea and most of the European countries.

Chapter 5 Quotations and Offers

Now we are desirous of opening up the market in your country. If you are interested in any of our items, you may contact us directly. We can assure you of our most favorable prices and the finest quality.

It will be highly appreciated if you can reply us at your earliest convenience.

Yours sincerely,

Sample Letter 5-2: A detailed quotation to an enquirer

The following letter uses very simple language to give the quotation. The listing of the important information is very effective.

Dear Stella,

Please note that the following prices are quoted excluding your commission. Please check with your buyer if those prices are workable or not. Thank you.

Item No.: SP001
Fabric 100% Nylon
Construction: 134 x 84/70D x 160D
Width: 59/60″
Finished : Teflon (for kids)
Price : FOB Shanghai USD1.32/M
Remark: This price is quoted in using the "DUPONT" Teflon, so this quality can be with the "Dupont" Hang Tag.
Capacity for one 40 feet container: 130,000 M
Delivery: 21 days after receipt of L/C and upon lab-dips confirmation

Thank you for your kind attention and awaiting your further instruction.

Best regards,
Allen Qian

Sample Letter 5-3: Seller making a voluntary offer

This letter is a combination of congratulation and introduction of writer's own products. The writer approaches the reader voluntarily when he hears the opening of the reader's new business. His voluntary offer will be appreciated.

Dear Sirs,

We learnt that you opened a store for the sale of silk neckties and we wish you a success.

We are taking the liberty of sending you our quotation for high-quality silk neckties. Our company is specializing in the production of silk neckties, and the products have gained great reputation in the market. Since it is the first transaction with you, we decide, as an exception, to cut the price by 2%. We assure you that the goods we are offering are an excellent value for money.

We hope to do business with you soon. We are sure you will be satisfied with our products and services.

We are looking forward to your favorable reply with keen interest.

Yours sincerely,
Miranda
Sales manager

Sample Letter 5-4: A counter-offer for lower prices

The following letter is a reply to an offer received. The writer does not state his demand directly in this letter, but implies that if he can receive lowered prices, he will begin business at once and will place repeat orders.

Dear Mr. Zhang,

It is long since we received your last letter. I requested for some discount in your prices, but you increased them. Why?

Please give me the last price so that I can start business with you. It is not that I need your goods just for one time. I am a regular customer who can buy in quantity and frequently. So please quote your best and last price.

Best regards,
(Signature)
General Manager

Sample Letter 5-5: Exporter accepting a counter-offer

This is a favorable reply to a counter-offer. Although we cannot find any polite words in the letter, the concession which the writer has made shows his sincerity in the business.

Gentlemen,

We have given your letter of Jan 30th very careful consideration.

As we have done business with each other so pleasantly for many years, we should like to comply with your request for lower prices and have agreed to reduce prices by 8.5% without lowering our standards of quality.

We look forward to your early order.

Sincerely yours,

Sample Letter 5-6: Seller rejecting a counter-offer

The following letter rejects a counter-offer received, but an explanation for the rejection is given, so no misunderstanding may arise. The writer makes a slight concession at the end to call for a larger order, which may be seen as a promotion strategy.

Dear Sirs,

We thank you for your letter of March 24. Your comments on our offer of socks have had our close attention.

Although we are keen to meet your requirements, we very much regret that we are unable to comply with your request to reduce the price as our prices are closely calculated. Even if there is a slight difference between our prices and those of our other suppliers, you will find it profitable to buy from us because the quality of our products is superior to that of other foreign makers available in your district.

However, we are desirous to develop business with you. In order to help you to push the sale of our products, we are prepared to allow you a 3% discount provided your order calls for a minimum quantity of 3,000 pairs.

If the proposal is acceptable to you, please let us have your order at an early date.

Yours faithfully,
Tom Brown

5.6 More Useful Sentences

1. Giving a Quotation or an Offer
- We usually quote on the basis of CIF/CFR/FOB terms without commission.
- Our offer is CIF New York with a commission of five percent for you.
- In reply, we are sending you a firm offer, subject to your reply reaching us before February 26, 2011.
- As requested, we take pleasure in offering you 300 dozen deerskin handbags.
- We are prepared to offer 100 metric tons of groundnuts at the market price for immediate shipment.
- Referring to your e-mail of 10 October, 2011 in which you inquired for shirts, we have pleasure in giving you an offer as follows.

2. Giving a Positive Response
- We put forward for your consideration an offer for our new products, and hope you will take advantage of this opportunity.
- We appreciate your enquiry of September 15, against which we have just sent you the following offer.
- We can allow a 2% discount on all orders of US$6,000 in value and over, and a 3% on orders exceeding US$20,000.
- We may consider allowing you a 3% commission on condition that your minimum quantity for the first order reaches 300 dozens.
- We are interested in making you an offer on our hand-made carpets, which are well received on the overseas market.
- Upon checking your offer, we would like to say that your price seems a little higher than we had expected.
- However, in view of the long connection between us in this line of business, we have decided to reduce the price by 5%, which is the furthest we can go to help you.
- After going carefully into this transaction, though your price is on the high side, we accept it exceptionally with the view of expanding our business in future.

3. Giving a Negative Response
- Our marketing research reveals that the prices you quoted appear to be on the high side even for tools of your quality.
- We do not deny that the quality of your TV sets is slightly better than that of other brands, but the difference in price should, in no case, be so big.
- Much as we would like to cooperate with you in expanding sales, we very much regret that we just cannot see our way clear to entertain your counter-offer.
- After careful thought, we must say frankly that our price is moderately fixed and we are not in a position to grant the reduction you asked for.
- Unfortunately we are not in a position to accept your offer since another supplier in your market offered us the similar article at a price 3% lower.

- In reply, we very much regret to state that our users here find your price too high and out of line with the prevailing market level. Should you be prepared to reduce your limit by, say 68%, we might come to terms.
- It is to our regret that we cannot make use of your kind offer at present as similar but well-established products of the same quality are available at much lower prices.
- Your request for a reduction in price has been noted. However, we are of the opinion that if you could increase your order to 50,000 pieces we would allow a 5% discount.
- We must point out that the falling market here will leave us little or no margin of profit. We must ask you for a better price in respect of future supplies.

4. Giving New Proposals or Requests
- The above prices are understood to be on CIF Karachi basis. Discount of 5% may be allowed if the quantity for each specification is more than 1,000 sets.
- We hope that you will quote us your rock-bottom price, otherwise we can have no alternative but to place our orders elsewhere.
- We would very much like to place further orders with you if you could bring down your prices at least by 15%. Otherwise we can only switch our requirements to other suppliers.
- To have this business concluded, I'm afraid you need to lower your price at least by 10 percent.
- We have to ask you to consider if you can make a reduction, say 5%, in your price.
- May we suggest that you perhaps make some allowance, say, two percent off your quoted prices?
- As our clients urgently need the goods, may we request you to shift your delivery time from "in May" to "in March"?
- We are prepared to accept your offer provided that you can meet our usual requirement on packing/payment/shipment as given below.

5. Persuasive Expressions
- We also point out that very good quality Canned Mushrooms is available in our market from several European manufacturers and their prices are about 5%–10% lower than yours.
- After you have examined them you can know the goods are both excellent in quality and very reasonable in price.
- In order to promote our business, please accept the above terms.
- We are considering placing even larger orders if you can grant us 10% discount.
- In view of our long term business relations, we suggest you accept our counter-offer.
- Please kindly trust us that our price is quite realistic. In fact, we have received lots of orders from various sources at our level.

5.7 Writing Tips

Some English majors have proposed the following points to note in writing letters for the establishment of a business relationship. Read the following list quickly and then discuss with your partner whether they are appropriate and try to add some more ideas to the list.

When writing a letter to make an offer, you should bear the following points in mind.

(1) Expressing your thanks for your counterpart's interest in your products if the buyer previously sends a letter of enquiry.

(2) Showing clearly your willingness to do business with the offeree according to terms stated, and emphasizing the special advantages of his products so that the reader may be more interested in the products or service.

(3) Stating the transaction terms as clearly and completely as possible so as to avoid the misunderstanding resulting from ambiguity.

(4) Adding the term of validity to the offer which can assure the offeree of your sincerity to do business with them, but if the price fluctuates frequently and dramatically you can choose to make a non-firm offer.

(5) Expressing your expectation to get the offeree's favorable reply.

(6) In a quotation letter or offer letter, the description of the goods, prices, terms of payment and delivery-terms should be explicitly and carefully stated and expressed so as to avoid ambiguity or misunderstanding.

While writing counter-offer letter, the writer must comply with the following principles.

(1) Thanking the seller for his offer and expressing regret at inability to accept.

(2) Explaining the reasons for his rejection politely and convincingly.

(3) Suggesting other opportunities to do business together clearly and definitely. His statements should not be ambiguous or confusing.

Notes and Explanations

1. offer *n.& v.* 报盘

    to make（或 give）an offer for/on/of 为……报价

    Please make us an offer CIF London for 20 metric tons of Brown Cashmere.

    请按伦敦到岸价报给我方 20 吨棕色山羊绒的价格。

    We confirm your offer of 2,000 kilos Black Tea.

    我方收到并接受你方 2 000 公斤红茶的报盘。

2. counter offer *n.& v.* 还盘，还价（counter offer 也可以写作 counteroffer 或 counter-offer）

    The price you counter-offered is not in line with the prevailing market.

    你方还盘价格与市场通行价格不符。

    We are sorry to tell you that we can not accept your counter-offer.

    非常抱歉地告诉贵方，我方不能接受你方还价。

3. joint venture company 合资企业

    joint 的其他一些用法还有：joint capital（合资），joint stock（合资，合股），equity joint venture（合资经营）。

    其他一些有关企业的说法有：cooperative venture（合作经营），wholly foreign venture（外商独资企业）。

4. effect *v.* 完成，实现

    to effect shipment 装船

    to effect payment 付款，支付

    to effect insurance 投保

    effect 也可以用作名词，表示"效果，影响"，例如：

to take effect from/on 自（在）……时开始生效
to come into effect from ... 自……时开始生效
The new regulation will take effect from its date of promulgation.
此新规章自公布日起开始生效。

5. be subject to 以……为条件的，以……为前提
   This offer is subject to our final confirmation.
   这一报盘只有经我方最后确认才能生效。
   Subject to your shipment in May, we will order 10,000 tons.
   如果你方能 5 月份装运，我们将订购 10 000 吨。

6. in favor of …/in sb.'s favor 以……为受益人
   We have made arrangements with Bank of Japan, Tokyo, to open a credit in your favor.
   我们已经安排由东京日本银行开立以你方为受益人的信用证。

7. acknowledge v. 承认，告知收到
   It is universally acknowledged that the quality of our goods is of the best quality.
   大家一致公认我方产品的质量是最好的。
   We acknowledge the receipt of your letter dated October 20.
   我们收到了你方 10 月 20 日的来信。
   acknowledge A as B 承认 A 为 B
   Stephen acknowledged Henry as his heir.
   斯蒂芬接受亨利为他的继承人。

8. to express regret at (for, over) 对……表示遗憾，为……表示抱歉
   to hear with regret of (that) 听到……后觉得惋惜

9. make a concession 做出让步
   We will make some concession in price.
   我们将在价格上做些让步。
   In order to conclude the business, how about meeting each other half-way and each make a concession?
   为了做成这笔交易,我们双方都做些让步怎么样？

10. on condition that 假如，在……条件下
    I will lend you the money on condition that you pay it back in one month.
    假如你在一个月内能还我钱，我就借给你。

11. see one's way to do sth. 有可能做某事
    I hope you can see your way to effect the payment at once.
    我希望你能设法立刻把款给付了。

12. out of line 不守常规，越轨的，不适宜的
    I must say your behavior at the meeting was a bit out of line.
    老实说，你在会上的举止有点儿不恰当。
    Prices and wages were badly out of line at that time.
    那时候，物价与工资严重不协调。

1. Complete the following sentences according to the Chinese given

   (1) We would like to take this opportunity to _____ （与你们做成几

笔生意）．

(2) We will settle the payment in accordance with the _____（国际惯例）．

(3) The corporation declined to state its revenues or otherwise explain _____（经营范围）．

(4) Enclosed is our latest _____（带插图的目录）．

(5) Besides, we will send you a sample product _____（另函邮寄）．

(6) Our newly developed products are _____（质量上乘，价格合理）．

(7) We will _____（立即装运）effect shipment without delay upon receipt of the covering L/C.

(8) The commodities you have ordered can be provided _____（现货）．

(9) On receiving our _____（付款通知）notice of payment, please kindly send a draft payable in our city as soon as possible.

(10) As our clients are now asking us for these goods, we would be grateful if you could replace the damaged merchandise _____（由你们负担费用）．

2. Read the following letter and answer the questions.

Dear Mr. Kny,

　　I am glad to hear from you, and much concerned about your requirement in the letter.

　　Regarding our last quotation, you feel that the price is too high for you to accept. I do think it is the common issue we face currently. As you know, the price for raw material has gone up beyond our prediction. We are proceeding to improve craft to lower the cost effectively.

　　The market goes big for these products day by day. Most clients have urged us to complete their orders in spite of the high price. They all agree that these products are of most potential high profits in the near future.

　　Provided we offer you a 15% discount, could you double your volume? If not, I would like to kick off 10% price to start an initial friendly cooperation with you.

　　Your further comment is highly appreciated.

　　　　　　　　　　　　　　　　　　　　　　　　　　　　　　　　　　Yours truly,
　　　　　　　　　　　　　　　　　　　　　　　　　　　　　　　　　　William Zhang

---

(1) Why is the writer concerned about the requirement he has received?

(2) Does the writer of the above letter admit that his price is high? How have you got to know it?

(3) How does the writer explain for the high price of his product?

(4) Why does the writer mention other clients' requirements for early execution of their orders in the third paragraph?

(5) Why does the writer ask whether his customer can double the volume if a 15% discount is granted?

(6) What does the last sentence of the letter imply?

3. Put the following sentences into the right order and make it a complete sales letter.

Dear Ms. Smith,

(1) As we are one of the leading electronic products dealers and have many branches in China, and are in a position to handle large quantities, your prompt attention to this matter will bring you a big business with us. (2) Your advertisement in the September issue of *Business Weekly* aroused our attention. (3) When quoting, please state your terms of payments and discounts that you would allow on purchase of no less than 1,000 dozen of individual items. (4) If the quality of your products is satisfactory and the prices attractive, we expect to place regular orders for fairly large numbers. (5) We also prefer that you send us samples of each category in order to enable us to make a sound decision. (6) Would you please quote us for the supply of the items listed on the estimate sheet enclosed, giving your lowest possible FOB San Francisco prices?

(7) We look forward to your prompt and favorable reply.

Yours sincerely,
Tony Smith

4. Translate the following Chinese letter into English.

敬启者：

事由：男式羊毛衫

贵方2011年6月8日报盘收悉，非常感谢！

我们非常抱歉地奉告，贵方报价偏高，与现行市价不一致。由于类似质量的货物在此处能以比较低的价格买到，故请贵方降低所报价格，比如降低5%，这样，贵我双方或许能达成交易。考虑到我们之间长期的贸易关系，我方才作出如此还盘。

由于市价日趋下跌，我们真诚地希望贵方能考虑我方的还盘，并尽早赐复。

彼的得·约翰逊
2011年6月20日

Chapter 6

Sales Promotion

> *Your goals for this chapter are to understand:*
> ☑ some basic knowledge about sales promotion;
> ☑ how to write sales promotion letters;
> ☑ some commonly-used patterns used in sales promotion letters;
> ☑ some points for attention in writing sales letters.

6.1 Lead-in

Before you begin your learning of this chapter, please discuss with your partner(s) about the following questions.

(1) Do you know the difference between sale and marketing?
(2) What is the purpose of a sales letter?
(3) What advice can you offer for a successful promotion of products?

6.2 Basic Information

As the buyer's market has prevailed in most businesses, sellers can not wait for eager customers to come to their offices any longer as they did several years ago when there was the seller's market. Instead, companies are puzzling their brains to devise every possible means to gain customers' attention. In a broad sense, all these activities conducted to push sales can be called sales promotion. To define it, sales promotion is the process of persuading a selected group of potential customers to buy certain products or services.

Nowadays all companies and manufactories know the important role that sales promotion plays in the development of its business. They know very few goods sell themselves and most goods need to be promoted in some way. So it is quite necessary for business people to learn to write effective promotion letters.

Sales promotion letters are a direct form of advertising, aiming at selling certain kinds of commodities or services to targeted customers so as to expand business. By this means, enterprises can draw potential customers' attention and interest, convince them that they can benefit from the products or services offered, and thereby arouse their motivation to buy them. Sales promotion letters fall into two main categories: unsolicited sales letters and solicited sales letters. Unsolicited sales letters are also known as direct-mail advertising. They are a form of advertising sent by mail directly to prospective buyers. Solicited letters are replies to enquiries for information about some products or services.

When the exporter fails to receive the expected order or enquiry after sending the information asked for, then it is necessary for him or her to write a follow-up letter. The purposes of follow-up letters are to provide further information, recap important points, reiterate the benefits of a product or service, or demonstrate continued interest in a client or potential customer by announcing a special offer. In such a letter, the writer may express regret or even surprise that no order has been received and discreetly inquire into the reason. Meanwhile, the writer can also introduce some new selling points or arguments favorable to the promotion of sales. When written correctly, follow-up letters can be effective tools in resuming a business relationship.

6.3 Analysis of Model Letters

Read and analyze the following letters. While reading, please try to find answers to the following questions.
(1) Why does the writer mention ordinary washing machines in the second paragraph?
(2) Do you think it is proper to enclose an order form with a reply letter?
(3) How does the writer show his sincerity in Model Letter 6-3?

Model Letter 6-1: Seller's unsolicited promotion of a washing machine

Dear Sirs,

Great interest was aroused at the recent Industry Exhibition in London by the new Jin Song Washing Machine. Numerous inquiries and orders have also come — the new machine is the realization of every washing machine owner's dream.

You are well aware of the shortcomings of ordinary washing machines — rough outer covers and a tendency to make some noises, just to mention some of the customers' complaints. Our Aiqi Washing Machine offers you a machine that is beyond criticism in the qualities and completes reliability.

We could tell you a lot more about the machine, but prefer you to read the enclosed copies of reports from racing drivers, test drivers, motor dealers and motor manufactures.

You are already aware of our terms of business, but to encourage you to lay in a stock of the new machine; we will allow a special discount of 5% on any order received on or before 31st August.

Your faithfully,

Model Letter 6-2: Seller's solicited promotion of machine tools

Dear Sirs,

Thank you for your enquiry of August 16 concerning the supply of machine tools.

We are pleased to say that we are the largest manufacturer of machine tools in China with a history of over 90 years. Our products cover a wide range of specifications. Our quality and prices compare favorably with those of similar products.

We are sending our full set of sales promotion literature for your reference. We deem it to your benefit to push the sales of our products in your market. And we are prepared to give a quantity discount of 3.5% if your order exceeds 2,000 sets.

We suggest that you take advantages of the enclosed order form in case you wish to place an immediate order.

Your faithfully,

Encl: An order form

Model Letter 6-3: A follow-up letter delivered when no more orders follow

Dear Sir,

We notice with regret that it is some considerable time since we last received an order from you. We hope this is in no way due to your dissatisfaction with our service or with the quality of the goods we have supplied. In either of these situations we should be grateful to hear from you, as we are most anxious to ensure that customers obtain maximum satisfaction from their dealings with us. If the lack of orders is due to changes in the types of goods you handle, we may still be able to meet your needs if you let us know in what directions your policy has changed.

Not having heard otherwise, we assume that you are selling the same range of sports goods and so enclose a copy of our latest illustrated catalogue. We feel it competes favorably in range, quality and price with the catalogues of other manufacturers. At the same time we take the opportunity to mention that our terms are now much easier than formerly, following the withdrawal of exchange control and other official measures since we last did business.

Yours truly,
Hans Meyer

6.4 Writing Guidelines

Both Model Letter 6-1 and 6-2 are sales letters aiming at pushing the sale of the products in question. Model Letter 6-3 is a follow-up letter aiming to resume a suspended business relationship. The two sales letters show that they usually include the following four essential parts which are closely related to each other.

(1) In the first part, you should refer to an inquiry or a previous communication if there is any.

(2) In the second part, you need to introduce the selling points, such as the good quality of products or favorable business terms available.

(3) In the third part, you can advise the reader to order the goods or try to motivate the reader to take advantage of the good chance.

(4) Besides these, you may also give an introduction of your own company to ensure the reader that you can provide the best service, or you can also introduce other clients' evaluation of your products to convince the reader that your products are really worth buying.

A follow-up letter, in general, consists of the following four parts.

(1) At the very beginning, you can make a reference to a previous transaction or an exchange of information in the past.

(2) Then you may ask tactfully why the expected enquiry or order has not come.

(3) Next you can provide additional information to stimulate the recipient's interest in your products. In this part, you may also offer some preferential terms to motivate your letter recipient.

(4) Finally you should close the letter in a friendly way, in which an expectation may be expressed.

6.5 More Sample Letters

The following letters comply basically with the above writing guidelines, but they are different from the models in 6.3 in one way or another. Read them to see how each letter is structured and worded to achieve its respective communicative purpose.

Sample Letter 6-1 An ordinary sales letter

The following letter uses some facts to convince the reader that the Power Brand Shaver is an excellent product and is worth importing. The favorable terms offered at the end can further motivate the reader to place an order.

Dear Sirs,

We're enclosing with this letter a copy of our illustrated catalogue and price list for our Power Brand Shavers.

The superior quality of our products helped us to acquire a sales volume of US$3,560,000 in Los

Angeles last month, and the number is expected to increase this month. Moreover, our products are well known and universally acknowledged in the UK, Italy, Spain, France and many other European countries. Our recent market survey reveals that consumers are also very satisfied with the design of our products, which is not only visually attractive but also easy to be held.

Apart from the excellent quality and the attractive designs, the quality of our Power Brand Shavers can be guaranteed within 3 years after purchase, which is absolutely impossible for the similar products.

We are confident that a trial order would convince you that this line can also be popular in Germany. In order to help you to push the sales, we can allow a special discount of 5% on any order received by the end of July.

We would welcome your earliest orders.

Yours faithfully,

Sample Letter 6-2: Introducing a new product

This is a letter distributed to many customers at one time. It is a cover letter giving the general information about their Celluar Phone. More details about the product may be found in the brochure.

Dear Customers,

We are delighted to send you our 2011 Celluar Phone Brochure, which we hope you will find of interest.

Our brochure features our latest Celluar Phones, which we manufacture ourselves. With over twenty years' experience in the production and sale of telephone equipments, we are confident that our products will give you full satisfaction.

Please let us know if you wish to receive details on one particular type or on a wider range as we would be pleased to send you additional information. We very much look forward to hearing from you.

Very truly yours,

Sample Letter 6-3: Selling more to a steady customer

This letter aims to sell more to an old customer. The reference to a previous transaction may help to pave the way for the following promotion. The favorable terms introduced at the end may be helpful for eliciting another order.

Dear Madam,

We figure that the computers we sold you last month are satisfactory to you. Now that you are acquainted with the quality of our computers, you might like to find out what other appliances we can supply.

Enclosed is a catalogue giving the details of all the appliances we deal in. If you find any items interesting to you, please do not hesitate to contact me. We would be very pleased to be at your service.

In order to popularize our products, all the catalogue prices are subject to a special discount of 5% from August to October. For orders exceeding the value of USD15,000, we can offer an additional discount of 3.5%.

We would appreciate a prompt reply.

Cordially yours,
(Signature)

Sample Letter 6-4: Offering a special favor to a valued client

This is a very friendly letter, the purpose of which is to sell more to a regular customer, and at the same time to expect future larger business transactions. The suggested arrangements for warehousing are very favorable and the receiver of the letter may be motivated into an order.

Dear Sirs,

Due to the rise in the world price of paper, from 1 January of next year, prices for our products are due to increase by 10% across the board.

Since you are a valued customer of long standing, we wish to give you the opportunity to beat the price increases by ordering now at the current prices. In addition, we are willing to give you a discount of 5% on all orders of more than GB£ 20,000.

We are aware that you do not have sufficient warehousing for large quantities of reserve stock. In that case, we would be prepared to hold paper for you to be delivered at your convenience. There will be no charge for warehousing at this end.

We believe that you will see the advantages of this arrangement, which will save you at least 15% on paper purchases in the coming year.

We look forward to your favorable response to the proposal.

Yours faithfully,
Tony Smith
Chief Seller

Sample Letter 6-5: A follow-up letter

The reference to previous business transactions lays a good foundation for the following sales promotion. The preferential terms which follow may leave an even better impression on the reader and may finally move the reader into the action of placing an order.

Dear sirs,

Looking through our record we note with regret that from 2008 to 2009 you bought from us a large quantity of typewriters in Models SF-101 to 105, ST-201 to 202, but during the year 2010 we did not have the pleasure of receiving an order from you.

We think you will be interested to know that we have a residue stock of 307 sets of Model ST-202, which you bought from us in substantial quantity previously. It is just next newest to the latest Model ST-203. You are well aware that it is efficient and durable, economical and practical in use for middle school students. We are prepared to clear the stock by allowing you a general discount as follows:
(1) 9% for an order 100 sets to 199 sets;
(2) 12% for an order 200 sets to 299 sets;
(3) 15% for an order 300 sets and above ;
(4) On the current price of HK$280 per set CIF Hong Kong. This offer is subject to your reply reaching us on or before 20th June.

We give you the first chance and hope you will take advantage of this exceptional offer. Looking forward to your favorable reply.

Your truly,
Manager

6.6 More Useful Sentences

1. Introducing the Company or Goods
- Boomba Machinery Co., Ltd is one of the largest manufacturers of machinery in China.
- With more than 20 years' experience in manufacturing and service, we are able to supply dozens of

- models of plastic machinery, metallic processing machinery and food processing machinery.
- "Chint" is a famous brand which has won the United States authentication.
- Have you ever heard of our Flying Horse Sewing Machines which are fine in quality and low in prices? The functions of our machines are many-sided.
- Just imagine how comfortable you are when you stretch out those tired limbs on our newly developed "White Cloud" water bed.
- We have pleasure in recommending you the following goods similar to the samples sent by you.
- With a view to supporting your sales, we have specially prepared some samples of our new makes and are sending them to you, under separate cover, for your perusal.
- We take pleasure in enclosing the latest designs of our products, which are superior in quality and moderate in price and are sure to be saleable in your market.
- We are sending you a sample book with a price-list of our new products, the high quality of which, we, trust, will induce you to place trial order with us.

2. Introducing New Selling Points
- We have shown some flexibility in price negotiation in order to make the conclusion of business possible.
- According to our investigation, the market is now showing a decline, so we are expecting an adjustment of the price at the end of this month.
- You will get a 30% increase in production upon using this machine and also it allows one person to perform the task of three people.
- The gloves are made of superior genuine leather and can be supplied in various designs and colors.
- The product is the result of years of research, and is likely to revolutionize all the chemical methods in use at present.
- The quality and specifications are much improved at very little extra cost and are enjoying best sales.
- The high standard craftsmanship will appeal to selective buyers.
- Our products have the following advantages: durability, precision, delicacy, efficiency and accurate function, which enable you to open up the European market without worrying about furious competition.
- Owing to the punctual shipment, reasonable prices as well as excellent quality, our company occupies the leading position in the field of chemical industry.
- We take pleasure in enclosing the latest designs of our products, which are superior in quality and moderate in price and are sure to be saleable in your market.
- We are quite confident that once our products are put on your market, they will overtake sales of all competitive brands.
- By virtue of its superior quality, this item has met with a warm reception in most European countries. We deem it to your advantage to buy this item for a trial sale in your market.
- Due to our excellent quality, efficient management system and good after-sales service, we have already earned a long-lasting good reputation in the world market.
- It is only to clear our season's stocks that we offer so excellent a quality at this price. We would remind you that a similar offer in the near future is most unlikely.
- We inform you that we are able to offer you the same discount of 10% of our recent price.

3. Introducing Preferential Terms

- Since this is our first transaction with you, we decide, as an exception, to cut the price by 2%.
- Special terms are allowed to you if you place trial order before the end of the current month.
- The price we quoted is accurately calculated, but in order to encourage business, we are prepared to allow you a discount of 2%.
- On condition that you could place an order for our West Lake Brand color TV 10,000 sets, we are prepared to offer this special price of US$200 per set and a 5% discount.
- You would be entitled to a 5% discount only if the invoice value is paid within 30 days of that date.
- In order to popularize the products illustrated in the catalogue, all the prices are subject to a special discount of 10% during the month of May.
- We have made the decision to reduce the price of our products from August 1st. This price will be cut off from 5%–10%.
- By sending the card before 30 August, you will obtain a special discount of 2 percent at our introductory stage.
- Considering its quality and workmanship, the price is moderate. What's more, since it's still in promotion, we can offer you a 10% discount.
- For an old customer like you, we are willing to allow a 5% commission on each machine, plus a discount of 7% in all orders received before the end of July.

4. Persuading the Reader into an Order

- You would benefit by ordering now, as there is every indication that the prices are rising.
- We would suggest that you send us your trial order as soon as possible, as there is a brisk demand for this article.
- In view of the large demand for this commodity, we would advise you to work fast and place an order with us as soon as possible.
- As this product is now in great demand and the supply is rather limited, we would recommend you to place an order as soon as possible.
- It is not our intention to rush you into a decision, but as this article is in great demand, we would advise you to avail yourselves of our offer in your own interest.
- You will note that we are making you a special reduction in prices owing to your support in the past. We can maintain this reduction only for a short time so we recommend your early orders.

6.7 Writing Tips

Some English majors have proposed the following points to note in writing sales letter or follow-up letters. Read the following list quickly and then discuss with your partner whether they are appropriate and try to add some more ideas to the list.

In writing promotion letters, it is quite necessary to comply with the following principles.

(1) You should do your utmost to get the reader's attention with the first paragraph or sentence. To achieve this purpose, you can start your letter with a question like: Would you like to see your factory's production increase by 10% or more?

(2) You must try to convince the reader of the value of your product or service. When you have

succeeded in getting the reader's attention, you must hold that attention by describing your product. In this part, you can use colorful and descriptive words and utilize sound reasoning and solid evidence to support your own ideas.

(3) Avoid negative remarks. Remember never to show even the slightest hint of reproach. If you do not receive a response after a first letter, do not imply in later letters that the reader is forgetful, thoughtless, or negligent, as this will probably make him or her feel defensive.

(4) The writer may offer to the reader a chance to take alternative steps when he is not quite sure about the prospective customer's needs.

(5) Because people are herd animals, they don't like to be the only person buying something. So you must let your customer know that others have bought your products and they evaluate your goods highly.

(6) The writer ought not to duplicate previous sales pitches but should include new points that will arouse the reader's interest.

(7) At the end of the letter, you should make a firm promise of service and anxious hope for a reply or an order. Besides, the writer should express thanks for the reader's time, emphasizes the advantages of doing business with the writer, and proposes the next step at the end of the letter.

Notes and Explanations

1. recap 重申
2. selling points （销售时强调的）商品优点，卖点
3. beyond criticism 无可挑剔的
   beyond 的类似用法还有：beyond sb.（为某人所不能理解），beyond oneself（精神错乱，忘乎所以）。
4. across the board 全面地，彻底地
   We are aiming to increase the productivity across the board.
   我们正力争全面提高生产力。
   an across-the-board pay hike 全面的工资提高
   an across-the-board policy decision 包括了一切在内的政策决定
5. on offer
   (1) 供出售的
   The share is on offer in parcel of 50.
   股票以每五十张为一宗出售。
   (2) 削价出售
   Baked beans are on offer this week at the local supermarket.
   当地超级市场本周烘豆罐头大减价。
   under offer （指待售房屋）已有人出价要买
   The office block is under offer.
   办公大楼已有人出价购买。
6. in view of 鉴于，由……看来，考虑到
   In view of our long-standing business relations, we can consider a price reduction.
   鉴于贵我双方长期的业务关系，我们可以考虑减价。
   下列词语与"in view of"同义，可以替换使用：in the light of, seeing that, in consideration of 等。

7. the rush of orders 订单蜂拥而至的情况
   to rush on/for sth. 大量购买（货物等），争购
   a rush on umbrellas 争购雨伞（如下大雨时）
   rush-hour （上下班时的）交通拥挤时间，高峰时刻
8. dead ad. 全然地，完全地
   dead calm 死一般地沉静
   dead a. 全然的，彻底的
   come to a dead stop 猛然停住
   dead centre 正中心
   a dead sleep 熟睡
9. just to mention some of the customers' complaints 仅举数例顾客的投诉
10. with a view to 为了，鉴于，带着……的目的（希望）
    With a view to improving his ability to speak French, he spent most of his holidays in France.
    为了提高法语口语能力，他的大部分假期是在法国度过的。
    This subject is one that should be handled with a view to the long-range interests of the country.
    这是一个应从国家的长远利益来考虑的问题。
11. be excellent value for money 物超所值
    表示类似意思的其他方式还有：be above the money's worth, be above the price in value 等。
12. discreetly 审慎地，小心地
    His utterances were discreetly academic.
    他的言论严谨，具有学术性。
13. stretch out
    (1) 伸出
    The little boy stretched out his hands to catch the toy.
    小男孩伸出双手去抓玩具。
    (2) 伸直四肢
    He stretched out on the grass in the sunshine.
    他舒展着身子躺在阳光下的草地上。
    (c) 使够用
    I don't see how I can stretch out the housekeeping to the end of the month.
    我不知道要怎样安排家用才能维持到月底。

1. Multiple choices.

(1) We thank you for all past favor, and we are always _____ your service.
    A. in   B. for   C. at   D. on
(2) _____ please find our latest catalogue and price list for the items we are handling.
    A. Enclose   B. Enclosed   C. To enclose   D. To be enclosed
(3) We would like to know what you can offer _____ this line as well as your terms of sales.
    A. in   B. for   C. at   D. with

(4) We are pleased to send you herewith our Proforma Invoice No. 12 _____ triplicate as requested.
　　A. for　　　　　　B. with　　　　　　C. in　　　　　　D. of
(5) There is brisk demand in our country for your items Art No.102, which has given us enough confidence to place a repeat order _____ them.
　　A. with　　　　　B. at　　　　　　　C. for　　　　　D. on
(6) _____ requested, we are sending you our quotation sheet in duplicate and wish you to place your order with us.
　　A. As　　　　　　B. After　　　　　　C. For　　　　　D. On
(7) We are staging an important private exhibition _____ by a series of technical lectures for our home and overseas customers at the National Exhibition Hall.
　　A. accompanied　　B. accompanying　　C. to accompany　　D. accompany
(8) We have pleasure _____ advising you that we are well placed to supply MP3 players which have already met with a warm reception abroad.
　　A. with　　　　　B. in　　　　　　　C. to　　　　　　D. of
(9) We allow a trade discount of 35% and a special discount of 5% _____ orders received on or before 31st May.
　　A. for　　　　　B. on　　　　　　　C. with　　　　　D. at
(10) Owing to your delay in delivery, we are no longer in the position _____ your goods. We hereby cancel our order.
　　A. accept　　　　B. accepting　　　　C. to accept　　　D. accepted

2. Translate the following Chinese sentences into English.

(1) 任何询盘我们都会迅速而完善地处理，并提供足够的信息。
(2) 今向你方发电子邮件以表示我们愿意和你方建立业务关系，以便提供机会发展双方贸易的愿望。
(3) 请速告知这些货物的伦敦离岸价和广州保险，运费加成本价，我们将非常感谢。
(4) 按照你方要求，我方现作如下发盘，以你方的回复10日内到达为有效。
(5) 我们通常要求的付款方式为即期不可撤销信用证。
(6) 上述询价已于1月15日发往你方，但迄今未见你方报价，望早日发盘为感。
(7) 因其他买方接受我方付款条款，相信贵方会同意在此条款上与我方达成交易。
(8) 我方6月22日寄去报盘信，想必你们早已收到，但迄今未见你方回函。

3. Correct the grammatical mistakes in the following sentences.

(1) The quality of our products are well known and are universally acknowledged.
(2) We are confident that a trial order would convince you that our goods are an excellent value of money.
(3) This is an exceptional opportunity for you to buy high-quality cameras at prices we can repeat.
(4) We would mention that we have good connections in the trade and are fully experiencing with the import business for this type of product.
(5) The L/C evidences shipment of 2,000 tons of steel may be used against presentation of the shipping documents.
(6) We take pleasure in informing you of that we are an enterprise manufacturing various electric fans.
(7) The quality of the fridge has been proved by a scrupulous test, which have been clearly explained in our illustrated catalog.

(8) If you have interest in dealing with us, please notify us your requirements together with your banker's name and address.

(9) Our curtains are special because they are made of good quality clothes.

(10) If you would like to receive more informations, please log onto our website at www.bmbooproducts.com.

4. Fill in the blanks with appropriate words.

Dear Sirs,

It's __(1)__ that we haven't received any replenishment orders from you since last July. We __(2)__ that the global financial crisis may be your main __(3)__.

The crisis gets most trading corporations into trouble. However, to our surprise, this year we are receiving much more orders. After __(4)__ the matter, we found that it's due to the high performance-to-price ratio of our products that our market share has been increased __(5)__. During economic depression, consumers tend to be more __(6)__ and prefer high performance-to-price ratio products. Although our refrigerators are not very beautiful in designs, they are quite __(7)__ and __(8)__ with __(9)__ to capacity, power consumption and maintenance expense. It's no doubt that a repeat order may help you get in on the ground floor in the unfavorable market environment.

In order to jointly pull through the crisis with our old customers, all the catalogue prices are __(10)__ to a special discount of 5% during the second quarter this year.

We're looking forward to your earliest reply.

Yours faithfully,

(1) A. regretful	B. regret	C. regrettable	D. regrets
(2) A. are sure	B. guess	C. convince	D. guessed
(3) A. worry	B. trouble	C. reason	D. concern
(4) A. investigate	B. investigating	C. to investigate	D. investigation
(5) A. dramatical	B. dramatically	C. dramatially	D. dramally
(6) A. reasonable	B. calm	C. rational	D. sensible
(7) A. practical	B. practice	C. practicable	D. practicing
(8) A. economy	B. economic	C. economically	D. economical
(9) A. respect	B. review	C. view	D. aim
(10) A. intended	B. meant	C. inclined	D. subject

Chapter 7

Orders and Execution

Your goals for this chapter are to understand:
- ☑ the basics about orders and order execution;
- ☑ the writing skills for writing order letters and execution letters;
- ☑ some commonly-used patterns in order letters and execution letters;
- ☑ some points for attention in writing order letters.

7.1 Lead-in

Before you begin your learning of this chapter, please discuss with your partner(s) about the following questions.

(1) Do you know what an order is?

(2) What do you think are the most important points in an order letter?

(3) What do you think is the most important principle that a businessman should comply with in executing an order?

7.2 Basic Information

An order is a request made by the buyer to the seller, asking the seller to supply a specified quantity of goods on the terms agreed upon by both parties. Very often, it is only after the exchange of a number of letters, faxes or e-mails that the two parties involved come to terms and the buyer finally places an order.

Most of the time an order is an acceptance of an offer, but it may also be sent voluntarily by a buyer. A buyer may give his or her order by letters, faxes or e-mails. He or she can also use printed order forms which ensure that no important information will be neglected. Many companies use special forms for ordering merchandise or service.

An order letter is a common form of business commutation in the international business. It is usually carefully worded lest any misunderstandings may arise. All relevant information should be included in an order letter. Usually an order should include the name of the commodity, the quantity, the article number, the specification, the total amount, the price terms (CIF, FOB), the mode of packing, the delivery date and the port of destination. In international business, orders are almost always made in writing with care.

In most cases, on receiving an order from the buyer, the seller, no matter whether he accepts the order or not, should give a reply to express his thanks for the order and tell the buyer what is under way. If he accepts it, he should reply to confirm the order and begin to execute it to the buyer's content. For small and routine orders, a printed acknowledgement or a postcard may be enough, but a short letter stating the expected delivery date is more helpful for creating goodwill. If the goods ordered cannot be supplied, the seller had better explain the situation and reasons in writing and check if suitable substitute goods are available to offer.

If not, he should reject it and give the reasons so that the good business relationship is sustained. In such a circumstance, letters rejecting orders must be written with the utmost care and with an eye to goodwill and further business. It is advisable to recommend suitable substitutes or make counter-offers instead of a simple declination.

7.3 Analysis of Model Letters

Read and analyze the following letters. While reading, please try to find answers to the following questions.

(1) Why does the writer of Model Letter 7-1 list the items, the quantity and the price in such a way?

(2) In Model Letter 7-2, what does the writer care for most, the acknowledgement, the requirement for opening the L/C or his own plan for execution of the order?

(3) Model Letter 7-3 gives a negative message, but the goodwill can still be easily detected. How does the writer achieve this?

Model Letter 7-1: Importer placing an initial order

Dear Sirs,

We acknowledge receipt of your letter dated May 10th, along with your Proforma Invoice in duplicate. We take pleasure in placing our initial order with you for the following items:

Item	Quantity	Price FOB NY
Teacups	2,000	US$30.00 per hundred
Tea Saucers	2,000	US$30.50 per hundred
Tea Plates	2,000	US$30.00 per hundred
Teapots, 2-pint	4,000	US$30.50 each

Since this is the first time we have explored the Philippine market for your products, it is, therefore, absolutely essential for you to see to it that all the goods delivered are up to the export standards and that all of them are thoroughly inspected prior to shipment.

We will open an irrevocable L/C with your company as beneficiary as soon as we receive a notice that the goods are ready for shipment.

Yours faithfully,
H. Simon & Co., Ltd.

Model Letter 7-2: Exporter acknowledging receipt of an order

Dear Sirs,

Re: Your Order No. 163

We are pleased to have received your Order No. 16808 for Canned Fish and are sending you herewith our Sales Confirmation No. AC-202 in duplicate. Please sign and return one copy for our file.

We trust that an L/C in our favor covering the above-mentioned order will be opened immediately. We wish to point out that the stipulations in the relevant Credit should strictly conform to the terms stated in our Sales Confirmation in order to avoid subsequent amendments. You may rest assured that we shall effect shipment with the least possible delay upon receipt of the Credit.

We appreciate your co-operation and look forward to receiving your future orders.

Yours sincerely,
Carrie Enterprises Limited Encl.

Model Letter 7-3: Exporter declining an order

Dear Mr. Sun,

Re: Your Recent Order of White Crystal Sugar

We feel thankful for your Order No.15808-A received this morning for the captioned goods, but regret that owing to the shortage of stocks, we are unable to accept the same, nor can our manufacturer undertake to entertain your order for future delivery on account of the uncertainty of raw materials.

We will, however, revert to this matter and contact you by e-mail, once the supply position improves.

Meanwhile, please feel free to send us your specific enquiries for any other sugar and you can rely on our best attention at all times.

We expect to work with you soon in the future.

Yours sincerely,
Martin Coopers

7.4 Writing Guidelines

The first model letter is a letter for placing an order. An analysis of the model shows that order letters often include the following parts.

(1) In part one, the writer may refer to a previous contact, for example, having received the offer or visited their showroom etc. If a contract has been signed before, he can mention the contract in this part.

(2) Part two is the most important part, in which all the details about the order are given.

(3) In the third part, the writer may make his requirements related to this order or give some further explanations about it. This part may include the expected delivery date, arrival date or terms of payment.

(4) At the end an expectation for smooth execution may be expressed.

Model Letter 7-2 is about execution of orders. An analysis shows that they are usually made up of the following parts.

(1) Acknowledging receipt of the order. Following this, the writer may also repeat the main points of the order lest any misunderstanding may occur.

(2) Writer's response to the order received such as acceptance or declination. If the order is accepted, more detailed arrangements for the execution of the order are given. If the order has to be declined, enough explanations should be added.

(3) Expectation or a friendly close. In this part the writer may assure the reader that he has bought wisely and encourage him to place more orders.

Model Letter 7-3 is also a response to an order letter, but it, instead of accepting, declines the order politely and gives justifications. Such a letter often includes the following elements.

(1) Expressing thankfulness for the order received.

(2) Stating your decision that you are not in a position to execute it.

(3) Giving explanations for the declination to avoid misunderstanding. This kind of matter should be handled with great care so as not to cause any harm to future business. Or you can suggest a substitute in order not to disappoint your partner.

(4) Expressing hope for future co-operation.

7.5 More Sample Letters

The following letters comply basically with the above writing guidelines, but they are different from the models in 7.3 in one way or another. Read them to see how each letter is structured and worded to achieve its respective communicative purpose.

Sample Letter 7-1: A cover letter for an order form

This is a brief cover letter for an order. It is very short and simple because the details of the order are in the order form enclosed. This is a wise way to place an order because by filling in a form no important message may be neglected.

Dear Sirs,

Thank you for the catalogue and price list you sent us recently. We enclose our Order Form No. 987 for four of the items.

We note that you can supply these items from stock and hope you will send them without delay.

Faithfully yours,

Encl: Order Form No. 987

Sample Letter 7-2: Placing an order for pillowcases

This letter is a bit more complicated than Sample Letter 7-1, but all the items are arranged clearly. Please note the use of bullet points and the number in words.

Dear Sirs,

Thank you for your letter of 16th August with which you enclosed your catalogues and price-lists. We therefore place our official Purchase Order No. 8046 for a range of your products to the value of US$18,600 (Eighteen thousand and six hundred US dollars only). Please ship the following merchandise:

- Quantity   Pattern No.   Catalogue No.   Prices (FOB Shanghai)

  6,000 Pillowcases   15-05   45   US$1.60 each

  5,000 Pillowcase   22-01   65   US$1.80 each

- Delivery: During October.
- Payment: By L/C to be opened in accordance with our agreement.
- Packing: Packed in strong bales, with gunny bag cover and water-proof material.

Please acknowledge this order immediately on receipt and inform a definite delivery date.

Looking forward to your early reply.

Faithfully yours,

Sample Letter 7-3: Seller accepting an order at old prices

In the following letter, the writer agrees to accept the order at old prices. Meanwhile the seller takes advantage of this opportunity to introduce his other range of products, which may keep the future co-operation going.

Dear Sirs,

We welcome your Order No. 508 for 100 dozen printed T-shirts. The prices you mentioned are the old ones. The current prices should be 5% higher. However, we accept your order and wish to assure you that dispatch will be put in hand immediately when we receive your L/C.

Our T-shirts and knitting wears enjoy favorable reception in the world market because of their fine quality and excellent craftsmanship. No wonder your customers have remarked favorably on our products. You may be sure that we shall do our best to maintain our reputation for quality and reliability.

We enclose a quotation for summer wears, such as bathing suits, all cotton vests and shall be pleased to receive further orders from you.

Your sincerely,
Margaret Taylor

Sample Letter 7-4: Executing an order

The writer is considerate because he has made good arrangements for the order. In the letter he gives all the necessary information about the execution. At the end he also promises to provide further information needed, so his friendliness is obvious.

Dear Sirs,

ORDER NO. 0987

The captioned order has now been completed and sent to Ningbo Docks where it is waiting to be loaded onto S.S. "East Wind", which sails for Kobe, Japan on 10 June and arrives on 15 June.

Once we have the necessary documents we will hand them to Chartered Bank, your bank's agents here, and they will forward them to the Union Trust Bank in Japan.

We have taken special care to see that the goods have been packed as per your instructions, the six crates being marked with your name, and numbered 1–6. Each crate measures 6ft×4ft×4ft and weighs 15 kg.

If you require any further information, please feel free to contact us. Thank you very much for your trial order and we hope it will lead to further business between us.

Yours faithfully,

Sample Letter 7-5: Seller declining an order politely

The writer has to decline the order received because of the reasons given in the letter, and he has also made a suggestion. But if he can propose a specific source from where the receiver of the letter can obtain the goods, that would be much better.

Dear Mr. Jarvis,

Thank you for your order No. PO9754 dated 15 July, 2011 for the shipment of 5,000 leather jackets by the end of September.

After careful consideration on your request, however, we have come to the conclusion that we are not presently in a position to deliver your order as requested. For the next four months our entire production capacity has already been committed.

We are indeed sorry for not being able to meet your present order and hope you will be able to meet your requirements from some other sources.

We hope that you will understand our situation.

Yours sincerely,
DAISY Kwan
Sales Manager

Sample Letter 7-6: Suggesting a substitute

The aim of this letter is to express the seller's inability to accept the order; however the writer seizes the opportune moment to suggest a substitute. It is a wise way of sales promotion.

Dear Sirs,

Thank you for your order for Bassinet Model C enclosed in your letter of 10 August, 2011.

We regret to say, however, that Bassinet Model C as required is not available in stock at this time. Instead we should like to recommend our new product Model D which we think is more attractive in design and practical for use, despite a little difference in price. The best price we can offer for Model D is USD56 each CIF New York. The sample picture with description will be forwarded to you by airmail today.

We are looking forward to your early reply.

Yours faithfully,
Henry M. Jones

7.6 More Useful Sentences

1. Giving decisions to Place an Order
- We agree to your quoted prices, as stated above, and anticipate receiving the goods on or before 15 May, 2004.
- Your prices and quality turned out to be satisfactory and we are sending you an order for the following items.
- In view of the fact that the prices you quoted are acceptable, we hereby place the following order with you.
- Enclosed is our Confirmation of Order in duplicate, of which please return us one copy duly signed.
- We are pleased to give you an order for the following items with the understanding that they will be supplied from stock at the prices named.
- We are writing to confirm our e-mail this morning ordering the following items.
- We have studied your catalogue and have chosen 3 models of calculating machines for which we enclose our order.
- We have the pleasure of sending you an order for 5,000 reams of paper, at USD48 per ream CIF New York, based on your quotation of 10th June.
- I am hereby authorized to place an order for 1,000 sewing machines, at USD260 each CIF London.

2. Making Requirements Related to an Order
- The material supplied must be absolutely waterproof, and we place our order subject to this guarantee.
- We place the order on the condition that the goods are dispatched in time to reach us by 4th

September.
- We need the goods urgently and it is imperative that the ordered goods reach us by the end of this month.
- Please send us the ordered goods by the first available steamer sailing for Ningbo before June 15th.
- Would you be so kind as to deal with this order as one of special urgency?
- We would stress that this is a trial order and if we are satisfied with your shipment you can expect regular repeat orders.

3. Acknowledging Receipt of an Order
- Thank you very much again for your trial order.
- We are pleased to acknowledge your order No. 4567.
- We highly appreciate your letter of March 12 together with your Order No. 8978.
- We thank you for your trial order of Oct. 17 for ten thousand sets of our "Diamond" electric fans.

4. Accepting an Order
- Thank you for your order No. 1032 and it is now being processed and should be ready for dispatch by September 30th.
- Your order is receiving our immediate attention, and you can depend on us to effect delivery well within your time limit.
- You may rest assured that this order will have our careful attention.
- We assure you that we shall effect shipment on the date specified in your order.
- Your order is booked and will be handled with great care.
- We have accepted your order for 20,000 yards of Article No. 50.
- We accept your order as you proposed, and enclose Sales Contract No. 24526.

5. Rejecting an Order
- There is a great demand for this quality and our stock is exhausted. It will be 3 months before it is available again.
- While thanking you for your order, we have to explain that supplies of raw materials are becoming more and more difficult to obtain, and we have no alternatives but to decline your order.
- We very much regret that we are not in a position to accept your order for special packs of printers as offered last year.
- We regret to inform you that the goods you want to order are no longer available.
- We are sorry that the model you require is no longer being manufactured.

6. Executing an Order
- We confirm that delivery will be made on July 5th.
- At present, we do not have in stock the goods you ordered. As per your request, we are sending you substitutes of the nearest quality.
- The goods you ordered are now ready for shipment and we are awaiting your shipping instructions.
- Delivery will be made immediately on receipt of your letter of credit. We have today dispatched by S. S. "Qingdao" a consignment of 1,000 cases canned beef and enclosed shipping documents.
- At present, we do not have in stock the goods you ordered. As per your request, we are sending you

substitutes of the nearest quality.
- The chief difficulty in accepting your orders now is the heavy backlog of commitments. But you may rest assured that as soon as we are able to accept new orders, we shall give priority or preference to yours.

7.7 Writing Tips

A class of Business English discussed about how to write letters concerning orders and their execution. Here are some points which they have concluded from their discussion. Do you agree to these writing rules?

When you write letters related to placing an order, you ought to note the following points.

(1) Completeness and accuracy are of special importance in placing an order, so you should remember to include all the essential details, for example, the price, the expected delivery date, arrival date or terms of payment. It should be carefully written because any error in such a letter may bring about unexpected trouble or even loss.

(2) It is advisable that while writing price terms and total amount, the writer should repeat the figures in words to avoid any misunderstanding.

(3) In an order letter, you may require your counterpart to execute the order as you wish. But at the same time, it is best for you to inform your counterpart of your arrangements for the payment.

When writing letters in reply to an order, you are advised to remember the following points.

(1) No matter whether you accept it or not, remember to acknowledge an order promptly.

(2) If you accept the order, it's advisable to make a repeat of the terms stipulated in the order.

(3) In case the order can not be accepted, a reply is also necessary. To avoid misunderstanding, you should justify yourself by giving explanations about why you can not meet your counterpart's demand.

(4) As a rejection to an order is often thought to be a rude action, rejecting an order should be handled with great care. It is advisable that the writer suggest some substitutes or other channels for the purchaser.

Notes and Explanations

1. come into terms   达成协议，妥协，和解
2. CIF   到岸价
   CIF 是"Cost, Insurance and Freight"的缩写，即包括成本、保险费、运费，一般译成"到岸价"。另外一个常用的价格术语是 FOB，是"Free on Board"的缩写，表示"离岸价"、"船上交货价格"。
3. delivery date   交货日期
4. to one's content   让某人满意
   We will effect payment immediately to your content.
   为了让你们满意，我们将立刻付款。
   content 也可以用作形容词，常用于下列结构：be content to do sth.（乐于做某事），be content with （沉迷于，满足于）。
5. routine order   常规订货，日常订单
6. proforma invoice   形式发票

形式发票是一种非正式发票，是卖方对潜在的买方报价的一种形式。买方常常需要形式发票，以作为申请进口和批准外汇之用。

7. see to it that 务必使，一定做到

   Please see to it that the door is safely locked.

   请务必做到把门锁好。

8. open an irrevocable L/C with your company as beneficiary 开立一张以贵公司为受益人的不可撤销信用证

9. entertain 愿意考虑或接受（某事物）

   He refused to entertain our proposal.

   他拒不考虑接受我们的提议。

   entertain sb. to sth. 用……款待某人

   They entertained us to a big cake.

   他们用一个大蛋糕来招待我们。

   entertain sb. with sth. 使某人快乐

   He entertained us for hours with his stories and jokes.

   他给我们讲故事、说笑话，让我们高兴了好几个小时。

10. revert (to) v. 回到（原话题或思路）

    revert to this matter 重新讨论这一问题

    revert 还可以表示"恢复"（原状、原先的做法或习惯）。

    We shall do our utmost to revert the damaged goods to its original state.

    我们将尽量把受损害的货物恢复到原始状态。

11. put in hand 开始（着手）

12. enjoy favorable reception 受到好评

13. as per 根据，按照

    As per the contract, the construction of the factory is now under way.

    根据合同规定，工厂的建设正在进行中。

14. commit 做（不合法的、错误的或愚蠢的事情）

    commit sb./oneself to sth. (to doing sth.) 使某人不能不做某事，向某人保证

    He committed himself to opening an L/C in our favor immediately.

    他承诺立即开立以我方为受益人的信用证。

15. to place the order subject to this guarantee 是在获得这样保证的前提下订购货物的

    be subject to 易受……影响的，屈服于……的，让步于……

    The goods in the cases are subject to damage, so it is essential to handle them in great care.

    这些箱子里面的货物容易受损，因此搬动时务必小心。

    Our delivery date is subject to change without notice.

    我们的交货时间可以在没有事先通知的情况下随时调整。

16. have no alternatives but to 没有其他方法，只能……

    Now they have no alternative but to supply the goods in compliance with our request.

    现在他们只能根据我们的要求提供货物。

17. S.S.是"steamship"的缩写，意为"轮船"。

18. under way 正在进行中

    Preparations for the celebration of National Day are under way.

    庆祝国庆的准备工作正在进行之中。

19. a ready marker   立即可以投入使用的市场，已成形的市场
20. be unduly inconvenienced   遇到太多的不便
21. We hope to be favored with your new order.   我们希望有幸得到你们的新订单。

1. **Translate the following English sentences into Chinese.**

    (1) We thank you for this order, and hope we may have the pleasure of supplying you again in the near future.
    (2) Your order is receiving our immediate attention and you can depend on us to effect delivery well within your time limit.
    (3) Owing to your delay in delivery, we are no longer in the position to accept your goods. We hereby cancel our order.
    (4) As requested, we are sending you our quotation sheet in duplicate and wish you to place your order with us as soon as possible.
    (5) There is brisk demand in our country for your items Art No. 102, which has given us enough confidence to place a repeat order for them.
    (6) After a careful consideration of your request, we have come to the conclusion that we cannot but decline the said order.
    (7) This is something we cannot afford as we will be heavily committed to orders for the latter half of the year.
    (8) We regret not being in a position to accept your order, but hope that you will understand our situation.

2. **Complete the following sentences according the Chinese given.**

    (1) We find it intolerable to ＿＿＿＿＿＿＿＿＿＿＿＿＿＿＿＿（照你们的要求办）as ours is the best possible price if you take the quality into consideration.
    (2) Please furnish us with your own samples of handkerchiefs ＿＿＿＿＿＿＿＿＿＿＿＿＿＿＿＿＿＿＿＿＿＿＿＿＿＿（在设计和质量上最接近我们样品的）.
    (3) All quotations are ＿＿＿＿＿＿＿＿＿＿＿＿＿＿＿＿＿＿＿＿＿＿＿＿（需要我方的最终确认）. Unless otherwise stated or agreed upon, all prices are net without commission.
    (4) We enclose a trial order. If the quality is ＿＿＿＿＿＿＿＿＿＿＿＿＿＿＿（达到我们所希望的要求）, we shall send further orders in the near future.
    (5) We are pleased to enclose ＿＿＿＿＿＿＿＿＿＿＿＿＿＿＿＿＿＿＿＿＿＿＿＿（订购 20 000 部手机的订单）.
    (6) ＿＿＿＿＿＿＿＿＿＿＿＿＿＿＿＿＿＿＿＿（关于你们的询盘）, we have pleasure in informing you that we have booked your order for 1,500 alarm clocks.
    (7) We are sending you our S/C in triplicate, one copy of which please ＿＿＿＿＿＿＿＿＿＿＿＿＿＿＿＿（请签字并返还一份以供我们存档）.
    (8) As some items under your order are ＿＿＿＿＿＿＿＿＿＿＿＿＿＿＿＿＿＿＿＿（在我们的业务范围以外）, we can only accept your order partially. We hope this will not bring you any inconvenience.

(9) As the goods are _____ （与信用证不符）, we can not help filing a claim against you.

(10) We are not in the position to accept _____ （你们的降价要求） as our products are of the finest materials and the highest craftsmanship.

3. **Translate the following letter from English into Chinese and pay attention to the use of words and the features of sentences.**

> Dear Mrs Hollyway,
>
> We are in receipt of your order of the 20th May. But it's a pity that we are not in a position to supply the brown serge Art. No. M89761, at the time required because we have completely sold out this color and no further lots will be received from the dyer before the end of July.
>
> Enclosed is a sample of a similar cloth, of exactly the same color, which we have in stock. Although our usual price is two cents per yard more than that for M89761, we are prepared to quote it at the same price. Please tell us whether we may substitute this cloth for M89761.
>
> You have not instructed us as to the shipping of these goods, nor as to how you wish them packed. If you prefer to leave this to us we will act to the best of your interest, but if you have any special preference in this matter we should be glad if you would inform us as early as possible.
>
> Yours sincerely,
> Sally Guan

4. **Fill in the blanks with appropriate words to make the letter complete.**

> Dear Sirs,
>
> Our committee provides advice and assistance to tea firms __(1)__ seek to export their services, goods to foreign areas __(2)__ to import goods and services abroad. We also assist tea firms in establishment of joint ventures and carry the procedures for examination and approval of joint ventures and foreign sole investment firms. Our committee can provide tea companies __(3)__ information on the world market and specific commercial opportunities as well as organize trade missions, seminars and business briefings.
>
> Our committee facilitates and encourages investment from other countries into targeted sectors of tea economy and maintains active promotion of tea through its network of contacts in domestic and foreign areas.
>
> Nowadays, we are seeking foreign investment in the field of capital construction, __(4)__ improving of tap water system and highway construction. __(5)__, we are setting up a tea zone in Long Jing Village, the largest tea producing and wholesaling base in our province. We invite Brazilian companies with most favorable policies to set up their firms in any form on tea processing and tea selling. Any information on investment projects into tea-making and on business cooperation __(6)__ firms in Zhejiang is highly appreciated and will pass on to anyone __(7)__ have approached us with interest in similar project. You are also invited to our city for investigation and business tour.

___(8)___ you have any questions, please feel free to contact us.

Thank you for your attention and looking forward to your prompt reply.

Sincerely yours,

Da-min Zhang

Chapter 8

Terms of Payment

Your goals for this chapter are to understand:
☑ some basic knowledge about payment in international trade;
☑ how to write letters concerning payment;
☑ some commonly-used patterns in payment-related letters;
☑ some points for attention in writing payment letters.

8.1 Lead-in

Before you begin your learning of this chapter, please discuss with your partner(s) about the following questions.

(1) How do we usually make payments when we buy something in a domestic market?
(2) What do you think are the main difficulties in international payments and settlements?
(3) Do you know Alipay? Can it be used in international payment?

8.2 Basic Information

Payment plays an important role in the course of business. If payment is not ensured then all will be meaningless.

Payment in foreign trade is often more complicated and difficult than that in the domestic market because a great distance separates the exporter and his customer, and in many cases, several parties will have to be involved in order to get the payment successfully effected.

Different payment methods involve different extent of risks. The exporters always try for less risky payment terms, whereas the importers may demand easy payment terms. Therefore, it is always a tough job to keep a balance between trying to persuade your customer to accept your request and keeping sensitive to maintain relations with them.

Basically there are four methods of obtaining payment for export shipment: (1) Remittance; (2) Open account; (3) Documentary collection; (4) Documentary credit.

Remittance is one of the most convenient and common terms of payment in international trade. There are generally three types of remittance: Telegraphic Transfer (T/T), Demand Draft (D/D), and Mail Transfer (M/T), of which T/T is the mainstay means.

In an open account trade arrangement, the goods are shipped to a buyer without guarantee of payment. Quite often, the buyer does not pay on the agreed time. Unless the buyer's integrity is unquestionable, this trade arrangement is risky to the seller.

Collection is an arrangement whereby the seller draws a draft on the buyer, and/or shipping documents are forwarded to his bank, authorizing it to collect the money from the buyer through its correspondent bank. Collection is still based on commercial credit instead of bank credit and the banks act only as a collector of funds under a transaction and provide a channel to transfer funds between the buyer and seller.

Among the various ways of payment, letter of credit (L/C) is the most commonly-used means of payment in international trade because it is reliable and safe. It can ensure that the exporter can get paid as soon as he has fulfilled his part of the sales contract and has shipped the goods even if the buyer has not received the goods, and ensure that the importer is assured of title to the goods before he pays for them. A commercial L/C goes through the following main stages.

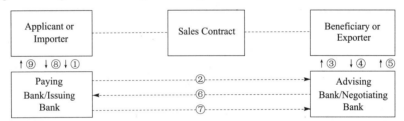

① The importer applies to a local bank for opening an L/C in favor of the exporter and provides a certain amount of deposit and formality fees.

② The opening bank sends the L/C opened to the advising bank.

③ The advising bank transfers the L/C to the exporter.

④ After examining the L/C, the exporter delivers the goods according to the stipulations of L/C. After shipment, the exporter makes out a draft and draws up the documents in accordance with the L/C, and delivers them to the negotiating bank within its validity.

⑤ If the documents are in conformity with the L/C, the negotiating bank will advance the purchase price to the exporter.

⑥ The negotiating bank transfers the draft and documents to the opening bank or the bank appointed by the opening bank applying for payment.

⑦ The opening bank will pay to the negotiating bank after examining the documents.

⑧ The opening bank informs the applicant of the same and asks him to make payment so as to get hold of the shipping documents.

⑨ The applicant makes payment to get hold of the shipping documents, and takes delivery of the goods against the documents.

When payment is made by L/C, the seller, on receiving the relevant L/C, should examine it thoroughly to see whether the clauses stipulated in it are in full conformity with the terms agreed upon by both parties and whether he is in a position to comply with these clauses. If any discrepancies or some unforeseen special clauses to which the seller does not agree are found in the L/C, the seller ought to write a letter to the buyer, asking him to make amendments.

When the importer fails to make the payment promptly, the seller may have to send a letter of payment demands. It is really a tough job to write such type of letters because it requires sophistication and communication skills as well as pressure, so the writer should take special care in writing these letters.

8.3 Analysis of Model Letters

Read and analyze the following letters. While reading, please try to find answers to the following questions.

(1) The following three letters have different purposes. What are their respective purposes?
(2) How is each letter structured to fulfill its communicative purpose?
(3) What are the most impressive points in each letter?

Model Letter 8-1: Requesting a change in method of payment

Dear Mr. Kojima,

We have been doing business with you since last year and we are quite satisfied with the quality of your products.

We would be happy to place another order with your company, provided that you kindly revise the payment method. Instead of payment by L/C, which is inconvenient to us, we hope you can accept payment by thirty days check against delivery. Please give our request your most serious consideration.

Concerning our credit standing you may refer to Maxima Clothes Factory and HSBC, Hong Kong Branch.

We look forward to your reply.

Yours Sincerely,
Irene Yeung
Sales Manager

Model Letter 8-2: Urging the establishment of L/C

Dear Sirs,

Re: Our Sales Confirmation No. AJ106

The goods under the captioned S/C have already been ready for shipment. The date of delivery is approaching, but we have not received your covering L/C yet. Please do your utmost to rush the L/C so as to enable us to effect shipment within the stipulated time.

In order to avoid subsequent amendments, please see to it that the L/C stipulations conform to the terms of the Contract. Moreover, we wish to invite your attention to the fact that the Contract is concluded on FOB Shanghai basis, therefore, your responsibility is to dispatch the vessel to the loading port in due course.

We are looking forward to receiving your L/C soon.

Yours sincerely,

Model Letter 8-3: A 10-day notice before collections on delinquent account

Dear Mr. Johnson,

I have written to you several times over the past three months requesting an explanation on why you have failed to bring your account with us currently.

By ignoring these requests, you are damaging the excellent credit record you had previously maintained with our company. In addition, you are incurring additional expense to yourself and to us.

Unless I hear from you within ten days, I will have no other choice but to turn your account over for collection. I am sorry that we must take such drastic action but I am afraid you leave us no alternative. You can preserve your credit rating by remitting your check today for the amount stated above.

Yours sincerely,

8.4 Writing Guidelines

Here are some points which may be helpful in writing letters concerning negotiations over terms of payment.

(1) Acknowledging receipt of the other party's letter, fax or e-mail and their concern with and preference for terms of payment.

(2) Providing information about your usual practice in terms of payment and include details about instrument, methods, time and amount of payment.

(3) Giving reasons or other convincing evidence to prove the merit of your request.

(4) Stating that your decision is based on the best cooperation and long-term relationship. This is a friendly move which can arouse the other party's enthusiasm for agreeing on your proposed payment terms.

When writing a letter urging to open an L/C, you need to include the following points.

(1) A reference to a relevant contract or agreement.

(2) The importance of receiving the L/C in time.

(3) A request for the opening of the expected L/C.

(4) Your expectation for a favorable reply or a friendly close.

When the importer has got his L/C opened, usually he must notify the establishment of the L/C. A letter of this type is usually made up of the following three parts.

(1) Notifying the establishment of L/C.

(2) Asking for delivery of the relevant consignment.

(3) A friendly close or an expectation for smooth delivery.

The following points may be helpful for writing a letter for amending an L/C.

(1) Expressing thanks for your counterpart's opening of the L/C.

(2) Presenting the explanations for an amendment.

(3) Specifying requirements of the amendment.

(4) Expressing expectation or making a repetition of the request at the end.

While writing a letter of payment demand, you should include the following essential parts.

(1) An indication of the overdue payment waiting to be settled — the sum of the money that should have been paid and the date when the payment should have been made.

(2) Suggestions for another date of payment.

(3) Additional remarks which may induce or press the reader to take immediate actions.

(4) Sometimes in a payment demand the writer may list some trivial possible excuses to give the reader an out so that the good business relationship may still be maintained.

8.5 More Sample Letters

The following letters comply basically with the above writing guidelines, but they are different from the models in 8.3 in one way or another. Read them to see how each letter is structured and worded to achieve its respective communicative purpose.

Sample Letter 8-1: Negotiating payment method

The following letter discusses about the method of payment. Both the reasons for a new payment method and the specifications of the suggested method are provided. This letter is simple but effective.

Dear Sirs,

Thank you for placing an order with us for 2,000 sets of 12V Power Tools. Our sales contract is attached to this letter. The products contain customized design according to your specifications. For this reason, in the sales contract we require a down payment.

The detailed clause of the payment terms in the S/C reads: The down payment up to 30% of the total contract amount shall be remitted to the seller no later than February 25, 2011. The balance shall be paid to the seller by T/T within 7 working days after receipt of the copy of shipping documents.

We expect your early confirmation.

Yours faithfully,

Encl: A Sales Contract

Sample Letter 8-2: Urging the establishment of L/C

It seems that this letter aims to confirm the order received, but while we read on, we can feel clearly that its focus is on urging the establishment of the relevant L/C.

Dear Sirs,

Thanks for confirming your recent order for 1,200 PCS of Ladies' Down Jacket with our company. Our Sales Contract (S/C K09127) has been sent to you on Nov. 27, 2011 by fax. Please sign the copies and return one copy to us for our record at your earliest convenience.

According to the sales contract, the confirmed and irrevocable L/C in our favor should be opened 30 days before the shipping date. I understand that now it's your busiest moment for arranging new season's orders. However, in order to avoid any delay of this order, please extend your cooperation on establishing this L/C to us immediately.

Upon receipt of your L/C, we will start production to ensure punctual delivery.

Should you require any further information on the L/C establishment, please contact us without any hesitation.

Yours faithfully,

Sample Letter 8-3: Application for Issuing an L/C

This is an application letter for the opening of an L/C. It is rich in its content, but because of its clear arrangement of the main information, the reader of the letter won't find it difficult to read.

Dear Ms Morgan,

<u>Application for L/C in favour of Julian Montero srl</u>

We have contacted Julian Montero, the Argentine supplier of the wine we are importing. We will be importing 500 cases of white and red wine and the total value of the contract is US$50,000.00 (Say fifty thousand US dollars only).

Please open a letter of credit to cover the shipment. Details are as follows:
(1) Beneficiary: Julian Montero srl, San Nicolas 1746.
(2) Sr. Montero's bank: Bank of Argentina, Buenos Aires.
(3) Irrevocable Letter of Credit 30 days. To be confirmed by your correspondent bank in Argentina.
(4) The letter of credit must cover the enclosed list of wines which specifies the brands and quantities we have ordered.
(5) Four clean copies of the Bill of Lading.
(6) No partial shipment permitted.
(7) Shipping terms: CIF.

We look forward to receiving a copy of your letter to your correspondent bank in Argentina as soon as possible. Please let me know if there is any further information you require.

Yours sincerely,
Vivian Eastwood
Manager

Sample Letter 8-4: Notifying the establishment of L/C

Superficially the purpose of this letter is to notify the other side of the establishment of the L/C, but actually the writer is expressing his wish that the shipment be effected immediately.

Dear Sirs,

We have received your letter of December 8th in connection with your Sales Confirmation No. YK165.

In reply, we are pleased to tell you that we have today established with the National Bank the confirmed, irrevocable L/C No. 8762 in your favor for the amount of FRF52,000 payable by sight draft accompanied by a full set of the shipping documents.

As the season is drawing near, our buyers are in urgent need of the goods. Please arrange shipment of the goods ordered by us upon receipt of the L/C. We would like to stress that any delay in shipping our order will involve us in no small difficulty. We hope you will let us know at your earliest convenience the name of the carrying vessel and its sailing date.

Thank you in advance for your cooperation.

Faithfully yours,
Robert Trumper

Sample Letter 8-5: Requesting an amendment to an L/C

Please note that in the following letter the details of the relevant L/C are given clearly at the very beginning. The problem, the reasons why an amendment is necessary and the suggested shipment date are stated in separate paragraphs so that the reader won't be confused.

Dear Sir,

<u>100 M/T Tons Cocoa Butter</u>

We are in receipt with thanks of your L/C No. K03987 issued by the Chartered Bank covering your order of 100 M/T of Cocoa Butter.

Much to our regret, however, you failed to open the said L/C as per the terms of the Contract, which stipulated: "Shipment: to be made in late June, 2011".

As you have been well informed in our previous correspondence, we are not in a position to advance delivery of the above goods to May owing to heavy commitments.

Therefore, you are kindly requested to amend the shipment date of your L/C to June 30 and validity to July 15, thus enabling us to execute the order smoothly.

We wish to have your understanding in this connection and await your amendment.

Faithfully yours,

Sample Letter 8-6: Warning to overdue account

This letter is short, but the writer's attitude towards the overdue payment is clearly expressed. The writer applies the stick and carrot to persuade the other side to pay the overdue balance immediately.

Dear Mr. Ho,

We feel very disappointed not having received any reply from you concerning our letter on 5 October, regarding the non-payment of the overdue balance HK$7,400.00.

Although our business relations in the past few years have always been pleasant, we cannot allow the amount remain unpaid indefinitely. We are reluctantly compelled to turn the matter over to a collection agent if you can't settle it by the end of this week.

Please treat this matter with the utmost urgency.

Yours sincerely,
Joannne Chan
Financial Controller

Sample Letter 8-7: A reply to a demand payment letter

As this is a positive reply to a demand payment letter, the receiver of the letter will be satisfied. In such a short letter, both the reasons for the delay and the settlement of the overdue payment are covered.

Dear Mr. Loake,

Thank you for your letter dated 5 October, reminding us that we did not settle our payment due on 30 September. After checking, we found that our accounting department made an oversight in settling the check to you.

Please find attached the check for the amount HK$8,000. We are sorry for the inconvenience caused and hope you will realize that we had no intention in delaying our payment.

Yours sincerely,

8.6 More Useful Sentences

1. Discussing Payment Terms

- Payment is to be made against sight draft drawn under a confirmed, irrevocable letter of credit without recourse for the full amount of purchase.
- For payment we require 100% value, irrevocable L/C in our favor available by draft at sight.

- Based on our company's rule, we only accept the L/C for all the new customers.
- Payment by L/C is our usual practice with all new customers.
- This transaction is done on the basis that you effect the payment covering the total value of the goods by T/T 15 days prior to the date of shipment.
- As our present purchase is sizable, we would like you to accept the terms of payment by installments.
- If you want to expand your business in our market, you have to take flexible ways in adopting payment terms.
- Instead of L/C at sight, we prefer to pay by D/P at sight for all our coming orders.
- It is expensive to open an L/C and tie up the capital of a small company like ours, so it is better for us to adopt D/P or D/A.
- We propose to pay by bill of exchange at 30 days' documents against acceptance.
- As agreed, we only accept 100% value, confirmed and irrevocable L/C payable at sight.
- Our terms of payment are by confirmed, irrevocable L/C in our favor, available by draft at sight, reaching us one month ahead of shipment, remaining valid for negotiation in China for a further 21 days after the prescribed time for shipment, and allowing transshipment and partial shipment.

2. Seller's Acceptance
- Your request for D/P payment has been considered and we are pleased to grant this facility.
- As a token of our sincere cooperation, we agree to payment by D/P at sight.
- As a special sign of encouragement, we shall consider accepting payment by D/P during this sales-pushing stage.
- In view of our long business relations, we exceptionally accept delivery against D/P at sight, but this should not be taken as a precedent.
- In compliance with your request, we will make an exception to our rules and accept delivery against D/P at sight.
- It was only in consideration of our good relationship that we give you an accommodation by agreeing to D/P instead of L/C.
- To meet each other halfway, we are prepared to accept payment of 50% by L/C and the balance by D/P at sight.
- It is understood that our previous payment method of the L/C at sight is inconvenient for your business. As a long-term business partner, we agree to use D/A for all the coming orders to support your business.
- In view of the small amount of this transaction, we are prepared to accept payment by D/P at 30 days' sight for the value of the goods shipped.
- We are prepared to accept payment by confirmed, irrevocable L/C available by draft at sight instead of T/T reimbursement.

3. Seller's Refusal
- We regret to tell you that we cannot accept your request for payment by D/P. It may be considered once trust has been established through regular business.
- We very much regret our inability to accept payment by D/P, since we haven't known much about your credit status.

- We regret our inability to make any arrangement contrary to our usual practice.
- We regret that we are unable to grant your request, as it is our usual practice to ask for sight L/C. In case you insist on payment by D/P, we will be unable to accept your order.
- We regret having to inform you that although it is our desire to pave the way for a smooth development of business between us, we cannot accept payment by D/A.
- We have considered your proposal carefully but we are very sorry to inform you we cannot agree on it.
- With regard to terms of payment, we regret being unable to accept D/P terms. We insist on L/C payment.
- Although it is our desire to pave the way for a smooth development of business between us, we cannot accept payment by D/P.

4. Asking for the Establishment of L/C
- It would be advisable for you to establish the covering L/C as early as possible so as to enable us to arrange shipment in due time.
- Much to our regret, we have not yet received your L/C against our S/C No. 98734, although it should have reached us by the end of March, as stipulated.
- As the goods against your Order No. 65264 have been ready for quite some time, it is imperative that you take immediate action to have the covering L/C established.
- To cover our shipment, we request you to establish a commercial letter of credit in our favor for the contracted amount through a Japanese bank.
- Please do your utmost to expedite the covering L/C, so that we may execute the order smoothly.
- We hope that you will take your commercial reputation into account in all seriousness and open the L/C at once; otherwise you will be responsible for all the losses arising as a result of your failure to do so.

5. Requesting L/C Amendment
- Your L/C has been received, but we would request you to amend it as follows.
- On examination of the L/C stipulations, we found the following discrepancies that do not conform to the terms of our contract. Therefore you are kindly requested to make the following amendments.
- We have received your L/C No. 9086. Among the clauses specified in your L/C we find that the following three points do not conform to the sales contract.
- We would request you to extend the validity of your L/C No. 0609 to 31 May for the shipment covered by it has not been prepared.
- Please extend by fax the shipment date and validity of your L/C to 15 August and 1 September respectively, thus enabling us to effect shipment.
- Will you persuade your customer to arrange for a one-month extension of L/C No. KM906?
- We regret to inform you that due to late receipt of the L/C, we require an extension of shipping date from May 1 to May 15. The validity date of the L/C should be extended accordingly.
- We consider it necessary for you to insert the wording "partial shipment" and "transshipment permitted", lest shipment should be delayed to the detriment of your interest.
- Please amend the L/C to read "Partial shipment and transshipment allowed".

6. Demanding Payment

- Please charge this order to our Account Number 833-876.
- According to our records, you have failed to make any repayments whatsoever and the sum of US$ 45,000 is now overdue.
- I certainly would not like to reduce your credit limit for future purchase, nor to contact a collection agency, which I shall be forced to do it if we do not receive payment in the very near future.
- As arranged, we are handing you our bill of exchange for US$120,000 and ask you to protect it upon presentation.
- This has made it impossible for us to ship the goods within the lifetime of L/C that expires on 8th of March.
- Much to my regret that we have made repeated applications for payment of this amount without avail.

7. Responding to a Payment Demand

- Upon checking the cause of this delay, we have found that our accounting department made an oversight in making remittance to you.
- Your draft of 30th June has been accepted and will be given our protection.
- Enclosed please find our check for USD5,000 in full settlement of this invoice.
- We have deducted the commission of 3% from the total amount due and enclose a remittance bill for $ 1,000 in full settlement of account.

8.7 Writing Tips

Here is a list of points to note suggested by some Business English students. Please read the rules to see whether they are correct or not.

If you write letters discussing payment methods, you'd better bear the following points in mind.

(1) Do not only say that which payment method can not be accepted. Tell your partner which method is preferred.

(2) Tell your reader why you prefer this method of payment to others. The more explanations you give for your request, the better your partner will understand you and more gladly will he accept your proposal.

(3) Tell your reader what you will do next if your proposal is approved. You may tell him or her that you will take action immediately so as to expedite the transaction.

While writing letters to urge for the establishment of an L/C, you should keep the following points in mind.

(1) It is necessary to reiterate some important points agreed upon in the related contract so that no important points may be neglected in the L/C.

(2) It should be written in a concise, polite and impersonal way. Good explanations and convincing reasons should also be provided in such letters.

(3) Always remember that the aim of such a letter is to persuade the buyer to fulfill their obligations of opening the L/C.

If you ask for an amendment to a received L/C, you should note the following points.

(1) Cite the L/C reference number and order information.

(2) Say explicitly the word "amend" or "amendment" to show your purpose of this letter.

(3) Provide the other side with the contents you want to add to the L/C.

(4) Tell the other side the expected date or deadline for receiving the amended L/C and at the same time express thankfulness your counterpart's cooperation.

(5) It is quite necessary to give explanations for the request for amendment as amendment may cost the importer a sum of money and some trouble. The explanations should be enough to convince the reader that amendment is inevitable.

(6) If you ask for an extension of an L/C, you should give special attention to the following three different concepts of "time" in an L/C: ① the expiry date; ② the date of shipment; ③ the period for presentation. When asking for an amendment in the validity term, you should remind the other side of an extension for all the three dates.

When you write payment demand letters, you ought to remember that the following points are important.

(1) In the first place you should send a statement of account with the letter and make reference to the date of the first statement and to the amount of money overdue.

(2) The tone of the first one or two payment demands should be polite, pleasant, firm and rational. It is not wise to make the letter sound offensive, rude or even insulting. But when they are ignored once and again, the writer can send the debtor a threat to take legal actions. Please note that the warning is usually introduced by a display of regret.

(3) The writer may bring forward some proposals for the settlement of payment if the debtor does have some difficulties in effecting the payment.

(4) It is also suggested that the repeated letters demanding payment be typed on pink or even red paper sheet so as to draw the owing side's attention.

Notes and Explanations

1. Alipay 支付宝
支付宝最初作为淘宝网为了解决网络交易安全所设的一个功能,该功能为首先使用的"第三方担保交易模式",由买家将货款打到支付宝账户,由支付宝向卖家通知发货,买家收到商品确认后指令支付宝将货款放于卖家,至此一笔网络交易完成。

2. remittance 汇付,汇款
其他与remittance有关的短语有:make remittance[汇款,开发(支)票];outward remittance(汇出汇款),inward remittance(汇入汇款)。

3. open account 赊账,记账交易

4. documentary credit 跟单信用证

5. documentary collection 跟单托收

6. telegraphic transfer (T/T) 电汇

7. D/D 是 "demand draft" 的缩写,意为 "即期汇票"。
即期汇票,即见票即付的汇票。即期汇票一般以提示日为到期日,持票人持票到银行或其他委托付款人处,后者见票必须付款的一种汇票。这种汇票的持票人可以随时行使自己的票据权利,在此之前无须提前通知付款人准备履行义务。

8. sight draft 即期汇票

9. D/P at sight　即期付款交单
   D/P 是"document against payment"的缩写，意思是"付款交单"。
10. D/A 是"document against acceptance"的缩写，意为"承兑交单"。
    所谓承兑，简单地说，就是承诺兑付，是付款人在汇票上签章表示承诺将来在汇票到期时承担付款义务的一种行为。承兑行为只发生在远期汇票的有关活动中。
11. M/T 是"mail transfer"的缩写，意为"信汇，邮汇"。
12. in favor of　以……为受益人，为……带来益处
    Cheques should be drawn in favor of the treasurer.
    支票应以会计为收款人。
    Price control would gradually disappear in favor of a free market.
    价格控制将逐渐消失而代之以自由市场。
13. opening bank　开证行（也叫 issuing bank）
14. advising bank　通知行
15. negotiating bank　议付行
16. correspondent bank　代理行
17. payment demands　催款信
18. a current account　往来账户，活期存款户
19. in conformity with　符合，按照，和……一致
    In conformity with your instructions by fax last night, we have today dispatched the goods as mention below.
    按昨夜贵方传真要求，我们已于今日将下列货物赶紧发出。
20. customized design　定制设计
21. a down payment　现付，成交即付的现款
22. down jacket　鸭绒衣
23. irrevocable L/C　不可撤销的信用证
    不可撤销信用证是指开证行一经开出、在有效期内未经受益人或议付行等有关当事人同意，不得随意修改或撤销的信用证；只要受益人按该证规定提供有关单据，开证行（或其指定的银行）保证付清货款。
24. covering L/C　相关的信用证
25. bill of lading　提单（可缩写为 B/L）
    提单是证明承运人已接管货物和货物已装船的货物收据，对于将货物交给承运人运输的托运人，提单具有货物收据的功能。
26. FRF　法国法郎
27. commitment　承诺，保证，承担的义务
    the heavy commitment of the orders　履行订单的任务很重
    The President affirmed America's commitment to its European allies.
    总统申明美国履行对其欧洲盟国承担的义务。
28. C.O.D.是"cash on delivery"的缩写，意为"货到付款"。
29. in due course　在适当的时候（也可以说 in due time）
30. in connection with　有关，涉及
31. involve us in no small difficulty　使我们遭遇不小的麻烦
32. collection agent　托收行
33. precedent　以后可以援用的先例

34. pave the way for   为……铺平道路
35. meet halfway   妥协，让步
36. in all seriousness   严肃地
37. contracted amount   合同中注明的金额
38. to the detriment of   不利于，对……有害
39. without avail   不成功
40. give our protection   兑现
41. in full settlement of this invoice   付清该发票的全部金额

Exercises

1. **Multiple choices.**

    (1) As specified on all our invoices our terms of business are 30 days net, so your account for the invoice No. 13009 has now been _____ for 20 days.
        A. outstanded   B. standing out   C. outstanding   D. outstood
    (2) If you are unable to _____ your account by the end of next week, I am afraid we will be forced to take legal actions.
        A. decide   B. solve   C. pay   D. settle
    (3) As we have always received your payment punctually, we wonder if there is any special reason to have caused your account to be one month _____.
        A. overpass   B. overdue   C. due   D. standing over
    (4) If you wish to make inquiries _____ our financial standing, you may refer to our bank, the Chartered Bank, Hong Kong Branch.
        A. with respect   B. regarding   C. for   D. to
    (5) We trust that a letter of credit in our favor _____ the above-mentioned goods will be established immediately.
        A. including   B. relating   C. covering   D. about
    (6) We apologize for the inconvenience you have _____ and assure you that we shall be more careful never to make such a mistake again.
        A. suffered   B. covered   C. accepted   D. received
    (7) The above mentioned are our usual terms of payment and also the payment methods commonly used in our foreign trade _____ in China.
        A. practice   B. habit   C. customs   D. rule
    (8) I would very much appreciate it if you could bear with us patiently, as I am sure that liquidation on our part would not be _____ your interest either.
        A. for   B. in   C. on   D. at
    (9) In view of the difficult situation we are in, you are requested to _____ the L/C to allow transshipment of the goods in Hong Kong.
        A. repair   B. prepare   C. amend   D. change
    (10) This has _____ in unfortunate delays in paying outstanding accounts.
        A. brought   B. made   C. caused   D. resulted

2. Complete the following sentences according to the Chinese given.

(1) Our terms of payment are normally 30-day bill of exchange, _____（承兑交单）.

(2) We are sorry that we are unable to _____（提前装船）due to our heavy commitments.

(3) Please cooperate to extend the dates of the shipment and the validity of the L/C to May 15th and 30th respectively,_____（允许转船和分批装运）.

(4) We only accept payment by confirmed, irrevocable letter of credit available by draft at sight for the full amount of the invoice value and that it should be established _____ _____（以我方为受益人的）.

(5) We _____（借此机会）to assure you of our prompt and careful attention in handling your future orders.

(6) We usually accept payment by irrevocable letter of credit _____（凭装运单据议付）.

(7) Kindly remit us the payment immediately as we expect to _____（为你们结清账目）.

(8) To _____（支付该笔交易）, we have arranged an L/C to be opened in your favor.

(9) We want to _____（真正订购）the series on page 190 in your catalogue.

(10) The order is so urgently required that we must ask you to _____（加速装船）.

3. Fill in the blanks with words or phrases given. Change the form where necessary.

| specify | beyond | talk | appreciate | strict | regard | entitle |
| offer | accommodate | remit | reference | list | express | |

Dear Sirs,

Your check in the amount of $100,000 is being returned to you because it has been made out for the wrong amount.

As we have explained previously, the 5% discount we __(1)__ can only be applied when your payment is mailed within 10 days of delivery. By waiting __(2)__ that period, you forgo the opportunity to deduct the discount from the amount of your invoice.

Since your payment of the above __(3)__ invoice was not made within the __(4)__ time period, you are not __(5)__ to a discount on this order. We are __(6)__ of your business and are most willing to __(7)__ you in any way possible. Our policy, however, in __(8)__ to open account terms, is __(9)__, and in fairness to all of our customers, must be even handed.

Please __(10)__ your check for the full amount of the invoice. Your cooperation in this matter is appreciated.

Thank you for your understanding.

Yours faithfully,
Karen

4. Suppose you have just received a letter pressing for overdue payment. Write a reply to this letter. In your letter, you must include the following particulars.

(1) Express your disappointment with your counterpart's failure to effect the payment overdue.

(2) Point out the damages that your counterpart may suffer from their failure to make the payment.

(3) Make your suggestions for the settlement of the matter.

Chapter 9

Packing and Marking

Your goals for this chapter are to understand:
☑ some technical terms used in packing and marking;
☑ how to structure a letter concerning packing and marking;
☑ some sentence patterns used in letters concerning packing and marking;
☑ some points for attention in writing letters related to packing and marking.

9.1 Lead-in

Before you begin your learning of this chapter, please discuss with your partner(s) about the following questions.

(1) Why should commodities be packed?
(2) How much do you know about the purposes of marking?
(3) Can you list some marks frequently used in international trade?

9.2 Basic Information

Packing is of particular importance in international trade because goods have to travel long distances before reaching their destination — often across oceans or across continents. Proper packing can not only serve as a form of protection, but also facilitate loading, unloading and stowage, and prevent pilferage. Furthermore it can promote sales. So although packing may contribute nothing to a product's value, its influence on distribution costs is considerable. It may be a way of selling a product or at least of providing product information to the customer.

There are various types of packing in international trade. In terms of its function, packing can be divided into two kinds — transport packing and sales packing. The former, also known as outer packing, large packing, export packing, protects goods that a company will move and store in the warehouse and also permits the company to use transportation vehicle space effectively. It also provides information and handling ease. The latter, also known as inner packing, small packing, immediate packing or packing for display, provides information important in selling the product, in motivating the customer to buy the product, or in giving the product maximum visibility when it competes with others on the retail shelf.

On the packs some shipping marks are usually stenciled. The purpose of these marks is to help exporter, customs, carriers, and importer to distinguish one consignment from another. The mark usually consists of the initials of the receiver of the goods, the port of destination, and serial numbers of the package. For example:

> ABC CO.
> LOS ANGELAS
> NO.1-N

They can also be made on order by some companies. For example:

The shipping marks must be exactly the same as those shown on the commercial invoice, bill of lading, etc. They should be in both English and the language of the country of destination. As the purpose of these shipping marks is to identify your goods from those of other shippers, they should be made boldly, with waterproof and salt-proof ink. The final destination point should be made to stand out so that the package can be easily located for customs clearance and delivery. In the case of cautions for handling, exporters are encouraged to use universally recognized cautionary marks such as a wineglass on the commercial invoice and bill of lading, etc. for "fragile", as well as words. Some countries indicate exactly the shipping marks to be used. Such specifications include the size of lettering, their position on the containers, the method of applying the marks, and the types of weights and measures to be used.

9.3 Analysis of Model Letters

Read and analyze the following letters. While reading, please try to find answers to the following questions.

(1) In Model Letter 9-1, the request for an elaboration is made in a conditional sentence. What's its superiority to an imperative sentence?

(2) Why is the suggested packing method stated in a separate paragraph in Model Letter 9-2?

(3) The purpose of Model Letter 9-3 is to inform the other side of the marking requirements, then why does the writer start the letter with reference to the contract and L/C?

Model Letter 9-1: Asking to revise packing instructions

Dear Sirs,

Re: Packing for T-shirts

We thank you very much for your letter of July 6, 2011 and your order No. 9854 for 5,000 dozen T-shirts.

However, after examining the terms in the order, we have noticed that other than the clause worded as "seaworthy packing", there are no detailed requirements for packing the goods. We feel it may cause confusion and misunderstanding in the execution of your order and may even result in disputes. If you could elaborate a bit more on this particular provision, we would appreciate it very much since it will not only give us more precise instructions on what to do, but also provide better coverage when insurance is to be involved.

We are looking forward to your detailed packing instructions.

Yours faithfully,

Model Letter 9-2: Request for improvement in packing

Dear Sirs,

We thank you for your above order of October 15 and have pleasure in informing you that we can accept all the terms but the packing.

We would like to recommend you our latest package, which is economical and strong. The packing mentioned in your order was of the old method we adopted several years ago. From then on we have improved it with the result that our recent goods have all turned out to the complete satisfaction of our clients.

Our Men's shirts are now packed in a polybag and then in a cardboard box, 5 dozen to a carton, with a gross weight about 20 kgs. Each carton is lined with a polythene sheet, so that the content is protected from moisture.

We are looking forward to your prompt reply and wondering if our proposal meets your requirement.

Your faithfully,

Model Letter 9-3: Requirements for marking

Dear Sirs:

We enclose the countersigned copy of Contract No. 53808 of 3 April, 2011 for 500 bales of printed cottons. The L/C is on its way to you. Please mark the bales with our initials, with the destination and contract number as follows:

KT
LONDON
53808

This will apply to all shipments unless otherwise instructed. Please advise us by fax as soon as shipment is effected.

Yours faithfully,
Tony Smith
Chief Buyer

9.4 Writing Guidelines

Letters in packing and marking are not complicated. Most letters deal with requirements in packing or marking and others talk about whether the expected requirements can be met.

The guidelines for writing letter concerning the requirements in packing or marking can be generalized as follows:

(1) At the start, you should express your thanks for the previous letter or order and/or introduce the matter of packing.

(2) Then you ought to state in detail some particular requirements about packing/marking, or modify the packing/marking requirements for the goods ordered.

(3) If necessary, you should give the reasons for your requirement so that your counterpart can understand you and co-operate with you more willingly.

(4) At the end you can express your hope for early confirmation etc.

A letter giving a reply about packing/marking usually consists of the following parts.

(1) First, you should acknowledge receipt of the letter inquiring about packing/marking.

(2) Give the details of your answer. Here you should state clearly whether you can comply with your counterpart's requirements.

(3) If you can meet your counterpart's requirements, you may mention your plan for packing/marking briefly. If you can't, you should give your reasons why you can't pack or mark the goods as requested.

(4) In the end you ought to ask for confirmation or agreement, and at the same time, express your expectation for good co-operation.

9.5 More Sample Letters

The following letters comply basically with the above writing guidelines, but they are different from the models in 9.3 in one way or another. Read them to see how each letter is structured and worded to achieve its respective communicative purpose.

Sample Letter 9-1: Requests in inner packing

The requirements in inner packing is the most important part of the letter, that's why they are separately placed so that enough attention may be attracted to it.

Dear Sirs,

In reply to your fax message of May 26, 2011 we regret having forgotten to mention the inner packing requirements of Bee Brand Brown Sugar we ordered at the Guangzhou Spring Fair this year. Now we have discussed the matter with our customers. They request as follows:

As brown sugar is moisture absorbent especially in hot rainy seasons, it should be packed in kraft paper bags containing 20 small paper bags of 1 kg net each, two kraft paper bags to a carton lined with water-proof paper.

We hope the above requirements will be acceptable to you and look forward to your early reply.

Yours sincerely,

Sample Letter 9-2: Packing requirements for bamboo products

The following is an order letter, and the packing requirement is part of the order. Because of its importance, the packing clause is placed in a separate paragraph.

Dear Zhang Dan,

For soonest possible shipment we are in need of the following articles:
- 300 pcs art-No. WDT 1-201 Bamboo pole, diameter 18/21 mm, 300 cms;
- 500 pcs art-No. WDT 1-205 Bamboo pole, diameter 9/15 mm, 500 cms;
- 150 pcs art-No. WDT 02-301 Bamboo-Fence, H175xW75 cms.

The above mentioned bamboo poles are to be packed in bundles of 100 pieces only. These poles are required in natural (not lacquered) color.

Regarding the quotation for several Bamboo Products dated 4th of May we have talked with our customer and he will keep us informed during the next few days of the quantities required.

Awaiting your reply.

Best regards.
JOHAN LUKET & CO.
Manyer jr.

Sample Letter 9-3: A request for amendments in packing and marking

In the following letter, the problem in packing is first pointed out, and then the reason for an amendment is given briefly, and finally the new requests are stated quite clearly. Everything in the letter is arranged logically.

Dear Miss Jenkins,

S/C No. 90SP — 24975

We acknowledge receipt of your letter dated the 3rd, August and the enclosed contract. After going through the contract we find that the packing clause in it is not clear enough. The relative clause reads as follows:

Packing: Seaworthy export packing, suitable for long distance ocean transportation.

In order to eliminate possible future trouble, we would like to make clear beforehand our packing requirements as follows:

The Tea under the captioned S/C should be packed in international standard tea boxes, 24 boxes on a pallet, 10 pallets in an FCL container. On the outer packing please mark our initials SP in a diamond, under which the port of destination and our order number should be stenciled. In addition, warning marks like KEEP DRY, USE NO HOOK, etc. should also be indicated.

We have made a footnote on the contract to that effect and are returning herein one copy of the contract after duly countersigning it. We hope you will find it in order and pay special attention to the packing.

We look forward to receiving your shipping advice.

Yours faithfully,

Sample Letter 9-4: Stressing the importance of good packing

The focus of the following letter is to stress the importance of trustworthy packing. It starts with a complaint, which may help to impress upon the reader the necessity of good packing.

Dear Sir or Madam,

We have taken delivery of the goods, but regret to inform you that of the 30 cases of machine parts you shipped to Shanghai on April 18, five were seriously damaged. In consideration of the long and friendly relationship between us, we refrain from lodging a claim this time. But we feel it necessary to stress the importance of trustworthy packing for your future deliveries to us.

As machine parts are susceptible to shock, they must be wrapped in soft materials and firmly packed in seaworthy cases in such a manner that movement inside the cases is impossible. The bright metal parts should be protected from dampness and rust in transit by a coating of antirust grease.

We trust that you can meet the above requirements and thank you in advance for your co-operation.

Yours faithfully,

Sample Letter 9-5: Advising packing and shipping marks

The following letter is in reply to an inquiry about packing and marking. The replies about packing and marking are stated separately so that the message is clear.

Dear Sirs,

We thank you for your letter dated May 2 inquiring about the packing and the shipping marks of the goods under Contract No. P211, and are pleased to state as follows:

All powders are wrapped in plastic bags and packed in tins, the lids of which are sealed with adhesive tape. Ten tins are packed in a wooden case, which is nailed, and secured by overall metal strapping.

As regards shipping marks outside the wooden case, in addition to gross, net and tare weights, the wording "Made in Japan" is also stenciled. Should you have any special preference in this respect, please let us know and we shall meet your requirements to the best of our ability.

We assure you of our close co-operation and await your further comments.

Yours sincerely,

Sample Letter 9-6: Advising the buyer of packing and marking

The purpose of the following letter is to confirm the details in packing and marking agreed upon by both parties in previous correspondence. Please note the clear arrangement of the main information.

Dear Sirs,

We are pleased to inform you that your Order No. 4319 will soon be ready for shipment as long as you have confirmed the following details for packing and marking of the goods as discussed in our earlier correspondence.

Packing: all 5,000 dozen T-shirts are packed 250 pieces to one standard export carton, lined with waterproof material. The T-shirts are wrapped with polyester bags, rolled up and packed into the cartons. The total 240 cartons are then packed into one 20ft container for convenience of shipment.

Marking: the cartons are marked "USE NO HOOKS", and the logo of your company comes above the line of the destination port. The bottom line consists of your order number and total number of cartons of the consignment.

We hope the packing and marking are up to your requirements. Please confirm as soon as possible so that we can pack accordingly for early shipment.

Yours faithfully,

9.6 More Useful Sentences

1. Enquiry about Packing/Marking
- Are your Soya Beans supplied in bulk or in gunny bags?
- Can the cartons be well protected against moisture by polythene sheet lining?
- We wonder whether the bicycles can be wrapped in strong waterproof material at the port and packed in lightweight crates.
- We appreciate the quality of your Alarm Clocks but should like to know how they are packed and marked.
- We would appreciate it very much if the full details regarding packing and marking are strictly observed.

2. Replies to Enquiries about Packing/Marking
- The coffee will be packed in clean sound bags of uniform size made of woven material, without inner lining or outer covering of any material properly sewn by hand and/or machine.
- It will be packed in wooden cases, each containing 12 five-pound tins, net weight 60 pounds, gross weight 70 pounds.

- The wheat is to be packed in new gunny bags of 100 kgs. Each gunny bag weighs about 1kg.
- It is to be packed in new strong wooden cases suitable for a long voyage and well protected against dampness, moisture, shock, rust and rough handling.
- Cases or other outside containers must be externally of the smallest cubic dimension consistent with adequate protection of the goods.
- Each set is packed in one export carton, each 810 cartons transported in one 40 ft container.
- Our improved packing will catch the eye of the buying public, which will help push the sales.
- Our cartons are strong enough to stand rough handling in the course of transportation.
- When the various products are complete in our warehouse we will pack them into bundles of suitable size for shipment.
- We usually have our screws packed in double gunny bags of 60 kgs each.
- Shirts are packed in wooden cases of 20 dozen each.
- Coats are packed in wooden cases, each containing 10 dozens.
- Goods are to be packed in cases of 50 dozen each, with the exception of case No. 6 containing 35 dozens and case No. 9 40 dozen respectively.
- We have now adopted carton packing instead of wooden cases as the former is just as seaworthy as the latter while the cost is less and the weight lighter.
- We shall pack the goods in our usual packing if you have nothing particular in this regard.

3. Packing Requirements

- Please see to it that the packing is strong enough to stand rough handling.
- Please use hard fermented plastic padding for fixing these fragile goods.
- Please wrap the carpets in thick grease-proof paper and reinforce at both ends to avoid wear by friction.
- The packing must be in line with local market preference.
- The machine must be well protected against dampness, moisture, rust and shock.
- Effective measures must be taken to protect this product, as the goods are particularly subject to breakage.
- Ropes or metal handles should be fixed to the boxes to facilitate carrying.
- Our cotton prints should be packed in cases lined with kraft paper and water-proof paper.
- The goods should be packed in a manner that ensures safe and sound arrival of goods at the destination and facilitates handling during transshipment.
- The eggs should be packed in cartons with beehives lined with shake-proof paper board.
- We would ask you to be particularly careful to seal each box into a watertight bag before packing into cases.
- Please see to it that straws are not allowed here as filling material.
- Please use normal export containers unless you receive special instructions from our agents.
- Packing in sturdy wooden cases is essential. Cases must be nailed, battened and secured by overall metal strapping.
- As the commodities will probably be subjected to a thorough customs examination, the cases should be of a type which can easily by made fast again after opening.
- We would like to let you know that the machines must be packed in special crates with reinforced bottom.

- They should be packed in wooden cases containing 30 pieces of 40 yards each.
- It is required that the goods be packed in cans, 12 cans to a cardboard box, 10 cardboard box to a case.
- It is essential that they be packed in wooden cases lined with tin plate, with iron hoops at both ends.
- Packing must be suitable for ocean shipment and sufficiently strong to withstand rough handling.

4. Marking Requirements

- Please see to it that the shipping marks indicated in our order and the gross and net weight are to be stenciled on each crate.
- The marks should be in black, with red or orange for dangerous cargo.
- The marks should be in both English and the language of the country of destination.
- The final destination point should be made to stand out so that the package can be easily identified with the corresponding shipping documents.
- A mark of origin should be placed on imported goods, if its absence would create a false impression about the origin of such goods.
- On outer packing please mark our initials CBBX, under which our order number and port of destination are stenciled.
- Packages must bear full marks and shipping numbers stenciled in good quality stencil ink in large plain characters on two sides and one end of each package. All bales must be marked "USE NO HOOKS".
- The goods are to be marked with our initials inside a diamond.

5. Agreement to Packing/Marking Arrangement

- We have examined the polythene bag you sent us and find it acceptable if you could omit the brand name on the bag as agreed before.
- Our Trip Scissors are packed in boxes of 1 dozen each, 100 boxes to a carton lined with waterproof paper.
- As requested, we have included a packing note with your commodities, and have pleasure in enclosing further copy of the note.
- We regret to learn your dissatisfaction with the packing for the last shipment but we can assure you of our special attention to the packing of your future shipments.
- Your specific requirements for packing have been transmitted to the department concerned for consideration and we will let you know the result later.
- We do not object to packing in cartons. Provided the flaps are glued down and the cartons secured by metal bands.
- We can meet your requirements to have the goods packed in wooden cases but you have to bear the extra packing charge.

6. Disagreement to Packing/Marking Arrangement

- We will take every step within our reach to improve the packing so as to protect the goods from breakage.
- As it will take us time to pack the goods according to your requirements, we are afraid that the shipment may not be effected at the contracted time.

- We have received the consignment under your S/C No. 9Sp-3085 but regret to find 10 cases broken, which evidently results from your poor packing and we reserve our right to lodge a claim after further inspection.
- Our improved packing with cartons has been universally accepted because there has not been a single complaint about the packing since the adoption of cartons.
- We can meet your special requirements for packing but the extra expenses should be borne by you.

9.7 Writing Tips

Some English majors have proposed the following points to note in writing letters about packing or marking. Read the following list quickly and then discuss with your partner whether they are appropriate and try to add some more ideas to the list.

In writing letters about packing and/or marking, you should bear the following points in mind.

(1) The instructions and requirements for the packing need to be clear and detailed for easy and possible handling. It is better to cover as many aspects as possible, including the packing material, manner of packing, packing specification, packing expenses to be borne, shipping marks and so on. Ambiguous phrases such as "seaworthy packing", "customary packing" or "seller's usual packing" are better to be avoided.

(2) The rights and obligations of the buyer and the seller, especially the clause of which party to bear the extra costs incurred from packing, need to be stipulated clearly. Generally speaking, packing costs are included in the price, and shall be borne by the exporter. If the importer has any special requirements for packing, which is beyond the exporter's ability, the additional charges should be borne by the importer.

(3) According to international trade practice, shipping marks are usually designated by the exporter, and it is not necessary to specify them in the contract, but they can also be definitely specified at the importer's request. If it is stipulated in the contract that the importer will designate the shipping marks, a deadline for the designated shipping marks should be set, and it should be also indicated that the exporter shall decide the shipping marks if the importer fails to provide the exporter with details of the shipping marks in time.

(4) It is advisable that you do not make unnecessary suggestions on particular packaging, since it might bring you trouble. Though well-intentioned, it might not turn out to be good for you. If you do need to recommend certain customary handling of one particular packing method, let the customer make the final decision and it would always be wise to ask such final negotiation terms and conditions to be present in the customer's orders or contracts in case of future disputes.

Notes and Explanations

1. facilitate *v.* 使容易，方便
   Well worded and structured letters may facilitate economic exchange.
   措辞和结构好的信件有助于经济交流。
2. outer packing   外包装，大包装
   inner packing   内包装，小包装

其他与 packing 有关的短语有：single packing（单件包装），collective packing（组合包装），vacuum packing（真空包装），waterproof packing（防水包装）。

3. stowage 装载，装载物

   其他与 stowage 有关的短语有：bottom stowage（压载，压舱货物），broken stowage（亏舱），stowage on deck（甲板上装载），wet stowage（湿储法）。

4. stencil *v.* 用模板印刷文字或图案

5. customs clearance 清关

   We will deliver exhibits to stands, assist unpacking and repacking and customs clearance against signature of exhibitors or their authorized agents.

   根据参展商做的标记或他们授权的代理的指示，我们将展品送至展台，负责拆箱、重新包装和清关。

6. seaworthy packing 适合海运的包装

7. economical 经济的，便宜的

   economic 的意思是"经济上的，经济学的"。注意两者的区别。

8. be lined with 被装/垫了衬里

   This box is lined with strong cloth.

   箱子里面用结实的布料做衬里。

9. countersign 会签

10. unless otherwise instructed 除非另有通知

11. keep sb. informed 使某人随时了解最新情况

    We'll keep you informed if any new message comes.

    如收到新信息，我们将随时告诉你。

12. an FCL container 满满一整箱

    FCL 是 "full container load" 的缩写，意思是"满箱货"，与"拼箱货"相对。

13. a coating of antirust grease 一层防锈的油

14. tare weight 皮重

    其他与 weight 有关的短语有：gross weight（毛重），net weight（净重）。

15. in bulk 大批，散装

16. polyester bag 涤纶袋

17. consignment 托运的货物

    其他与 consignment 有关的短语有：to sell on consignment（以托售、寄卖的方式出售），delivery on consignment（托销），consignment-sheet（收货清单），consignment invoice（发货单），freight consignment（托运货物）。

18. grease-proof paper 防油纸

19. kraft paper 牛皮纸

20. self-service retailing 自助零售

21. polythene sheet 聚乙烯薄膜

22. adhesive tape 自粘带

23. cubic dimension 立方

1. Translate the following Chinese phrases into English.

   (1) 一捆棉布
   (2) 一箱机器零件
   (3) 一卷卫生纸
   (4) 一包香烟
   (5) 一张牛皮纸
   (6) 小心轻放
   (7) 勿倒置
   (8) 请勿倒挂
   (9) 勿倾倒
   (10) 在干燥处保管
   (11) 在冷处保管
   (12) 远离锅炉
   (13) 请勿受热
   (14) 请勿受冷

2. Complete the following sentences according to the Chinese given.

   (1) It's sure that all our quotations are _____（随市场的波动而变化）.
   (2) If you have no interest in our products, please send the letter to _____（你方潜在的客户）.
   (3) Enclosed are a letter and _____（一张要求订购1 000双塑料拖鞋的订单）.
   (4) We admit that the quality of your products _____（达到我们的要求）.
   (5) We shall effect shipment immediately _____（保证准时装船）.
   (6) We will assign our production manager _____（安排发运货物）.
   (7) I can assure you that his order will _____（引起我们的密切关注）.
   (8) We shall strengthen quality inspection to _____（向你们保证货物的质量）.
   (9) We can _____（保证履行订单）.
   (10) _____（我方库存已空），so this order won't be executed until the end of next month.

3. Correct the mistakes in the following sentences that are picked from some students' homework.

   (1) All the cases must be lined with waterproofed paper.
   (2) All bags ought have an inner waterproof lining.
   (3) The goods ordered should be good quality and in attractive packing.
   (4) The goods must been packed in cartons, then on pallets.
   (5) Packing in new jute bags each containing about 300 lbs net.
   (6) The goods are to packed in seaworthy cartons.
   (7) Pens is packed 20 pieces to a box and 100 boxes to a wooden case.
   (8) Goods must to be packed in boxes of one dozen each, 100 boxes to a carton, and 4 cartons to a pallet.

(9) Dehydrated garlic flakes are to be packing in double polythene bags of 20 kgs net, over packed with a carton.

(10) Please convey the finished goods by your own transport to our forwarding agent's warehouse, where will be repacked for shipment.

4. Fill in the blanks with appropriate words from the following box.

| instructions | take | follow | practical | account | consideration | space |
| think | | packed | reduce | damaged | insist | cover |

Dear Sirs,

　　Thank you for your prompt reply to our request for packing __(1)__ for the goods you ordered on August 6. We would be most willing to __(2)__ and carry out the packing as you instructed. However, from our usual handling experience, we would like to point out that there is something not so __(3)__ in your request and therefore would like to make the following suggestions for your __(4)__.

　　(A) The requirement of placing 100 pieces of T-shirts only into each carton will waste too much __(5)__ in the carton, since a standard export carton would be able to contain 250 pieces of our products if __(6)__ as standing rolls instead of flat sheets. Since the products will be sold in basic economic package only, it would not harm them if they are rolled up for storage. This can simply cut down the number of cartons to be used from 600 to 240, and __(7)__ the cost of package to less than half of the original. We hope you also like this idea and would agree that we go ahead with our usual packing.

　　(B) The use of crates for every 4 cartons would also seem to be an unusual request since T-shirts are not fragile or heavy products that can be easily __(8)__. The use of crates will not only increase the costs of packing, but also increase the weight of the whole consignment, disproportional to the weight of the merchandise and therefore greatly increase the freight cost. However, if you do __(9)__ on the use of crates, would you be happy to __(10)__ extra costs incurred? A better choice would be to stack the 240 cartons into one 20 ft container instead, which can prove to be much safer and economical.

　　We hope to have your confirmation on the above at your earliest convenience.

　　　　　　　　　　　　　　　　　　　　　　　　　　　　　　　　　Yours faithfully,

Chapter 10

Delivery and After-sale Service

Your goals for this chapter are to understand:

☑ some basic knowledge about delivery and after-sale;
☑ how to write letters concerning delivery and after-sale;
☑ some commonly-used patterns in letters of delivery and after-sale;
☑ some points for attention in writing delivery-related and after-sale-related letters.

10.1 Lead-in

Before you begin your learning of this chapter, please discuss with your partner(s) about the following questions.

(1) Is after-sale service necessary for all kinds of commodities?
(2) Why is after-sale service important?

10.2 Basic Information

Delivery is the process of sending goods. Most goods are delivered through a transportation network. Cargo (physical goods) is primarily delivered via roads and railroads on land, shipping lanes on the sea and airline networks in the air. So delivery is often closely related to transportation, but is not simply equivalent to transportation because certain specialized goods may be delivered via other networks, such as pipelines for liquid goods, power grids for electrical power and computer networks such as the Internet or broadcast networks for electronic information.

The general process of delivering goods is known as distribution. Firms that specialize in delivering commercial goods from point of production or storage to point of sale are generally known as distributors, while those that specialize in the delivery of goods from point of sale to the consumer are known as delivery services. Postal, courier, and relocation services also deliver goods for commercial and private interests.

Most consumer goods are delivered from a point of production through one or more points of storage to a point of sale, where the consumer buys the goods and is responsible for its transportation to point of consumption. Products sold via catalogue or the Internet may be delivered directly from the manufacturer or warehouse to the consumer's home, or to an automated delivery booth. Small manufacturers may deliver their products directly to retail stores without warehousing. Building, construction, landscaping and like materials are generally delivered to the consumer by a contractor as part of another service.

Goods sold will remain at your own risk until the customer has accepted delivery of them. The customer will be deemed to have accepted delivery of the goods when they expressly communicate their acceptance to you or their conduct indicates that they have accepted delivery of the goods.

After-sale service means periodic or as-required maintenance or repair of equipment by its manufacturer or supplier, during and after a warranty period. It is an important part of non price competition. In general, after sales service means providing additional 'offerings' to the customer even after he/she has purchased your product.

A common example of after-sale service is the provision of a warranty for the good. A warranty allows the good to be repaired or replaced if it breaks down within a certain period of time after purchase. For many customers, after-sale service is what makes one supplier stand out from another, often more than product or price. Good customer service can attract new business and can create a loyal customer base.

The provision of after sales service varies in importance depending on the type of good. For example, after sales service and extended warranties are important for goods like electrical goods and new cars. If you currently are or will be competing in an industry where after sales service is of great importance, be sure to indicate this under the after sales service section of your operations plan. In addition, mention each service you intend to offer and how each will strengthen your business venture. If you decide to offer the service yourself, be sure to discuss the costs involved in offering each after sale service. If you decide to contract the work out to a private service business, be sure to discuss all contracting costs, deadlines, the names of each contracting firm, the contracting firms' current workload and their ability to handle your service requirements.

10.3 Analysis of Model Letters

Read the following letters. While reading, please try to find answers to the following questions.

(1) Model Letter 10-1 seems to be an enquiry about the date of delivery, but actually it aims to press for an early delivery of the ordered goods. How does the writer achieve such a purpose?

(2) What is the function of the proposed solution in Model Letter 10-2?

(3) Why does the writer of Model Letter 10-3 list the services in such a neat way?

Model Letter 10-1: Asking about date of delivery

Dear Sirs,

RE: SHEEP WOOL

With reference to our Order No. TC303 of 22 February for 50 M/T of Sheep Wool, we shall be glad to know when we may expect delivery, as they are urgently required.

When we made the initial inquiry, your department assured us that delivery would only take two months, and we placed the order on that understanding as we wished to have the wool before the end of October. Your delay in delivery may bring us much inconvenience.

Will you please inform us by fax or e-mail, of the earliest possible date when you can deliver these goods. Should the delay be longer than two or three weeks, we shall regretfully have to cancel the order.

Yours faithfully,
Tong Xiang Woolen Sweaters Co. Ltd.
Jia-kun Zhang, manager of the Sales Department

Model Letter 10-2: Being unable to advance delivery

Dear Sirs,

Thank you for your letter of 2nd, August requesting earlier delivery of goods under your purchase contract No. 9548.

We have contacted the shipping company and regret to tell you that we are unable to comply with your request. We have been informed that there is no available space on ships sailing from here to your port before 5 September.

We are very sorry for being unable to advance shipment. We will, however, do everything possible to ensure that the goods are shipped within the contracted time.

Yours faithfully,
Tony Smith
Chief Seller

Model Letter 10-3: Reply to an inquiry about after-sale service

Dear Sirs,

We are in receipt of your letter dated April 9, inquiring about after-sales service on equipment we sell. In reply, we would advise that we are pleased to render first-rate services to end-users through our agents all over the world in the following business.

(1) Installation, testing and adjustment of equipment.
(2) Training of technical personnel for operation, maintenance and management.
(3) Providing operation and maintenance instructions as well as catalogues.
(4) Maintenance and replacement of equipment and supply of spare parts and technical information through our agents abroad.
(5) Making periodic calls on end-users to find out the operation condition of equipment, aimed at enhancing the quality of products.

Please do not hesitate to contact us for further information in which you may be interested and we shall be glad to let you have the same upon receipt of your letter.

Yours truly,

10.4 Writing Guidelines

Analysis of a letter inquiring about delivery or after-sale service arrangement indicates that letters of such kind usually consist of the following components.

(1) First, you should refer to an order you have placed so that your counterpart can understand for which order you are talking about the delivery or after-sale service.

(2) Then make your inquiry about the delivery or after-sale service. At this stage, you may also state your requirements about delivery or after-sale service.

(3) You may make some further requirements related to the delivery, if you want.

(4) At the end you may express your hope for a smooth cooperation.

In a reply to an enquiry about delivery or after-sale service, you ought to include the following elements.

(1) Acknowledging receipt of the inquiry or letter.

(2) Giving information asked for, for example, the delivery date, the types of after-sale services to be rendered etc.

(3) Making necessary explanations if your reply is a negative one, or make a recommendation or substitute to appease the receiver of your letter.

(4) Expressing a good expectation to close the letter.

10.5 More Sample Letters

The following letters comply basically with the above writing guidelines, but they are different from the models in 10.3 in one way or another. Read them to see how each letter is structured and worded to achieve its respective communicative purpose.

Sample Letter 10-1: Urging delivery
The writer of the following letter states what he has done for the order at the beginning, which may pave a way for the following requirement for early delivery. The clear paragraphing of the letter makes the message easy to follow.

Dear Miss Zhang,

We wish to draw your attention to our Order No. A642 covering 5 sets of Model 810 machine, for which we opened the irrevocable L/C NO. BA789 in your favor this morning through Bank of China, Hamburg.

Upon receipt of the above-mentioned L/C, please do make delivery of the goods on time. You are supposed to ship the goods by a steamer of ABC Co. The main reason is that their steamers offer the shortest time for the journey between China and Germany.

We trust you will endeavor to ship the goods within the stipulated time and the consignment will arrive in good order.

Your close cooperation will be highly appreciated.

Yours faithfully,

Sample Letter 10-2: Requesting to advance delivery date
The request for early delivery is politely conveyed, but if more concrete reasons were provided, the following letter would be more persuasive and his demand could be satisfied more easily and possibly.

Dear Sirs,

We refer to our purchase contract No. 954.

Under the terms of the contract, delivery is scheduled for May 2011. We would now like to bring delivery forward to March/April 2011.

We realize that the change of delivery date will probably inconvenience you and we offer our sincere apologies. We know that you will understand that we would not ask for earlier delivery if we did not have compelling reasons for doing so. In view of our longstanding, cordial commercial relationship, we would be very grateful if you would make a special effort to comply with our request.

We look forward your early reply.

Yours faithfully,
Tony Smith
Chief Seller

Sample Letter 10-3: Promising to make the soonest delivery

After stating the arrangement for the delivery, the writer of the following letter focuses his attention on explaining why the delivery was delayed and at the same time publicizing his products.

Dear Sir,

We are in receipt of your letter of 2nd April, and very much regret the delay in delivering the above. We are now making the arrangements for immediate delivery, which means you will have the excavators by the end of April at the latest.

The Superline GSC is the most successful excavator we have so far produced. It was an instant success at its first appearance last year at the Leeds Building Exhibition and we were soon inundated with orders. Your own order received in Dec. and, according to the waiting list we had, it was not due for delivery until June.

Nevertheless, we have put the delivery date forward so that you could have the machines in March. In February, production was slightly set back by the late arrival of some special parts, and this has been responsible for the delay in the present case.

We trust that you will not be unduly inconvenienced by having to wait a few more days. The performance of the Superline GSC excavator will amply compensate you.

Yours faithfully,

Sample Letter 10-4: Notifying delivery date

The notification of the delivery date, which is the most important message in the letter, is placed at the very beginning. Meanwhile, the writer is requesting the details of the order.

Dear Sir/Madam,

Re: Delivery date

Please note that the delivery date is normally in 45–60 days provided that all information is submitted to the factory and upon lab-dips confirmation. Under this situation, we cannot confirm when we can deliver the bulk as until this moment we still have not yet received any details regarding your order. So, please immediately send the complete information of your order and after checking we'll inform you the best delivery date.

Sincerely yours,
(Signature)

Sample Letter 10-5: Appreciating prompt delivery

  This is an acknowledgement letter as well as an encouragement letter because the writer has not only expressed his thankfulness but also commended what the other side has done.

Dear Mr. Castro,

Thank you for your prompt deliveries to our Doe Plant.

In our business we must get our products to the stores on a regular schedule. We rely on dependable service from suppliers like you to help us keep our schedule and satisfy our customers.

We want you to know that we appreciate your efforts and look forward to continuing our business relationship.

Yours sincerely,

Sample Letter 10-6: A reply about after-sale service

  This is a polite reply to a request for after-sale service. The writer does not decline the request simply, but tells the reader what he should do next.

Dear Mr. Gilson,

I have got your letter of May 1 on our D-Lux vacuum cleaner you bought from our department store on February 1 last year.

I wonder if you had read the warranty of the cleaner before you sent us your letter as that was expired at the end of the third month from the day the cleaner was purchased. If you were more careful you might have read the manufacturer's address and you could turn to them for help.

I hope you can get your problem solved by yourself.

Yours faithfully,

Sample Letter 10-7: Arrangement for the replacement of battery cells

In the following letter, the writer not only notifies his counterpart of the arrangements for the replacement, but also gives some advice for maintenance of the hammer, so the writer is very considerate.

Dear Sirs,

We have your letter of August 10th, in which you notify us that some battery cells of the steam hammer were damaged and had to be replaced.

We now enclose our S/C No. 6433 for the replacement order which will be promptly executed when we receive your L/C.

Please allow us to remind you here of the importance of checking the specific gravity of the electrolyte in each cell of the battery every 100 hours. In warm weather, however, it should be checked more frequently due to more rapid loss of water from electrolyte. The electrolyte level should be maintained in accordance with the battery manufacturer's recommendations. Our experience tells us that in case of negligence in this regard the cells will often be damaged.

Yours faithfully,

10.6 More Useful Sentences

1. Pressing for Early Delivery
- Please be informed that the clients are in urgent need of the commodity contracted and are in fact pressing for an early delivery.
- Please deliver us the following by the first steamer sailing for London next month.
- Please ship the following goods by motor freight as soon as possible, and charge them to our account.
- Please deliver these goods immediately to the London dock.

2. Response to a Request for Delivery
- The goods have been dispatched by rail to your address.

- Delivery will be made immediately on receipt of your letter of credit. We have today dispatched by S. S. "Zhen Da" a consignment of 1,000 cases canned beef and enclosed shipping documents.
- Your order is receiving our immediate attention, and you can depend on us to effect delivery well within your time limit.
- We should have our merchandise ready to ship within 10 days of the original delivery date and we hope that you can hold off until that time.
- If your order remains in force we will expedite delivery to you as soon as we have received the merchandise.
- In accordance with your letter of the 6th June, we are sending off the fifty cases by the Tokaido line.
- In compliance with your request to our Mr. Jiang, we have pleasure in sending by separate post a sample of our 10s. 3-ply yarn.
- Agreeably to your request, we have sent you, through Messrs. Yamadawu & Co., 40 bales of cotton.
- This is to inform you that we are unable to make delivery on the above referenced purchase order on the date indicated.

3. Promises or Policies in After-sale Service

- Within 7 days after the item is delivered, our company will exchange the product according to your request if there are any quality problems.
- A purchase with any defect or fault can be exchanged for a new one of the same model within 15 days after you're in receipt of the item.
- If any quality problems occurs in your first year of ownership of your purchases, then repairs will be performed free of charge.
- Should your item be used more than one year, we will provide repairs with a low charge.
- For damages caused by customers' mal-operation, incorrect installation or misapplication, we shall charge customer for the product repair.
- We usually charge the replaced accessories at cost and the service in accordance with the specific condition.
- Items with the specific state laws or regulations shall be handled in line with the related laws or regulations.
- Our service commitment superior to the National Three-Guarantees terms will also be performed.
- Please call our toll-free hotline at 800-810-1991, and state the problems in detail so that our customer service specialist can keep a record of your problems.
- Please do send back your goods via Express Mail Service to our company. Allow one week from when we receive your returned product for the related procedures.
- Commonly, we'll receive the returned goods within 10 days after you send it out.
- We shall send to you the new product which has passed the quality inspection by regular postal parcel within one week after we receive your returned product.
- The returned item will be sent to manufacturer for repair within one week after it arrives.
- The purchase price you've paid for the item will be refunded. And shipping charges for the returned goods are not refundable.
- Merchandise with reimbursed invoice or without invoice cannot be refunded.
- If any merchandise beyond the coverage of Three Guarantees is needed to be replaced or refunded due to special reasons, you shall be responsible for all shipping charges.

- For any returned items that are incomplete, or the original packages of any such items are broken or lost, exchange and refunding will not be applicable.

10.7 Writing Tips

Some English majors have proposed the following points to note in writing letters concerning delivery or after-sale service. Read the following list quickly and then discuss with your partner whether they are appropriate and try to add some more ideas to the list.

While writing letters related to delivery, you should keep the following in mind.

(1) The best policy in delivery or after-sale service is to under-promise and over-deliver. For example, if you know you can deliver in three days, promise five. If you make empty promises and the reality does not match your claims, then you will lose business.

(2) If you ask for early delivery, you need to give detailed background information to justify your request, for example, it is your end-user's request, not your intention to inconvenience your reader.

(3) If you press for early delivery, you should mention the trouble or difficulty that delayed delivery may bring to both you and your partner, so that your partner will understand you better and co-operate with you more gladly.

(4) While you ask your partner to do something for you, you should also tell him what you can do for him in order to encourage your partner, for example, L/C will be opened soon, or money will be remitted at once etc.

When you write a letter concerning after-sale service, you ought to follow the following points.

(1) After every sale, you must give the customer a written invoice, statement, or receipt which contains the following minimum information: your full name, or registered business name, and VAT registration number (if any), the date on which the transaction occurred, the unit price, the total price of the transaction, the quantity of goods etc.

(2) Try to justify your request, for, example, other companies producing similar products offer after-sale service etc.

(3) Tell your partner that your purpose of asking for after-sale service is to help promote the sales of his products at your end.

(4) If you have several requests to make at the same time, make a list and arrange them in a neat way, so that your partner will not miss anything.

Notes and Explanations

1. submit   *v.*   呈送，屈服

   Please submit your application form in quadruplicate.
   请交申请表一式四份。
   They refused to submit to the unwise decision.
   他们拒绝服从这一不明智的决定。
   to submit sth. to sb.   向某人提交或呈递某物（以供考虑或裁决等）
   We must submit your counter-offer to our managing director for decision.

我们必须把你们的还盘提交我们的总经理，请他来做决定。
   submit oneself to   甘受，服从
   We ought to submit ourselves to international practice.
   我们应该服从国际惯例。
2. delivery   *n.*   交货
   与 delivery 有关的常用短语有：immediate delivery（即刻交货），deferred delivery（迟延交货），fixed-date delivery（定期交货），accelerated delivery（快速交付）。
3. excavator   挖掘机，开凿机
4. at its first experience   第一次的经历
5. inconvenience   *n.*   不便，麻烦
   put sb. to inconvenience   使某人感到不便
   cause inconvenience to a person   给某人带来麻烦
6. the date indicated   原规定的时间
7. to make alternative arrangements   交错布置，间隔布置
8. dispatch   *v.*   派遣，发货
   dispatch sb./sth. (to ...)   派遣（某人），发送（某事物）
   American warships have been dispatched to that area.
   美国军舰已派往那个地区。
   to send sth. by dispatch   （把某物）用快件送发
9. warranty   保证，担保
   与 warranty 有关的常用短语有：extended warranty（延长的保证期），short-time warranty（短期保单），long-term warranty（长期保单），product warranty（产品质量保证书）。
10. in special crates   在特制的板条箱中
11. endeavor to do sth.   努力去做
    Can we endeavor to prolong the brevity of human life?
    我们能延长短促的人生吗？
    其他与 endeavor 有关的短语有：endeavor to the best of one's ability（尽最大的努力，竭尽全力），make one's (best) endeavor（尽全力，竭力），to endeavor after happiness（努力追求幸福）。
12. expedite delivery   加快发货
13. mal-operation   不正确的操作

Exercises

1. Multiple choices.

(1) I apologize for the delivery problems you had _____ us last month.
   A. for　　　　　　B. with　　　　　　C. at　　　　　　D. of

(2) _____ your decision to place regular orders with us, we request that you furnish us with two references for the initial purchase.
   A. While appreciating　　　　　　B. As appreciating
   C. When appreciate　　　　　　　D. Because we appreciate

(3) If there were fewer management staff, more work _____

A. would be done B. be done
   C. have to be done D. should be done

(4) I wish to offer you my service _____ the sales of our products in your district.
   A. with B. of C. for D. according to

(5) In view of my experience and extensive business connections, I hope to be granted your sole agency _____ the territory.
   A. with B. of C. for D. to

(6) We trust that our experience in foreign trade and marketing will entitle us _____ your confidence.
   A. with B. of C. by D. to

(7) This is to confirm your booking _____ a single room from 20 July to 27 July
   A. with B. of C. at D. for

(8) _____ your excellent connections, we believe it will be possible to promote the sale of our products in your territory.
   A. Because of B. Thanks to C. With D. At

(9) Every six months we would like to receive _____ you a detailed report on current market conditions.
   A. from B. to C. of D. with

(10) Despite our pressing need _____ delivery and a lot of troubles caused to your loading work, at the last minute the goods has been dispatched successfully.
   A. from B. to C. for D. with

2. Translate the following Chinese sentences into English.

(1) 我方同意提前交付贵方所订货物。
(2) 恳请将货物交付时间通知我们。
(3) 我们相信能在下月底前将货物交付给你们。
(4) 恳请贵方告知我们你方交付货物的详细时间和方式。
(5) 贵公司如能给我方寄来你们最新产品的样品，我方不胜感谢。
(6) 由于不可抗力的原因，我们不能按照约定的日期交付合同载明的货物。
(7) 由于我们的供货商因台风原因生产受到严重影响，因此我们无法按你们的要求交货。
(8) 如果我们没有令人信服的理由，是不会要求你们提前交货的。

3. Translate the following letter into Chinese.

Dear Emily,
   Thank you for your reply of August 8th. We are very pleased to learn that your company will keep promise in accepting the payment for L/C 45 days. Actually this is an exceptional case and also the first time we deal with our customer in this term of payment.
   As for your last e-mail for checking the delivery date, please note the reply given by our production manager. Please also note that the delivery date is normally in 30 days provided that all the relevant information is submitted to the factory.
   Under this situation, we cannot confirm when we can deliver the goods as until this moment we still haven't received from you any details regarding your order. Therefore, please send us the

complete information of your order immediately. We'll inform you of the best delivery date after we check your order.

Best wishes,
(Signature)

4. Situational writing.

    Suppose that your boss has asked you to prepare a letter. In the letter, you should inform your client of a delay in delivery. At the same time, you ought to give explanations for the delay and propose a solution. You may add some details which you may think necessary.

Chapter 11

Shipment

Your goals for this chapter are to understand:
- ☑ some basic knowledge about shipment;
- ☑ how to write shipment-related letters;
- ☑ some commonly-used patterns in letters about shipment;
- ☑ some points for attention in writing letters related to shipment.

11.1 Lead-in

Before you begin your learning of this chapter, please discuss with your partner(s) about the following questions.

(1) What is the difference between delivery and shipment?

(2) Which do you think is the most widely-used method of transport in international business? Why is it so popular?

11.2 Basic Information

Shipment plays a very important role in international trade because, without shipment, business transactions cannot be concluded, delivery not effected and circulation of commodities between countries not realized. Shipment permits goods to flow between the various fixed points and bridges the buyer-seller gap, and it is the physical thread connecting companies' geographically dispersed operations. Transportation of goods may take place by road, railway, inland waterway, sea or air, but transport by sea is the most widely used form of transportation with advantages of easy passage, large capacity and low cost. That's why in this chapter we shall mainly deal with sea transport. In recent years, a new type of carriage has appeared, called the combined transport, operating on a road-sea-rail journey.

Cargo transportation by container ship is a modern way of transportation. Goods are packed and loaded into standard containers at the factory or the premises of the exporter and sent by rail or truck to the wharf on to the container ship which has special lifting machinery and special holds for the cargo to be transported to destination. According to International Organization for Standardization, there are several standard sizes of the containers:

8 feet × 8.5 feet × 40 feet

8 feet × 8 feet × 40 feet

8 feet × 8 feet × 20 feet

There are three parties involved in most movements of goods, the consignor — who sends the goods, the carrier — who carries them and the consignee — who receives them at the destination.

In sea transport, chartering of ships or booking shipping space is involved. And the contract entered into between the ship-owner and shipper may take the form of either a charter party or a bill of lading.

A charter party is the documents which state the terms and conditions of the contract signed by the ship-owner who provides the ship and the charterer who hires it. Ship chartering is usually arranged through shipbroker.

A bill of lading, generally abbreviated as B/L, is the most important shipping document. It is indeed a receipt for goods shipped on board a vessel, signed by person who contracts to carry them, and stating the conditions in which the goods were delivered to the ship. It is not the actual contract, but forms excellent evidence of the terms of the contract. It is a document of title to the goods, enabling the shipper or owner of the goods to endorse title to other parties, sell goods in transit, and present to banks with other documents in seeking payment under documentary credits.

If a transaction is concluded on a CIF basis, the exporter should, before or after effecting shipment, notify the importer of their dispatch. In case of CFR transaction, a shipping advice is also necessary for the importer to cover insurance of the relevant goods.

11.3 Analysis of Model Letters

Read and analyze the following letters. While reading, please try to find answers to the following questions.

(1) In Model Letter 11-1, why does the writer mention the approval of his end-user?

(2) What is the writer's purpose of listing the shipping documents in Model Letter 11-2?

Model Letter 11-1: Importer requesting shipment

Dear Sirs:

Re: Sales Confirmation No. B4288

Your e-mail of yesterday has been received with thanks.

We are pleased to inform you that the sample for 1×20' FCL China Black Tea Standard No B5432 under Sales Confirmation No. B4288 has been approved by our end-user who is one of the largest tea buyers in Europe, so please arrange shipment of the goods to Antwerp via Maersk as soon as possible.

When the shipment is effected, please advise us of the name of vessel, voyage No., container No. and seal No., ETD and ETA immediately. Taking this opportunity, we would like to emphasize that you must give special care to the quality and packing of the ordered goods.

It is our sincere hope that this order will lead to further business between us. We thank you in advance for your cooperation.

Yours truly,

Model Letter 11-2: Advising buyer of shipment

Dear Poeh,

Your Order for 3,000 kg Wool

We have the pleasure of informing you that the goods of 3,000 kg wool was shipped today in accordance with the stipulations set forth in the captioned order.

The following copies of shipping documents are enclosed so that you may find no trouble in taking delivery of the goods when they arrive.

- Our Invoice No. 250 in duplicate.
- Packing List No. 45 in duplicate.
- Non-negotiable B/L No. 9878.
- Insurance Policy No. 876-123.
- Survey Report No. 7865.

We trust the above shipment will reach you in perfect condition and we hope you will find them satisfactory.

We look forward to more opportunities to pay our most careful attention to your future correspondence, inquiries and orders.

Truly yours,

11.4 Writing Guidelines

Shipment-related letters are usually written for the following purposes: to request an early shipment, to amend shipping terms, to give shipping advice, or to dispatch shipping documents.

In the above models, the first letter is delivered for the purpose of asking for shipment. Analysis of the letter shows that it consists of the following components.

(1) Acknowledging or referring to an order placed, or a contract signed.

(2) Making the request for immediate shipment of the goods.

(3) Making some additional requirements related to the shipment.

(4) Taking advantage of the letter, the seller may also express the desire for further development of business.

A shipping advice can usually be divided into three parts.

(1) Notifying shipment of the goods first because this is the most important information.

(2) Giving further information relating to the shipment such as the name of the ship, the quantities delivered, the packing condition, the estimated time of departure and arrival etc.

(3) Expressing hope that the goods may arrive at the destination without delay.

A reply to a request for shipment is usually composed of the parts specified below.

(1) Acknowledging receipt of the letter asking for early shipment.

(2) Giving writer's opinion about the shipment, for example, asking for a delay in shipment, or partial shipment or transshipment etc. At the same time the writer may give sufficient explanations here to back up his proposal or request.

(3) Expressing expectations for approval or agreement.

11.5 More Sample Letters

The following letters comply basically with the above writing guidelines, but they are different from the models in 11.3 in one way or another. Read them to see how each letter is structured and worded to achieve its respective communicative purpose.

Sample Letter 11-1: A Reply to an Enquiry about booking space

The following is a reply to an Enquiry for shipping information. The writer gives detailed information about the types of containers they can supply. Besides, he introduces some savings available and gives some general information about their tariff.

Dear Sirs,

Thank you for your enquiry of April 30, asking us to quote shipping containers to any EMP for your goods.

We provide containers of two sizes, 10 ft and 20 ft. They can take loads up to two to four tons respectively. They can be opened at both ends, thus facilitating loading and unloading. For carrying goods liable to be spoiled by moisture or water, they have great advantages of being both watertight and airtight. For frozen or perishable goods, we offer special temperature-controlled containers to ensure that such goods arrive at their destinations in sound condition.

There is also a saving on freight charges, when separate consignments intended for the same port of destination are carried in one container, and an additional saving on insurance because of lower premium charged for container-shipped goods.

We enclose a copy of our tariff and look forward to receiving your instruction.

Yours faithfully,

Sample Letter 11-2: Proposing partial shipment

In the following letter, the writer gives adequate explanations for his partial rejection, so that his proposal may be easily accepted. Note that the last sentence in the first paragraph may help to call the reader's attention to the matter.

Dear Sir,

Your Order No. 890 for Rice

We have received your letter dated 30th May which requested us to ship all the 5,000 metric ton of rice in one lot. We are very sorry for our inability to do so.

When we offered the consignment it was clearly stated that we would make shipment of the goods in June. If you request to advance the shipment, what we can do at best is to ship 4,000 metric ton of rice in part in June and the remaining 1,000 metric ton in July. We hope the proposal will meet with your approval.

Should the arrangement be accepted, you are under the necessity of amending the covering L/C to allow partial shipments and meanwhile, inform us.

The earlier confirmation from you is appreciated as we hope that we will make arrangements accordingly.

Sincerely yours,
Henry Patrel

Sample Letter 11-3: Agreeing to advance partial shipment

The following letter aims to achieve two purposes. One is to agree to the received proposal about the advance of shipment date. The other is to persuade the recipient of this letter to keep the port of destination unchanged. They are placed neatly in two paragraphs and are discussed thoroughly.

Dear Sirs,

Thank you for your letter dated February 20, 2012.

For the purpose of assisting you to recommend our products to your clients as early as possible, we agree to your proposal to advance the initial shipment for 1/3 (one third) of the total quantity from July/Aug. to may/June. The remaining 2/3 (two thirds) will be shipped during July/Aug.

With regard to your request for alteration of the port of destination from Hamburg to Oslo, we wish to say that direct sailings from here to Oslo are at present few and far between, and the transshipment charges are very high. For the sake of avoiding any possible delay and extra expenses caused by transshipment, it is hoped, therefore, that you will comply with the original stipulation for destination.

Your prompt reply will be appreciated.

Yours sincerely,

Sample Letter 11-4: Pressing for immediate shipment

The purpose of the following letter is to urge for the expected shipment which should be effected earlier. The writer fulfills this purpose with three steps. First he starts the letter with a review of the agreement in shipment. Second he argues why immediate shipment is necessary and what trouble his counterpart will have if he fails to do so. Thirdly, he makes a positive requirement for immediate shipment.

Dear Sirs,

With reference to our Order No. 8409 of 1,000 metric tons of peanut oil, which is stipulated for shipment in August, 2011, we wish to remind you that up to now we have not received any definite information from you about the delivery date, although the time of shipment has expired.

As our buyers are in urgent need of the goods, the long delay has caused us considerable trouble and we may be compelled to seek an alternative source of supply. In case you should fail to effect shipment in September, we will have to lodge a claim against you for the loss and reserve the right to cancel the contract.

Please make your best efforts to dispatch the goods with the least possible delay for long-established relationship.

We look forward to receiving your shipping advice by fax within the coming week.

Yours faithfully,

Sample Letter 11-5: Asking to extend the date of shipment

The following letter aims to extend the date of shipment. In order to achieve such a purpose, the writer gives adequate explanations for his request and gives a specific proposal for the extention. The structure of the letter is clear and the language used is polite.

Dear Sirs,

We acknowledge receipt of your L/C No. AD6854 for the amount of USD4,000 to cover your Order No. 4878 for 20 metric tons of wheat.

The said L/C calls for shipment on or before August 31. As the earliest steamer sailing for your port is the M.V. "Victory" scheduled to leave Qing Dao on or about September 3, it is, therefore, impossible for us to effect shipment at the time you requested.

Under this circumstance, we have to ask you to extend the date of shipment to September 10. We realize that the change of delivery date will probably bring you inconvenience, for which we offer our sincere apologies.

In view of our cordial commercial relationship, we would be very grateful if you could make a special effort to comply with our request.

We are looking forward to your favorable reply and your understanding.

Yours faithfully,

Sample Letter 11-6: Explaining a delay in shipment

Although this letter discusses a delay in shipment, the tone is quite optimistic. The writer makes sincere apologies for the delay as well as some encouraging and satisfying arrangements for immediate shipment.

Dear Mr. Brown,

Thank you very much for your fax. We are sorry for the delay in shipping your order No. 976.

We normally pride ourselves on keeping to our delivery dates, but in this case our suppliers shipped to us late and the components did not arrive here till last Wednesday. I am glad to be able to say that your order is being packed for export now. We will ship the goods on June 9 ex Newark to Rotterdam. The shipment will arrive in London on June 17.

Again we are sorry for the delay and hope this will not cause you too much inconvenience. We hope you will understand our situation and we look forward to your prompt reply.

Your sincerely,
Jack Smith

Sample Letter 11-7: Accepting an order and discussing the date of shipment

This letter is simple and straightforward. No unnecessary information is supplied. Such a letter is usually delivered to one who has a close business relationship with you.

Dear Sirs,

Acknowledging your order of 10th April, we regret that we cannot ship the order until 28th April. Please let us know if this is satisfactory to you so that we can make shipment on that date.

Very truly yours,
John Ranson

11.6 More Useful Sentences

1. Shipment Terms
- Shipments are to be made during August/September/October from Shanghai to San Francisco or other Pacific coast with transshipment at Hong Kong.
- Our shipment terms are shipment within three months after receipt of L/C.
- As the purchase is made on FOB terms, you should ship the goods from London on a steamer to be designated by us. As soon as shipping space is booked, we shall advise you of the name of the carrying vessel.
- One of our customers placed an order for 30,000 dry batteries for shipment in five equal lots at intervals of three months.
- Please arrange to send the consignment by road to Liverpool, and it is going to be shipped by S.S. "Merchant Prince", due to sail for Alexandra on May 25.
- If you wish to have earlier delivery, the best we can do is to make a partial shipment of five machines in June and ship the remaining five in July.

2. Requesting Shipment

- Instead of S.S. "Manhattan Maru" as previously advised, you are now required to ship the goods of this order by S.S. "Calchas".
- We trust that you will make all necessary arrangements to deliver the goods in time.
- We request you to make serious efforts to get the ordered goods dispatched within the prescribed time limit.
- Please rush the preparation of the goods and try your best to ship the same without the least delay.
- We hope that by the time you receive this letter, you will have the goods ready for shipment.
- We would like you to try your utmost to effect shipment in accordance with the original schedule.
- For some special reason we request you to advance shipment of the consignment under order No 897 from October to September.
- It is stipulated that shipment is to be made before the end of this month, however, we shall appreciate it if you will arrange to ship the goods at an earlier date.
- You should fax us immediately of the earliest possible date of shipment for our consideration without prejudice to our right to cancel the order.
- We wish to call your attention to the fact that up to the present moment no news has come from you about the shipment under the captioned contract.
- It would be appreciated if you could arrange for the immediate shipment of our order.
- The relevant L/C has been issued by Bank of China. Upon receipt of the said L/C, please arrange shipment and inform us by fax of the name of vessel and the date of sailing.
- Please try your utmost to ship our goods by S.S. "Freedom" which is due to arrive at Hamburg on September 12, and confirm by return that the goods will be ready in time.
- Please ship as soon as possible seventy bales of goat skins to Messrs. White & Co. in London, and send me the Bill of Lading.
- We should be much obliged if you could effect shipment of the milk powder in two equal lots by direct steamer as soon as you receive our L/C.
- Your goods are nearly ready for dispatch, and we would be glad to have your immediate instruction.

3. Urging Shipment

- Your delay has caused us considerable difficulties and we must ask you to do your utmost to dispatch the overdue goods without any further delay.
- As the contract time of delivery is rapidly falling due, it is imperative that we hear from you without any further delay.
- We have placed this order because your delivery is so attractive. Therefore we ask you to do everything possible to ensure punctual shipment.
- We are now referring to the Contract No. 889 signed between us on 12th August for 3,000 cases Tin Plates, which is stipulated for shipment in September 10. However, up to now we have not received from you any news about this consignment.
- Our customers are pressing us for immediate shipment and therefore it is impossible for us to extend the shipment to the time you indicated.
- We are in urgent need of these goods and would have to request you to execute the order within the time stipulated.

4. Replying to Requests for Shipment

- The goods you ordered are now ready for shipment and we are awaiting your shipping instructions.
- The space has been booked on S.S. "Dong Fang", which is due to sail from your port to Ningbo at the end of next month.
- We are pleased to inform you that we have booked freight for our Order No. 1234 of 20,000 refrigerator compressors on S.S. 'Noah' with ETA 23 Nov. For delivery instructions, please approach Messrs Johnason & Co., Ltd., Milan.
- The goods have been packed and marked exactly as directed so that they may be rushed to the wharf for loading on the 'TOKYO MARU'.
- We have today sent to you by S.S. "Dong Feng" a consignment of Men's shirts for which we enclose our bill of lading and invoice.
- We inform you that we have forwarded by the "Twilight", freight paid, 200 bales cotton, marked OH.
- We are pleased to notify you that the cargo has been shipped by the S.S. "Scotland" for transshipment at Tianjin.
- A consignment of your tableware dispatched by Smith Transport Company is delivered in good condition on 17th July.
- We have pleasure in notifying you that we have booked shipping space for your goods under the order No. M45-01 on S.S. "Peace" for Colombia next week.
- We are pleased to inform you that we have booked shipping space for your order No. ... S/S ... The ETA will be ...
- Shipment can not be made within the prescribed/stipulated time.
- Since many repeat orders from our regular customers are rushing in, prompt shipment cannot be guaranteed after the middle of this month.

5. Shipping Advice

- We are pleased to advise you that we have forwarded by air one package of samples.
- We have the pleasure of informing you that the goods under Contract No. K123 have been shipped today by S.S. "Captain" from port A to port B.
- We have shipped the goods ordered last week by M.S. "Dongfeng" and hope the shipment will reach you in perfect condition.
- We are sending you today by the American Railway Express, prepaid, the following books.
- Under the terms of the relative L/C, we are sending the following shipping documents covering this shipment.
- We are glad to confirm our cable just dispatched informing you that we have shipped the following goods by M.V. "Pacific Bear" of the US Lines which left here today.

11.7 Writing Tips

Some English majors have proposed the following points in writing shipment-related letters. Read the following list quickly and then discuss with your partner whether they are appropriate and try to add some more ideas to the list.

(1) A letter of shipment, like other business letters, is usually composed of the following three parts. The first part introduces the matter concerned, the shipment of goods under the given order. The second part provides all the details of shipment that both parties concern. They may be put in more than one paragraph if necessary. The third part is where you state the response required from the recipient and the action you will take as a result.

(2) A letter of urging shipment should cover the following points: Order No./Contract No., the name and the quantity of the goods, the time of shipment, the need to rush the shipment.

(3) Shipping instruction is given by the buyer or his forwarding agent to inform the seller of the packing and the matters concerning the shipment of the goods. Such letters may include packing instruction, special requests concerning the nature of the goods if any, the name of the vessel, and the time of its arrival and departure, etc.

(4) Shipping advice means the seller gives the notice that goods have been shipped on board the ship. Such letters should include the following details of the transaction: Contract No./Order No., the name of the goods, quantity of the order, the name of vessel, ETD and ETA, shipping documents enclosed. The seller usually ends the letter with thanks for the order and a wish to receive more orders in the future.

(5) When stipulating the time of shipment, both parties should consider the availability of goods, ships and shipping space, the opening date of L/C and the nature of the cargo. Avoid ambiguous phrases as "immediate shipment", "prompt shipment", "to ship as soon as possible". Such expressions may be interpreted in different ways and even lead to misunderstanding or even disputes.

Notes and Explanations

1. shipping mark 运输标志，唛头
   其他与 shipping 有关的短语有：shipping agent（运输代理商），shipping bill/note（船运清单，装船通知单），shipping room［（工厂商店等的）发货仓库］。

2. shipping documents 运输单据

3. prompt shipment 立刻装运
   其他与 shipment 有关的短语有：forward shipment（远期装运），advance shipment（提前装船），ready shipment（即期装船，已备装船），timed shipment（限期装船），partial shipment（分批装运），consolidated shipment（合并装运），lift-on lift-off shipment（吊上吊下装运），bulk shipment（整装运输）。

4. commercial invoice 商业发票
   其他与 invoice 有关的短语有：firm invoice（正式发票），provisional invoice（临时发票，暂开发票），plain invoice（普通发票），uniform invoice（统一发票），purchase invoice（购货发票）。

5. packing list 装箱单
   其他与 packing 有关的短语有：packing box/case（货箱，垫料箱），packing charges（打包费），packing piece（垫片），packing press（打包机，压缩机），packing sheet（包装布，包装纸）。

6. certificate of quantity 数量证明书
   其他与 certificate 有关的短语有：certificate of origin（原产地证明书），certificate of quality（质量证明书）。

7. insurance policy 保险单（也可称为 policy of insurance 或 certificate of insurance）

8. delivery notice 交货通知

其他与delivery有关的短语有：immediate delivery（立即交货），delivery on arrival（货到交付），delivery book（交货簿），delivery port（交货港），delivery to docks（交到码头），delivery to domicile（送货到户）。

9. shipping advice　装运通知
10. port of shipment　装运港

    其他与port有关的短语有：port of delivery（卸货港），port of entry（进口港），port of exit（出口港）。
11. shipping agent　运输代理
12. immediate shipment　立即装运

    indefinite shipment　不定期装运
13. expedite　*v.*　加快，加速

    Please expedite shipment as much as possible.
    请尽快装运。
    Please do what you can to expedite the building work.
    请尽量加快建筑工作。
    Shipment is ready, please expedite credit.
    船已装完，请速开信用证。

Exercises

1. Translate the following Chinese phrases into English.

(1) 订舱　　　　　　　　　(2) 欧洲主要口岸
(3) 离岸净重　　　　　　　(4) 海洋运输货物保险
(5) 适于海运的包装　　　　(6) 装船通知
(7) 装船单据　　　　　　　(8) 装船须知
(9) 商品交易会　　　　　　(10) 虚盘
(11) 不可抗力　　　　　　　(12) 跟单信用证
(13) 装运港　　　　　　　　(14) 汇票
(15) 试购订单　　　　　　　(16) 保险单

2. Complete the sentences with appropriate prepositions.

(1) We are _____ the necessity of requesting you to allow transshipment at Paris.
(2) We usually effect insurance _____ All Risks and War Risk for full invoice value on CIF sales.
(3) We are _____ receipt of your letter of 16th November, and regret to state that we cannot agree with your views.
(4) Thank you for your letter of 10th March advising us that all the goods ordered on 1 January are available _____ collection.
(5) Please ship the following goods by motor freight as soon as possible, and charge them _____ our account.
(6) For FOB and CFR sales, insurance is to be covered by buyers, while _____ CIF sales, insurance is to be covered by sellers.

(7) Please let us have the particulars of your terms and conditions _____ the insurance policy, together with a proposal form.

(8) In accordance _____ your letter of the 6th June, we are sending off by the Tokaido line the fifty cases.

(9) Agreeably to your request, we have sent you, _____ Messrs. Yamada & Co., 40 bales of cotton.

(10) Please note that the above–mentioned goods should be shipped before October 20 and that the shipment should be covered WPA _____ 130% of the invoice value.

3. Translate the following Chinese sentences into English.

(1) 这是贵我双方达成的首笔交易，因此装运延误将会影响到我们今后的长期合作关系，务必请注意。

(2) 我们料到，提前装运的要求会给你们带来不便，但希望你们能理解我们的难处，并尽量满足我们的要求。

(3) 我们从船运公司处获悉，5月底前驶往汉堡的舱位已经订满，最早的装运时间是8月20日。

(4) 我方将用"济南"号货轮装运第122号合同项下的货物，该货轮定于5月5日前后从本港驶往贵港。

(5) 如果你们能接受我们的价格，你们必须立刻开立信用证，以便我们能早日装运。

(6) 我们很高兴向你方确认，我们已向中国人民保险公司投保3 300美元的一切险。

(7) 如果有关信用证不迟于5月3日到达我方，可保证准时装船。

(8) 我们真诚地希望你们能同意我们的要求，并殷切期盼贵方的答复。

(9) 我们希望你们能和你们的银行联系，安排好修改信用证的事宜，以使总金额增加至涵盖额外增加的保险费，然后通知我方。

(10) 按照贵方传真指示，我方今日按照惯例向被认可的保险者安排投保。

4. Translate the following short paragraphs into English.

(1) 请按我方要求以那瓦夏瓦港到岸价将货物装直达船出运；必须由船运公司直接签发提单。我方不接受货代提单或由其他第三方如物流公司和拼货公司签发的提单，因为此类公司收取高于印度正常标准的理货和拼货费用。若发生上述一切额外费用，均由贵公司负担。今后发货亦须照此办理。

(2) 如买方在2012年8月17日或之前未向卖方发出装运通知，则卖方可自行决定取消本合同，并要求买方赔偿因未发出装运通知而使其蒙受的一切损失。

Chapter 12

Cargo Insurance

Your goals for this chapter are to understand:
- ☑ what cargo insurance is;
- ☑ how to write insurance-related letters;
- ☑ some sentence patterns used in letters concerning insurance;
- ☑ some points for attention in writing insurance-related letters.

12.1 Lead-in

Before you begin your learning of this chapter, please discuss with your partner(s) about the following questions.

(1) How much do you know about insurance?
(2) Why is insurance necessary in international trade?

12.2 Basic Information

In international trade, the transportation of goods from the seller to the buyer has to go through the procedures of loading, unloading and storing. During this process it is quite possible that the goods will encounter various kinds of perils and sometimes may suffer losses. In order to protect the goods against possible loss, the buyer or seller, before the transportation of the goods, usually applies to an insurance company for insurance covering the goods in transit. Such insurance is called cargo insurance.

Cargo insurance refers to the fact that the insured covers insurance for the shipment with the insurer, i.e. the insurance company before shipment. It covers physical damage to or loss of the goods while in transit by land, sea or air. The insured pays premium to the insurance company on the basis of insurance amounts, insurance cover as well as insurance premium rate, and obtains the insurance policy. The insurer undertakes to make payment to the insured, i.e., the person who is insured against loss, should the event insured against occur according to the amount insured and the level of loss.

The China Insurance Clauses issued by People's Insurance Company of China (PICC) provides two types of insurance coverage — basic coverage and additional coverage for marine cargo transport. Basic risks include Free from Particular Average (FPA), With Particular Average/With Average (WPA/WA) and All Risks (AR). Additional risks include General Additional Risks and Special Additional Risks. Additional Risks cannot be taken out alone and should go with FPA, WPA or All Risks.

Being an indispensable part of a sales contract, the insurance clauses should be stipulated explicitly and reasonably. The insurance clause in a sales contract under different trade terms may vary. Normally, it should specifically stipulate the insured amount, basic risk and additional risks to be covered, the insurance document required and standard of insurance coverage, etc.

12.3 Analysis of Model Letters

Read and analyze the following letters. While reading, please try to find answers to the following questions.

(1) In Model Letter 12-1, is it necessary to introduce the consignment in such a detail?

(2) Is it necessary for the writer to mention the order No. and the ordered goods at the beginning in Model Letter 12-2?

(3) The purpose of Model Letter 12-3 is to advise insurance, then why does the writer introduce the arrangement for shipment?

Model Letter 12-1: An enquiry for insurance rate

Dear Sirs,

We shall recently have a consignment of raincoats under the order No. 34698 enclosed, valued at US$40,000 (forty thousand US dollars only) CIF Hong Kong, to be shipped from Shanghai by S.S. Chong Qing.

We plan to arrange the insurance on all the raincoats supplied against TPND, Contamination and Rain in addition to WPA at the rate of 10% for the sum of US$40,000 from Shanghai to Hong Kong with your company. Could you please let us know immediately the insurance rate covering the above-mentioned risks?

We look forward to your prompt reply.

Your faithfully,

Model Letter 12-2: Importer asking exporter to cover insurance

Dear Miss Zhang,

We wish to call your attention to our Order No. ZD-0130 for 300 M/T Canned Fish placed on a CFR basis.

As we now desire to have the shipment insured on your side, we shall appreciate it very much if you could kindly arrange to insure the same on our behalf against All Risks at invoice value plus 10%. Please charge the cost to our accounts.

It is our sincere hope that our request will meet with your approval.

Looking forward to your early reply.

Yours faithfully,
Louis Kohl

Model Letter 12-3: Agreeing to cover the insurance

Dear Sir or Madam,

This is to acknowledge receipt of your letter dated August 20th concerning Order No. 9876 for 300 cases of battery, requesting us to effect insurance on your behalf for the above order.

We are pleased to inform you that we have covered the above shipment against All Risks for USD1,500.00 with the People's Insurance Company of China. The Policy is being processed accordingly and will be forwarded to you by Fedex next Wednesday together with our debit note for the premium and expenses.

We are now making arrangements to ship your order by S. S. "Zhujiang", due to leave for Kobe from Ningbo on September 15th.

Yours faithfully,

12.4 Writing Guidelines

When writing enquires with regard to insurance rate, you should bear the following points in mind.

(1) First, you should offer some basic information about your order, such as time, destination, quantity, value and so on.

(2) Then you should state what risks are to be covered.

(3) Lastly you should say you are waiting for a prompt reply.

If you are writing a letter asking the other side to cover insurance, your letter should include the following points.

(1) At the beginning you should refer to the order waiting to be covered.

(2) Then you can mention why it is your partner's duty to effect insurance.

(3) Next you should introduce some relevant particulars such as the amount, the premium, quantity, etc. for your partner's information.

(4) Finally you should say "thank you" at the end of the letter.

When writing replies to a request for covering insurance, you'd better comply with the following points.

(1) You should acknowledge receipt of the letter on insurance matters at the beginning.

(2) Then you can express your willingness to insure the goods, stating clearly the usual terms of insurance including the insurance amount and premium, types of risks covered, etc. This part may consist of more than one paragraph, if necessary, and state the details of insurance concisely and fully.

(3) In the closing paragraph you could express your hope for an early reply and give assurance of your close cooperation.

12.5 More Sample Letters

The following letters comply basically with the above writing guidelines, but they are different from the models in 12.3 in one way or another. Read them to see how each letter is structured and worded to achieve its respective communicative purpose.

Sample Letter 12-1: An insurance company giving the insurance rate

In this letter, acknowledgement is given first, and a brief reply about the insurance rate is given in the second paragraph. The writer expresses his sincere expectation for further cooperation at the end.

Dear Sirs,

Thanks for your enquiry of October 2nd for our insurance rate, and we are pleased to note your readiness to insure with us a shipment of electronic planes from Dalian to Yokohama by sea.

We would advise that the rate we are now charging for the proposed shipment against All Risks and War Risk is 2% subject to our own Ocean Marine Cargo Clauses and Ocean Marine War Risk Clauses. We have enclosed copies of our quotation for your reference.

If you find our rate acceptable, please let us know the details of your shipment so that we may issue our policy accordingly.

Looking forward to your early reply.

Yours faithfully,

Sample Letter12-2: Asking exporter to cover insurance

The writer goes directly to the point about what goods are waiting to be insured and what risks are to be covered. The relevant details necessary for the insurance are all provided and there is no redundant information in the letter.

Dear Sir/Madam,

We wish you can insure the following consignment against all risks for the sum of US$ 80,000.(say eighty thousand US dollars) for us.

4 X/P Solar Heaters, marked: BTO CO.
     Singapore
     NO.1-N

These goods are now held at Number 3 Dock, Shanghai, waiting to be shipped by S.S. "Red Banner" due to leave for Singapore on Friday, 20 August, 2011.

We require immediate cover as far as Singapore. Please let us have the insurance policy as soon as it is ready. In the meantime please confirm that you hold the consignment covered.

Yours faithfully,

Sample Letter12-3: Asking for insurance at the exporter's end

The following letter is short and simple, but all the necessary information about the request for insurance is included. The letter is appropriately paragraphed, so the message is presented neatly.

Dear Mr. Meyer,

We wish to refer you to our Order No. NL-80098 for 500 electronic printers. As you see, this order is placed on a CFR basis.

Since we desire to have the shipment insured at your end, we shall be pleased if you will arrange to insure the goods on our behalf against All Risks invoice value plus 10%.

We shall of course refund to you the premium upon receipt of your debit note or, if you like, you may draw upon us at sight of the amount required.

We sincerely hope that you will approve our request.

Sincerely yours,

Sample Letter 12-4: Agreeing to cover the insurance

The writer of the following letter agrees to cover the insurance, but with reserve. He expects the receiver to pay the extra account. The language used is formal and the message conveyed is clear and definite.

Dear Sirs,

Re: Your Order No. 260 for 4,000 Cases of Power Tools

We have received your letter of May 2, asking us to insure the captioned goods for an amount of 130% above the invoice value.

Although it is our usual practice to take out insurance for the invoice value plus 10%, we are prepared to comply with your request for covering the goods for 130% of the invoice value, but the extra premium will be for your account.

We trust the above will be acceptable to you.

Yours faithfully,

Sample Letter 12-5: Buyer requesting seller to lodge a claim

The following letter gives reasons for the claim first and then makes the request for assistance. The request is specific and detailed so the reader will find it easy to follow. This letter is concise and straightforward.

Dear Mr. Jenkinhouse,

Subject: Our Order No. C541

When the S.S. "Lancaster" arrived at Shanghai on 30 November, it was noticed that one side of case No. 009 containing electronic toy planes was split. Therefore the case was opened and the contents were examined by a local insurance surveyor in the presence of the shipping company's agents. The case was invoiced as containing 30 "Challenger" electronic toy planes, 15 of which were seriously damaged. The surveyor's report is enclosed with statement from the shipping agent.

As you hold the insurance policy I should be grateful if you would take up this matter with the insurers.

Fifteen replacement planes will be required. Please arrange to supply these as soon as possible and charge them to our account.

Thank you in advance for your trouble on our behalf. If there are any queries please feel free to contact me.

Yours faithfully,

12.6 More Useful Sentences

1. Requesting Insurance

- Please cover us on the goods detailed below.
- We would be obliged if you could hold us covered for/on the cargo listed on the attached sheet.
- We would like to cover the risk of breakage for this lot of goods.
- We should be glad if you would provide cover of $10,000 on the goods ordered, in transit from Hong Kong to Shanghai.
- Would you please tell us whether you can cover All Risks for the consignments and, if so, on what terms?
- We would like to know whether you can undertake insurance on a batch of glassware against All Risks, including breakage and pilferage risks.
- We shall appreciate it very much if you will kindly arrange to insure the goods under our Order No. 4325 against All Risks at invoice value plus 8%.
- Please insure for us the following goods against All Risks and War Risk for the full invoice value plus 10% based on the warehouse to warehouse clause as per China Insurance Clauses of 1 January, 1981.
- Please effect insurance for my account of USD55,000 on my goods, against All Risks, from Hong Kong to Ningbo, and at the lowest premium possible, not exceeding 10 percent.
- Please insure the cargoes against All Risks and send the insurance policy to us with the shipping documents immediately after shipment.
- We leave the insurance arrangement to you but we wish to have the goods covered against All Risks and War Risk.
- We shall be pleased if you will arrange to insure the goods on our behalf against All Risks at invoice value plus 10%.

2. Replying to Requests for Insurance

- We have the pleasure in making acknowledgement to your letter of May 29th requiring us to insure you in the sum of $20,000 at 25% yearly on your goods stock.

- The cargo is to be insured warehouse to warehouse against All Risks.
- We can serve you with a broad range of coverage against all kinds of risks for sea transport, such as FPA, WPA, All Risks and Extraneous Risks.
- We will effect insurance against All Risks, as requested, charging premium and freight to the consignees.
- We have insured WPA and against War Risk at 130% of the invoice cost.
- We will have the insurance of the goods covered at 100% of the invoice amount.
- We will cover insurance WPA & War Risk according to usual practice in the absence of definite instructions from you. The premium for this cover is at the rate of 1.5% of the declared value of $8,200.
- We have arranged the insurance on all the leathers supplied against TPND, Contamination and Rain in addition to WPA at the rate of 10% for the sum of US$10,000 with the insurance company.
- Insurance on the goods shall be covered by us for 110% of the CIF value, and any extra premium for additional coverage, if required, shall be borne by the buyers.
- We will effect insurance against All Risks, as requested, charging premium and freight to the consignees.
- According to our usual practice, unless the buyers require, we usually do not cover these special additional risks.
- We usually effect insurance against All Risks and War Risk for the invoice value plus 10% for the goods sold on CIF basis.
- Regarding insurance, the coverage is for 110% of invoice value up to the port of destination only.

3. Discussing Insurance Terms
- We think FPA gives enough protection to all our shipments to your area.
- The premium for insurance covering All Risks and War Risk will naturally be much higher than that covering WPA.
- As a rule, the extra premium involved is to be for the buyer's account.
- Our usual practice is to insure shipments for the invoice value plus 10%.
- Please note that our insurance coverage is for 110% of the invoice value only. If more than that is asked for, the extra premium should be borne by the buyer.
- For goods sold on CIF basis, insurance is to be effected by us for 110% of the invoice value against All Risks based on warehouse to warehouse clause.
- If you wish to add other risks, you should pay an extra premium.
- We can provide this additional coverage with the extra premium for your account.
- If a higher percentage is required, we may do accordingly but you have to bear the extra premium as well.
- Our CIF price includes insurance premium against only WPA and War Risk. If you require insurance to be covered against breakage, an extra premium will have to be paid.
- Risks other than All Risks and War Risk can be accepted if the insurance company accepts. In case of affirmative, the extra premium should be borne by the buyers.
- If you wish to have the Risk of Breakage included in the coverage, you must bear the additional premium.

12.7 Writing Tips

Some students of Business English have proposed the following points for attention in writing letters concerning insurance. Read the following list quickly and then discuss with your partner whether they are appropriate and try to add some more ideas to the list.

(1) When writing a letter for covering insurance, the writer must see to it that he should write down clearly the following information: duration of coverage, insurance amount and premium, scope of cover etc.

(2) If a transaction is concluded on the FOB and C&F basis, the exporter should notify the importer immediately after he has made shipment so that the importer may cover the goods promptly. The seller should notify the buyer of the consignee of the contract number, name of the commodity, quantity, gross weight, measurement, invoice value and number of B/L, name of the vessel, the date of shipment, etc.

(3) On the basis of CIF, the exporter should cover the goods and notify the importer of insurance and transfer the insurance policy to the importer so that the importer is entitled to get the compensation in case damage occurs to the goods after shipment is made.

(4) It is a usual practice for the seller to effect insurance for the amount of seller's CIF invoice value plus 10% against proposed risks, say, WPA. Any additional insurance required by the buyer shall be at his own expense.

Notes and Explanations

1. additional risks 附加险（也可叫作 accessory risks 或 extraneous risks）
   附加险是相对于基本险而言的险种，是指附加在基本险合同下的附加合同。它不可以单独投保，要购买附加险必须先购买主险。一般来说，附加险所交的保险费比较少，但它的存在是以基本险的存在为前提的，不能脱离基本险。它和基本险一起形成一个比较全面的险种。

2. all risk 一切险
   其他与 risk 有关的短语有：overall risk（综合险），average risk（平均风险），avoidable risk（可避免风险），systematic risk（不可避免的风险），calculated risk（计划风险，预计风险），basic risks（基本险），credit risks（信用风险），social risks [（罢工、租税和物价变动等所引起的）社会风险]。

3. breakage 破损量
   其他与 breakage 有关的短语有：risk of breakage（破损险），breakage of packing（包装破裂险），breakage allowance（破损折扣）。

4. comply with 顺从，答应
   If you join the society, you must comply with its rules.
   如果参加这个协会，就必须遵守该协会的规章制度。

5. consignment 委托，委托物；寄售
   其他与 consignment 有关的短语有：to sell on consignment [以托售（寄卖）的方式销售]，consignment invoice（发货单），consignment-sheet（收货清单），consignment note（发货通知书）。

6. insurance premium　保险费
   insurer　保险人
   insurant　被保险人
7. insurance cover　保险范围
   其他与 insurance 有关的短语有：5 insurances & housing fund（五险一金），endowment insurance（养老保险），medical insurance（医疗保险），unemployment insurance（失业保险），employment injury insurance（工伤保险），maternity insurance（生育保险）。
8. invoice value　发票价值
   其他与 invoice 有关的短语有：make an invoice of（开发票），cash invoice（现购发票），credit sale invoice（赊销发票），duplicate invoice（发票副本）。
9. Ocean Marine Cargo Clauses　《海洋运输货物保险条款》
   Ocean Marine Cargo War Clauses　《海洋运输货物战争险条款》
10. particular　*n.* 信息，细节
    Her account is correct in all particulars.
    她的账目笔笔无误。
    descend to particulars　（在一般性讨论之后）转入具体讨论，转入细节
    enter into particulars/go into particulars　详述
    particular　*a.* 详细的
    particular description　详细的描述
11. war risk　战争险

1. Put the following sentences in the logical order.

(1) In your letter you request us to effect insurance on the shipment for your account.
(2) The ship sails on or about the 25th of January, 2012.
(3) For your information, we will ship the 500 printers by S.S. "May Flower".
(4) We are pleased to tell you that we have covered the shipment with the Asian Insurance Company of Hong Kong against All Risks for US$10,000.
(5) It will be forwarded to you by the end of this week together with our debit note.
(6) The policy has been prepared accordingly.
(7) We hope you will be satisfied with our arrangement.
(8) We acknowledge receipt of your letter dated 30th December.

2. Translate the following letter into Chinese.

Dear Ms. Thompson,
　　Thank you for your favorable e-mail of 25th October. As the goods are sold on CIF basis, insurance ought to be effected by us against All Risks and war risks based on warehouse to warehouse clause for the invoice value plus 10%.

Your request for insurance to be covered for 150% of the invoice can be met but the premium for the difference between 150% and 110% should be for your account. Based on our calculation, the difference is USD415.70. If you are willing to pay the difference, we will make corresponding arrangements soon.

We are looking forward to your immediate reply.

Yours sincerely,

3. Write a reply to the following letter.

Dear Sirs,

We wish to refer you to our Order No. 6128 for 800 cases of umbrellas, from which you will see that this order is placed on a CFR basis.

Since we now desire to have the consignment insured at your end, we shall appreciate it very much if you will kindly arrange to insure the goods on our behalf against All Risks at invoice value plus 10%. Upon receipt of your debit note, we will refund the premium to you at once.

We sincerely hope that our request will meet with your approval and await your early reply.

Yours faithfully,

4. Situational writing.

Suppose you have received a consignment of goods. You find that some of the goods have been damaged and you want to make an insurance claim, but the insurance policy is in the exporter's hand, so you hope the exporter can ask for the claim on your behalf. Write a letter to your supplier. You may add some details which you may think necessary.

Chapter 13

Agency

Your goals for this chapter are to understand:
- ☑ what agency is;
- ☑ why agency is important in international business;
- ☑ how to write letters concerning agency;
- ☑ the sentence patterns used in agency-related letters.

13.1 Lead-in

Before you begin your learning of this chapter, please discuss with your partner(s) about the following questions.

(1) Do you know what agency is?

(2) What role can an agent play in international business?

(3) What is the main factor which should be taken into account before the concluding of an agency agreement?

13.2 Basic Information

Not all international trade is handled through direct negotiations between buyers and sellers, that's why we need agency sometimes.

An agency is the one that signs contracts with a third party representing the principal or handles other kinds of affairs relating to the sales according to the instructions from his principal, in other ways around, the principal shall be responsible for the agent's business activities and the obligations incurred thereafter.

There are various reasons for appointing a foreign agent, one of the most important is that he knows more about local conditions and operate better in that very market. The agent knows what kinds of goods are in most need in his area and what price will be acceptable for the targeted customers. The agent is a valuable server and information offer to the exporter. An agent is more effective and economical because the principal only needs to pay when the agent is successful.

Agencies are mainly classified into two types, one is the sole agency and the other is the general agency. The sole agent may refer to a person or a firm acting specifically for a foreign principal with sole (exclusive) rights to sell on a commission basis certain commodities in a certain area. The general agent is regarded as the representative of the principal and in general the acts of the agent are taken as those of the principal.

13.3 Analysis of Model Letters

Read the following letters. While reading, please try to find answers to the following questions.

(1) Why does the writer of Model Letter 13-1 begin the letter with an introduction of his company and products?

(2) What advantages does the writer of Model Letter 13-2 set out to show that they are qualified for representing the recipients' products?

(3) Why does the writer mention the reasons for their decision to grant the sole agency in the first paragraph of Model Letter 13-3?

Model Letter 13-1: Looking for an agent

Dear Mr. Jonathon,

We are a life jacket manufacturer with a company based in Malaysia and factories in China. We have been in this line of business for over twenty years. Our products are mainly exported to Europe and North America, and they are very popular there.

We are planning to expand our business to Australia, and you have been highly recommended to us since you have enjoyed a high reputation in marketing of this field. We would like to ask if you are interested in representing us.

I hope you are in general agreement with the proposal.

Yours sincerely,

Model Letter 13-2: Applying for sole agency

Dear Mr. Swift,

We learned from the *Business Field* that you are looking for a reliable firm with rich experience in silk business to represent you in South Korea.

We have been in the silk market for over fifteen years. We import silk products from Taiwan for our purchasers. Since we have had such rich experiences in marketing products of your kind, and we know exactly about the local customers' needs and have confidence that we could expand your sales in South Korea. We have exhibition rooms in South Korea, which can help promotion of your products. Furthermore, we have an experienced sales team to promote your products energetically.

We look forward to your approval to our request to represent your products here.

Yours sincerely,
Kee Kwong
Sales Manager

Model Letter 13-3: Appointing an agent

Dear Sir,

We have received your letter of June 12th and are greatly interested in your proposal for an agency agreement between us. In consideration of your extensive experience in the photographic trade, we are glad to appoint you as our sole agent in South Korea.

We have drawn up a draft sole agency agreement in which the terms and conditions are set forth in details. Please examine it and inform us if they meet with your approval.

We hope the establishment of agency will further expand the business to our mutual benefit.

Yours faithfully,

13.4 Writing Guidelines

The above sample letters serve different purposes, but they may be categorized into the following three groups: letters aiming to find an agent, letters aiming to apply for agency or letters responding to an application for agency.

Generally speaking, a letter aiming to look for an agent is composed of the following parts.
(1) Giving background information or reasons why new agents are needed.
(2) Introducing agency to be granted.
(3) Showing expectations for a quick and favorable response to the offer as well as for good cooperation.
A letter intended to apply for agency consists of the following elements.

(1) Stating the purpose directly in the opening paragraph.
(2) Offering reasons for the application.
(3) Presenting supporting information.
(4) Expressing expectations for being granted the expected agency.

A letter which gives a reply to an application for agency usually contains the components listed below.

(1) Acknowledging receipt of the application.
(2) Responding to the application and giving decisions (acceptance or declination). If the reply is a negative one, an explanation is usually needed.
(3) Expressing expectations for further cooperation or a friendly close. If the response in part two is positive, then make some requests, otherwise, a good wish for understanding is expressed.

13.5 More Sample Letters

The following letters comply basically with the above writing guidelines, but they are different from the models in 13.3 in one way or another. Read them to see how each letter is structured and worded to achieve its respective communicative purpose.

Sample Letter 13-1: A voluntary offer of an agency

This letter offers agency voluntarily for the purpose of expanding business. Many detailed explanations are given to persuade the reader to accept the offer. At the end a request is made if the reader has to reject the offer.

Dear Mr. Jackson,

Because the demand for our Air Conditioner in your country is rising, we have decided to appoint an agent to deal with our export trade in your areas. When we last met at the Canton Fair, you were showing some interests in being an agency, and we may come to some arrangements.

There are great potential for our products in your market and there is little doubt that a really active agent could bring about a big increase in our sales. Since your wide experience in this business and your connections with the principal buyers in your country is generally known, we feel that your company is the one to do this, and we are extremely willing to offer you a sole agency.

If you are not able to accept it, we hope that you could recommend some other reliable and well-established firm, with whom we might approach. We do hope, however, that you are the one who will accept it. If you decide to do so, please state the terms that you would be willing to represent us.

Yours faithfully,

Sample Letter 13-2: Agreeing to an application for an agency

Because this is a positive reply to an application for agency, the writer has switched its focus to the arrangement for signing an agreement. The important points of the draft agreement are listed clearly for the reader's consideration.

Dear Sir,

Thank you for your letter of 23rd April proposing a sole agency for our products. We have examined our long and, I must say, mutually beneficial collaboration. We would be very pleased to entrust you with the sole agency in Hong Kong. We have drafted the agreement, and we would like you to go over and confirm the enclosed draft agreement with detailed terms and conditions, namely:

- That the agency commences on 1st August next and is terminated on 1st August, 2013, subject to renewal.
- That the agency is a sole agency for marketing our products in Hong Kong.
- That you undertake not to handle competing products of other local manufacturers.
- That we pay you quarterly a commission at 5% based on the net value of all the sales order received through you in Hong Kong.
- That all accounts are settled at the end of each year.
- That you keep a full range of our products in your showrooms.
- The area to be covered by the agency agreement is confined to Hong Kong.

It will be highly appreciated if you confirm these terms at your earliest convenience. A formal agreement will then be followed and copies sent for your signature.

Yours sincerely,

Sample Letter 13-3: Declining a request for a sole agency

The following letter gives a negative reply to an application, but it is still a friendly and polite letter because the writer gives adequate explanation for the rejection and an expectation for a trial collaboration is expressed.

Dear Mr. Sue,

Thank you for your letter of 1 May suggesting that we grant you a sole agency for our household linens. I regret to say that, at this stage, such an arrangement would be rather premature. We would, however, be willing to engage in a trial collaboration with your company to see how the arrangement works. It would be necessary for you to test the market for our products at your end. You would also have to build up a much larger turnover to justify a sole agency.

We enclose price lists covering all the products you are interested in and look forward to hearing from you soon.

Yours sincerely,
Allen Wang
Sales Manager

Sample Letter 13-4: Granting the sole agency

Now that the decision to grant agency has been made, the next step is to discuss the terms and conditions of the agreement, so in the third paragraph, the writer gives some basic information about the agreement and asks for a reconfirmation.

Dear Miss Hung,

It was our great pleasure to meet you on 11 October at your office in Macao.

After careful consideration, we are pleased to offer you an appointment as our sole agent for Macao. The sole agency will naturally be contingent on your maintaining qualified after sales staff. Please read the enclosed terms and conditions and let us know whether they meet with your approval.

The appointment will be valid for 3 years. The commission rate agreed is 5% on total sales of our goods. We will send you full range of our product samples for display in your showrooms.

Please reconfirm your acceptance of the above terms in written form as soon as possible, and we will send you the formal agreement in return.

Looking forward to a successful business relationship.

Yours sincerely,
Richard Chen
Regional Manager

Sample Letter 13-5: Informing of our agent

This is a letter notifying the reader of their new agent in India, so it is concise and short, and no details about the new agent are given.

Dear Mr. Lo,

It's my pleasure to inform you that as from 1 January, 2011, the Honda Company will be our general agent in India. Please direct all your inquiries concerning issues of sale and after-sale services to this company. The new agent will continue to provide good and reliable services as before.

We would be very pleased if an active business were to develop between your company and our agent.

Yours sincerely,
Leo Wong
General Manager

13.6 More Useful Sentences

1. Giving Reasons for an Application for Agency
- We specialize in finished cotton goods for the Middle Eastern market: Our activities cover all types of household linen. Until now, we have been working with your textiles department and our collaboration has proved to be mutually beneficial.
- We learn that you are looking for a reliable firm which has good relations in electric apparatus line to be your representative in Hong Kong.
- We have good knowledge of the local customers' needs and are confident that there is much we can do to extend your business here.
- Since we have dealt in equipment for hospitals for 20 years, we believe that we can offer expertise in obtaining orders and handling sales in this line.
- We do have very wide business connections, and our reputation as an agent is second to none.
- I saw your advertisement in *China Daily* and should like to have the agency for your products.
- We are convinced that there is a profitable market in our area waiting to be developed for your product and should like to act as your agent in this line.

2. Asking for Agency
- We are very interested in an exclusive arrangement with your factory for the promotion of your products in Jiangsu. We hope you could grant us as the sole agent.
- If you offer us this chance of agency we should make every effort to further your interests.
- We hope you will consider an offer for us to sell your products on exclusive sales basis.
- We are writing to inquire whether we could begin discussing arrangement whereby we handle your camera exclusively in the UK.
- If you are not already represented in Paris, we should like to offer our services as your agent.
- We ask to be the exclusive agent for your products in our territory.
- We wish to handle as an agent the goods you are exporting now, because we are commanding an extensive domestic market in this line.
- We now represent some best-known manufacturers in other countries and hope you will allow us to give you similar services.
- Since we see a bright prospect for the sale of your sports wears, we wish you to avail yourselves of

our services as selling agent.
- Considering we have a bright prospect for the sale of your newly-patented printer, we should like to act as your agent in the market here in this line of business.

3. Responding to an Application for Agency
- It is my great pleasure to advise you that you will now be representing our firm in your area.
- In view of your excellent performance in pushing the sales of our manufactures and the satisfactory business records, we have decided to appoint you as our sole agent for our Panda Brand Recorders in the territory of Iran.
- In view of your past efforts in pushing the sales of our products, we have decided to appoint you as our agent in your areas.
- For your reference, we would propose a sole agency agreement for a duration of three years with annual turnover of 5,000, 6,000 and 7,000 pieces for the first, second and third year respectively.
- We have noted your request to act as our agent in your district, but before going further into the matter, we should like to know your plan for promoting sales and the annual turnover you may realize in your market.
- The question of agency is still under consideration and we hope that you will continue your efforts to push sales of our products at the present stage.
- We do not think the time is ripe for you to act as an exclusive agency for our goods.
- We regret to inform you that we have already appointed someone else as our agent in Canada, and we are no longer in a position to consider a similar from you.
- If a bigger turnover can be realized to justify establishing the agency, we would like you to represent us.
- During the validity of the agency agreement, we shall not handle any other foreign products of the same line and competitive types.
- Your proposal is appreciated that you offer your services in sales of our products on a sole agency basis, but first of all we find it necessary to know the regular quantity you guarantee to sell monthly.

4. Expressing Gratitude for Agency Granted
- Thank you for your letter dated 5th May offering us an appointment as your sole agent in China.
- We express our heartfelt gratitude for your offering us this opportunity to take up your agency here.
- Thank you for your confidence. We are ready to accept your appointing us as your agent.
- Please be assured that as your agent, we will make greater efforts to push the sales of your products.

5. Offering Expectations or a Friendly Close
- Your prompt reply is highly appreciated.
- We await your returning a signed copy of the agency agreement.
- The agency will be for a trial period of one year, commencing on 1st August this year.
- With your excellent connections, we believe it will be possible to promote the sale of our products in your territory, and we hope your acting as our agent will be to our mutual benefit.

13.7 Writing Tips

Some English majors have proposed the following points to note in writing letters with relation to agency. Read the following list quickly and then discuss with your partner about whether they are reasonable and try to add some more ideas to the list.

The following are some tips which an inquirer or applicant for agency should pay special attention to in writing agency-related letters.

(1) It is advisable to offer source of information. The writer should tell the reader how he has got to know the recipient's name, address, telephone number etc.

(2) It is necessary for the writer to give reasons why he is interested in the agency and what request or competence he has for the agency so that the receiver may be convinced and will give a favorable reply immediately.

(3) In writing an enquiry or application, the writer should be confident and adopt an optimistic tone for his letter.

(4) In order to achieve the purpose of obtaining the expected agency, the writer can provide some testimonials such as your annual marketing turnover, your marketing channels etc.

While writing replies to a request or application for agency, the writer should follow the principles listed below.

(1) Replying promptly. The inquirer or applicant is usually anxious to know whether his inquiry or application is accepted or not, so it is polite of the replier to answer without delay.

(2) Writing with no arrogance. Any applicant's request for agency shows his confidence in marketing your products in his area.

(3) Declining mildly. Even if the writer has to decline an application, he should not give a definite "no". He should reject in a mild way or state that the application may be considered later on when the volume of business is large enough.

Notes and Explanations

1. sole agency 独家代理（也称作 exclusive agency）
2. principal 被代理人，委托人
   其他与 principal 有关的短语有：named principal（显名的委托人），undisclosed principal（未公开的委托人），unnamed principal（隐名的委托人），principal of business house（商行负责人），principal to the contract（合同的直接参与者）。
3. general agency 总代理
4. exhibition room/ showroom 样品间，陈列室
5. draw up/draft an agreement 起草协议
   The lawyer has drawn up the agreement.
   律师起草了协议书。
6. terms and conditions 合同条款
7. meet with your approval 得到你们的同意

The suggestion met with unanimous approval.

该项建议获得一致通过。

8. well-established　已经建立良好关系的，根基深厚的
9. subject to renewal　（代理协议等）允许续签
10. undertake

    (1) 承担（某事物），负起责任

    She undertook the organization of the whole scheme.

    她负责整个计划的组织工作。

    (2) 同意或答应做某事

    He undertook to finish the job by Friday.

    他答应在星期五以前完成工作。

    (3) 许诺，保证，担保

    She gave a solemn undertaking to respect their decision.

    她郑重地保证尊重他们的决定。

11. net value　净值
12. turnover　营业额

    其他与 turnover 有关的短语有：annual turnover（年营业额），capital turnover（资金周转），commodity/goods turnover（商品流转），foreign trade turnover（对外贸易额）。

13. del credere commission　保证收取货款的佣金，担保还款佣金

    有付款担保的代理商除了在委托人与卖家之间建立桥梁关系之外，还向委托人保证督促买家履行合同。有付款担保的代理商只有在买家未能履行合同义务，如无力偿还债务时才承担责任；但当买家拒绝履行合同义务，如不愿提货时，代理商不承担责任。一般来说，保证收取货款佣金会高于一般的代理佣金。

14. second to none　独占鳌头

    As a football player John is second to none.

    约翰是最好的足球运动员。

15. in return (for)　作为回报，作为报答

    return 用作名词时，其他与其有关的短语有：by return (of post)（回信由原送信人带回），make return for（报答），make a return（作报告），return to [回到（某个话题、某种状态），恢复，重新采取]。

Exercises

1. Multiple choices.

(1) We have decided to _____ you the sole agent for the sale of our fur in this area.

　　A. get　　　　　B. give　　　　　C. appoint　　　　　D. offer

(2) I wish to offer you my service _____ the sales of your products in your district.

　　A. of　　　　　B. with　　　　　C. on　　　　　D. for

(3) We do not think conditions are ripe to _____ you _____ the agency at the present stage as the sales volume mentioned in your letter is too small for us to grant you the agency.

　　A. assign ... to　　B. offer ... of　　C. entrust ... with　　D. allow ... with

(4) In view of my experience and extensive business connections, I hope to_____ _____ your sole agent for the territory.
    A. be assigned as   B. be appoint of   C. be given to   D. be allowed of
(5) After careful consideration, we decided not to _____ ourselves at this stage, when the record of transactions shows only a moderate volume of business.
    A. devote   B. bind   C. control   D. commit
(6) _____ your excellent connections, we believe it will be possible to promote the sale of our products in your territory and we hope your acting as our agent will be _____ our mutual benefit.
    A. Of … for   B. With … of   C. Of … to   D. With … to
(7) We would like to receive from you a detailed report _____ current market conditions and the users' comments _____ the quality of our products every month.
    A. about … about   B. on … on   C. of … about   D. about … of
(8) We trust that our experience in foreign trade and marketing will _____ us to your confidence.
    A. entitle   B. allow   C. permit   D. offer
(9) The commission agent may be a firm or a person who act _____ the instructions from his principal to sell goods _____ the best terms obtainable.
    A. over … on   B. with … on   C. upon … with   D. upon … on
(10) The general agent is regarded as the representative of the principal and in general the acts of the agent are taken _____ those of the principal.
    A. for   B. as   C. with   D. at

2. Translate the following English sentences into Chinese.

(1) We wonder whether you are agreeable to the agency agreement.
(2) Our corporation is established for the purpose of carrying on import and export business as well as other activities in connection with foreign trade.
(3) The whole matter hinges upon the question of the amount of commission you would require on orders obtained and executed.
(4) After a careful review of our business relations and your past efforts in pushing the sales of our products, we have decided to entrust you with the exclusive agency for our foot-wears in your district.
(5) Regarding your proposal to represent us in Tokyo for the sale of Chinese quilts, we have decided to appoint you as our agent.
(6) We should be glad to know on what terms you would be willing to represent us, also the terms on which business is generally conducted in your country.
(7) Agents play roles of manufacturers' marketing arm which can keep them informed of latest developments.
(8) As our executive agent, you should undertake neither to sell any competitive products of any other manufacturers nor re-export our products to any other areas outside your own.
(9) We have received your letter of January 18th and shall be glad to offer you a sole agency for the sale of our products in your country.
(10) The question of agency is still under consideration and we hope that you will continue your efforts to push the sale of our products at the present stage.

3. Fill in the blanks with the appropriate words from the following box. Change the forms where necessary.

| cooperate | learn | act | specify | other | represent | apply |
| recommend | right | contact | link | gratify | appreciate | request |

Dear Mr. Jackinson,

    We are a leading dealer in leather goods in Haining — the largest leather goods trading center in China. On the __(1)__ of Mr. Wang, an official from China Council for the Promotion of International Trade, we've __(2)__ something about your company's new brand "Downinghall". We're very interested in this brand, so we would like to __(3)__ as your sole agent in Shenzhen and Guangzhou.

    We'd __(4)__ it if you could let us know, if there is any, what would be your __(5)__ terms of being your sole agent, especially some details about the guarantee money, goods returning and the first delivery. __(6)__ than these points, we also want to know how to __(7)__ for this sole agent qualification exactly, the right procedures, or could you give us the __(8)__ information of the __(9)__ person or section that we should go up to.

    We hope we will have a good __(10)__ with you in the future.

    Your early reply is appreciated.

                                                                         Yours sincerely,

4. Situational writing.

    Suppose you have received a letter from Mr. Jennison, who is a businessman in Hamburg. In his letter, he expressed his wish to be your sole agent in Hamburg. Write a letter to him, in which you may approve his proposal. You may add some details which you may think necessary.

Chapter 14

Complaints and Adjustments

Your goals for this chapter are to understand:
☑ what are complaint letters and adjustment letters;
☑ how to write an effective complaint letter or adjustment letter;
☑ some sentence patterns used in complaint letters or adjustment letters;
☑ some points for attention in writing complaint letters.

14.1 Lead-in

Before you begin your learning of this chapter, please discuss with your partner(s) about the following questions.

(1) When do people usually complain?

(2) When someone complains to you, what do you usually do?

(3) Is it necessary for a seller to go into a long story of finding out how a mistake was made? Why or why not?

14.2 Basic Information

In international business, complaints and claims do not happen frequently but may sometimes occur. Many complaints can be made in person, but sometimes the complaint may be so complex that a phone call can not effectively resolve the problem; or the writer may prefer the permanence, formality, and seriousness of a business letter. In these circumstances, a formal complaint letter may be required.

A complaint letter is written to complain about, maybe, the quality of goods or services, the damage which has happened to the goods, or late or incomplete delivery of an order etc. In a complaint letter, reasons for the complaint are usually put at the beginning of the letter and then suggestions for the solutions to the problem follow, such as the compensation for defective or damaged merchandise or for inadequate or delayed services. It is suggested that such letters should not be aggressive because causes for the problems may be complex and diverse.

A claim letter aims to convince the reader that the claimer has a legitimate complaint which deserves a desired response. The claim letter should be professional and well-arranged, otherwise the writer cannot receive positive feedback in his favor.

Customers' complaints can cause you to lose future sales from customers as well as potential customers. On the contrary, if your customers' complaints are settled satisfactorily, you can turn them into more sales from these same customers and the people they influence. Of course, it's better not to let that happen. But once that has occurred, the manner in which you respond to your customer is of vital importance. In other words, how you handle your customers' complaints determines which of these two results you might get.

An adjustment letter usually refers to replies to complaint letters, and it should be written with care because it plays a key role in problem solving. When the requested compensation cannot be granted, writing a reply to a complainer tests writer's diplomacy and tact. The reply to a complaint can be either a mere reply, or an adjustment letter. It is not only meant to send a message for readiness to solve the problem but also with the intention to convince the other side that the mistake occurred is only a slip.

14.3 Analysis of Model Letters

Read the following letters. While reading, please try to find answers to the following questions.

(1) Why doesn't the writer of Model Letter 14-1 express thankfulness for the arrival of the goods at the beginning of the letter?

(2) Do you think the reason for a discount in Model Letter 14-2 is convincing? Why or why not?

(3) Why does the writer of Model Letter 14-3 repeat his apology at the end?

(4) Why does the writer of Model Letter 14-4 advise the recipient of the letter to lodge a claim with the insurance company?

Model Letter 14-1: A complaint about damaged goods

Dear Mr. Smith,

Damages on tea pots under S/C No. 6798

The shipment of 30,000 tea pots under S/C No. 6798 reached us on 25th April, 2011, but we have to say that, on opening the cases with great care, over 100 pcs of the tea pots were found damaged.

The person in charge at the Allan Glassware Company told me that the goods left the premises in perfect condition, and that they were carefully packed. The shipment documents held is proof enough that the goods were received by the carrier in good condition. Therefore, we can form a judgment that the damage must have happened in route.

This is not the first time that our goods have been damaged during transportation. You must look into this matter and give us a satisfactory reply by your first convenience. Meanwhile, we request you take some measure to prevent the reoccurrence of such matter.

Your sincerely,
Jerry Henry

Model Letter 14-2: A claim for inferior goods

Dear Mr. Hughes,

We received your goods on August 11, 2011, but found that they are not up to the standard. The goods we received are inferior to the samples in quality.

We, therefore, require you to grant us a special discount of 6% on the invoice value. We should be grateful if you could send us a check by return or, if you prefer, we can deduct the amount from your next invoice.

We appreciate your quick response.

Sincerely yours,

Model Letter 14-3: Making an adjustment for wrong delivery

Dear Sirs,

Your Order No. 1897 per S/S "Happiness"

Thank you for your letter of May 20th. We were glad to know that the consignment was delivered promptly, but it was a regret that we heard case No.1-90 did not contain the goods you ordered.

On going into the matter we find that a mistake was indeed made in packing, through a confusion of number, and we have arranged for the right goods to be dispatched to you at once. Relative documents will be mailed by courier service as soon as they are ready.

We will appreciate it if you will keep case No.1-90 and its contents until called for by the local agents of World Transport Ltd., our forwarding agents, whom we have instructed accordingly.

Once again we apologize for the trouble caused to you by the error.

Yours sincerely,
George Shelton

Model Letter 14-4: Rejecting a claim

Dear Mr. Long,

Order No. 54335

Thank you for your letter of May 3rd related to the quality of the Chinese traditional fans.

After a careful investigation, we didn't find any error on our part, because we took every effort to fulfill your order as shown in the enclosed certificate of packing inspection.

Since the quality is up to the standard and slight quality variation is unavoidable, we are sorry that we can't accept your request to return the goods.

Therefore we suggest that you lodge a claim with the insurance company. We will do whatever possible to assist you in processing the claim.

Though it is quite beyond our control, we still fell very sorry for the inconvenience you have suffered.

Sincerely yours,
Leo Jason
Customer Service Manager

14.4 Writing Guidelines

In the above four model letters, the first two are usually written by complainer, while the latter two are responses to complaints.

An analysis of the complaint and claim letters shows that they include the following essential elements.

(1) Referring to the receipt of the order at the beginning. In this part, a brief review about the order, invoice or delivery may by included.

(2) Identifying complaints or claims. The writer ought to specify the mistakes or errors made by the other side and mention what losses or negative effects these mistakes may bring about.

(3) Suggesting a solution exactly. A clear constructive claim for a solution to the problem is often included in a very polite tone.

(4) Ending the letter respectfully and implying that more orders may follow if the requirements are met.

A reply to a complaint letter or a claim letter usually includes the following basic elements.

(1) An acknowledgement of receiving the complaint letter or claim letter.

(2) An expression of regret or apology no matter whether the writer's company is to be blamed or not. This can help to relieve the reader's angry feeling.

(3) A statement of the investigation result. A specific description about the way the investigation is conducted and the people involved may make the investigation result more convincing.

(4) An explanation for the matter occurred. If you deny the request, explain the reasons why the request cannot be granted in a cordial manner, and try to offer some partial or substitute compensation or give some friendly advice to take the sting out of the denial. If you agree to grant the request, don't write in a way as if you are doing so in a begrudging way and explain what has caused the misunderstanding.

(5) An expression of confidence that you and the writer will continue doing business.

14.5 More Sample Letters

The following letters comply basically with the above writing guidelines, but they are different from the models in 14.3 in one way or another. Read them to see how each letter is structured and worded to achieve its respective communicative purpose.

Sample Letter 14-1: Complaint on a mail-ordered gift

The following letter starts with the writer's past pleasant experience with the Friendship Gallery and then goes on to the complaint. This arrangement makes the complaint and request for replacement more acceptable.

Dear Manager,

While working in China for the past three years, I had always purchased gifts from the Friendship Gallery for my Canadian friends. The quality and value had always been more than I could reasonably expect, and I have often recommended your store to others.

Last autumn, I was back in Canada, but I did not forget to mail-order some Christmas gifts from your usual annual Fall Sales. After examining the gifts supplied to my order of November 8, I found that there was a distinct hole in the middle of one of the silk scarves. Although I remember that you apply a no-return policy to this kind of merchandise, I sent this silk scarf in a separate mailing yesterday so that you may see the damage for yourself. When you receive it I am sure that you will share my surprise and dismay.

I understand from my past experience with the Friendship Gallery that this is an unusual situation. Will you kindly reconsider your no-return regulation with one of your loyal customers and replace the above mentioned silk scarf by mailing another one? I would be delighted to have it and present it to my friend for Christmas.

Yours sincerely,

Sample Letter 14-2: A claim letter on shortage of shipment

The writer's argument is very persuasive because he gives enough evidence to certify that the shortage of goods is not due to the writer's fault.

Dear Sirs,

We have just been informed by Jonson Company in Singapore, the consignees under B/L No. 670 dated April 20th, 2011 that four of the 150 cases shipped from Ningbo to Male per S/S "Chong Qing" are missing.

The consignees contacted your agents in Singapore about it and they were advised to approach us directly to investigate the matter. As matters stand, it is legibly indicated in the B/L: shipped in apparently good order and condition. The same indication appears in our Shipping Order and your Mate's Receipt. It is therefore obvious that the shortage is due to your fault, and we hereby notify you that we reserve the right to claim on you for the shortage, should it be subsequently confirmed.

Your early clarification and settlement of the case will be highly appreciated.

Yours faithfully,

Sample Letter 14-3: Proposal for settlement of a claim

The writer first argues that there is no problem with the quality of their products, and then makes a concession in the name of valuing the long-standing business relations.

Dear Sir or Madam,

Thank you for your letter dated October 18th, with the enclosure of Survey Report No. H-3326.

You claim that the quality of the goods shipped per S.S. "Red Star" is inferior to the original sample and request us to make a 10% reduction on the contract price. This does not seem reasonable to us, as we sent you an advanced sample prior to shipment, and not hearing from you any advice or objection, we presumed it to be acceptable to you. Meanwhile, quality of this rank is what we have sold for years without receiving any complaints from other customers. It is made in our own mills, and the source of our raw materials has never changed.

However, considering our long-standing business relations and since the goods were examined by a Public Surveyor upon arrival, we will meet you halfway by offering a discount of 5%.

We hope that our proposal will be entertained by you for the settlement of the pending case so that we may continue doing business with you in the future.

We look forward to your agreement to our proposal.

Yours faithfully,

Sample Letter 14-4: Acceptance of a claim

Before the letter states its decision to accept the claim and agree to make a compensation for the loss, it argues that there is no problem with the quality of the goods. This arrangement may make the receiver of the letter believe that the writer is doing him a favor.

Dear Sirs,

Re: Contract No. DY-223- Air Conditioner

We thank you for your letter of December 2nd, with enclosures, claiming for shortage in quantity and inferior quality on the consignment of the air conditioner shipped per S/S "Ocean Star".

On examination we found that some 20 boxes had missed packing as stipulated in the contract, resulting in breakage during transit. However, the quality of the consignment was up to standard. We really cannot account for the reason of your complaint about the quality. But since the air conditioner was examined by a public surveyor upon arrival at Shanghai and in view of our long-standing business relations, we cannot but accept your claims as tendered.

We therefore enclose our check No. 2254 for USD40,000.00 in full and final settlement of your claims ARC-I1 and I2.

We apologize sincerely for the trouble you have encountered, and will take all possible steps to ensure that such a mistake shall not be made again in our further cooperation.

Yours sincerely,

Sample Letter 14-5: Refusing an adjustment for damaged goods

The declination to the claim in the following letter is made in a tactful way, therefore, no misunderstanding will arise. Meanwhile, the seller expresses the sincerity for future cooperation by offering a discount.

Dear Sirs,

We wish to refer to our letter dated March 18th and your letter of April 21st, in which you made a claim on our shipment of water filter.

After further consultation with the manufactures of the goods, we regret to say that we are unable to come to any positive agreement which could solve the present problem.

Since the manufacturer suggested that the products are not precision instruments, which would need different packing, he came to the conclusion that there is no valid ground for complaint so long as such a defect does not in the least affect the use of the goods.

Therefore, we consider it difficult to file a claim against the manufactures. Nevertheless, we are prepared to straighten out the matter in an amicable way by paying you a rebate of 5% so as to start with a clean slate.

We hope that our proposal will be acceptable to you for the settlement of the pending case so that we may continue doing business with you shortly.

We look forward to hearing from you as soon as you can.

Yours faithfully,
Howard Ling

14.6 More Useful Sentences

1. Identifying Complaints or Claims
- The inspection reveals that both the quantity and quality of the hats delivered are not in conformity with those stipulated in the contract.
- We feel that the percentage of the goods of inferior quality was too high.
- On checking the goods received, we find that several items on your invoice have not been included; we enclose a list of the missing articles for your inspection.
- It was found by the inspection that there is a difference of 50 kgs between the actual landed weight and the invoiced weight.
- As we have pointed out repeatedly, prompt delivery is essential in this trade. However, we have not yet received the goods or any advice.
- When we discussed delivery dates, you assured us that you could deliver by October 5th. However,

the goods are now three weeks overdue.
- One of the cases was badly smashed and the contents were seriously damaged, apparently due to faulty packing.
- This is not the first time a delay in delivery has occurred, and this has compelled us to point out that business on such conditions can not be continued for a long time.

2. Making Requests
- We believe that you will spare no efforts to straighten this matter out immediately.
- We shall be pleased to know your explanation as to this discrepancy in quality, and also as to what is the best you can do for us in the matter.
- We would be obliged if you would replace the goods you delivered with the correct ones.
- Unless we can depend on the very best quality being supplied in every case, we shall be compelled to place our orders with some other firms.
- We have to ask for compensation from you for the amount mentioned above.
- Please let us know if you will take the goods back or make us an adequate allowance for the damage the goods have sustained.
- Unless improvement is made at your end we shall have to cancel all further orders according to the terms of our contract.
- If you do not refund all of the money we have paid, we shall have no choice but to seek legal advice in the matter.

3. Suggesting a Solution
- Although the quality of these goods is not up to that of our usual line, we are prepared to accept the goods if you will reduce the price, say by 20%.
- We are compelled to claim on you to compensate us for the loss, USD50,000, which we have sustained by the disqualified goods.
- We require you to replace the damaged goods and grant us a special discount of 6% to compensate for the loss.
- Since the free acidity exceeds the contract maximum by 0.3%, so we have to ask you to indemnify us for a loss of USD15,000.
- We will remit to you a sum of $300 in compensation for the loss arising therefrom and hope you to send the receipt at your earliest convenience.
- I propose we compensate you by 4% of the total value/total amount of the contract plus inspection fee.
- We will get this matter resolved as soon as possible and hope to compensate you for your loss to your satisfaction.
- We will make you a compensation of 5% and give you some preferential terms later on.
- We will give you a 20% allowance of the next shipment to compensate you for the loss.
- We are pleased to inform you that the goods will be ready for shipment next week, and hope that they will arrive in time.
- Please let us know what adjustment you think is satisfactory. Please propose/suggest a settlement which is fair and reasonable.
- We leave it to you to suggest a solution as we have full confidence in your fairness.

- If you don't accept our propositions, we might submit the matter for arbitration.
- Evidently the damage occurred during transit, we should therefore, suggest that you lodge your claim with the forwarders.
- The shipping documents can prove that the digital cameras, when shipped, were in perfect condition. They must have been damaged en route, so you should make a claim on the insurance company.

4. Admitting Mistakes or Faults

- The defective goods which you have mentioned must have been overlooked by our inspectors.
- We assure you that this was due to a clerical error and an oversight on our part, that all the goods were not included in the shipment.
- According to the Surveyor' report, the damage was due to rough/careless handling during the transit.
- We checked this on the computer this morning and found that there was a slip-up in our shipping department. It's certainly our fault. What would you like us to do about it?
- On going into the matter we find that a mistake was indeed made in the packing through a confusion of numbers, and we have arranged for the right goods to be dispatched to you at once. Relative documents will be sent to you by DHL as soon as they are ready.
- Owing to the rush of orders, it is impossible for us to make delivery as soon as we wish.
- We frankly admit that delivery was delayed, but it was really beyond our control and we are taking up the matter with the forwarders and will let you know without loss of time.
- The goods though not the very ones you ordered are in good quality and attractive designs, and we think you can sell them out at our price.
- We can understand the inconvenience and annoyance you have suffered, and will do our best to adjust the matter to your satisfaction.
- Such case does exist but it counts for little. It is our hope that you will waive the claim and we shall then see if we can do something for your orders to follow.

5. Not Admitting Mistakes or Faults

- Since your complaint does not agree with results of our tests, we suggest that therefore, that another through examination be conducted by you to show whether there is any reason for a claim.
- We regret we cannot entertain your claim, which is without any foundation.
- As the shipping company is liable for the damage, your claim for compensation should , in our opinion, be referred to them for settlement.
- We regret our inability to accept your claim because the case, when being loaded, left nothing to be desired.
- Such color deviation existing between the products and the confirmed sample is normal and permissible. Therefore, the claim for compensation is impracticable.
- As the goods have been insured, you may refer the matter to the insurance company or their agents at your end.
- We are willing to make you a reasonable compensation, but not the amount you claimed.
- The shortage you alleged might have occurred in transit, and that is a matter over which we can exercise no control.

14.7 Writing Tips

Some English majors have proposed the following points to note in writing complaint letters and adjustment letters. Read the following list quickly and then discuss with your partner about whether they are appropriate and try to add some more ideas to the list.

In writing complaint letters or claim letters, you should keep in mind the following tips.

(1) Make a complaint or claim without any hesitation or delay.

(2) Complaints should be made in a restrained and tactful way so that future business relationships won't be influenced.

(3) Explain the problem clearly by providing specific details. If possible, you can enclose some documents indicating the problems.

(4) Make specific requests. Clearly state what result or compensation you expect to gain.

(5) Use stronger tone in the following complaints if you fail to get a reply or a satisfactory correction from the other side within a reasonable time. But always remember that only when necessary can you tell the recipient that actions will be taken if the requirements are not met.

(6) Keep a copy of your investigation result and do not send original documentation.

Below are some suggestions that may help you write replies to complaint or claim letters more effectively.

(1) Take the complaint or claim seriously. A reference of the original letter of complaint is necessary. Express your sympathy over the writer's troubles and your appreciation that he has written.

(2) Give explanations for what has happened. Go deep into details when offering the facts.

(3) Do not run away from responsibility. Admit your mistake without justifying yourself and apologize sincerely if you are wrong. If the mistake is from the reader's side, point that out tactfully. If it is a third party's fault, give suggestions or offer assistance generously.

(4) State ways for solving the problem. You should tell the reader that you are ready to do what you can to meet the reader's requirements. If you deny the request, explain the reasons cordially and offer your way of settlement for other's reference.

(5) If you think the claim you have received is acceptable or reasonable, you ought to take it. If not, you should tell them why you think it is too much and make another suggestion to solve the problem.

Notes and Explanations

1. adjustment letter 投诉回复函
   投诉回复函是对投诉所给出的答复，它也可以是记录所作出的决定和所采取的行动的信函。其内容一般是承认失误，表示歉意，提出补偿等。有时候，即使写信方并没有错误，这样的信件也可以起到平息对方怒气、保持良好贸易关系的作用。

2. premise 房屋等的建筑物
   其他与 premise 有关的短语有：live on the premises（住在楼内），off the premise［只卖给在店外喝的（尤指酒店）］，on/in the premise［只卖给在店内喝的（尤指酒店）］，see sb. off the premise（送至门口，下逐客令），business premises（事务所），storage premises（库房，仓库）。

3. consignee 收货人

   consignor 发货人，托运人

4. hatchway 舱口，天窗

5. lodge a claim 提出索赔（也可以说 file a claim）

   lodge v. 提出（抗议、投诉等）

   lodge 常用于下列结构中：lodge sth. against sb. with a department（向某部门提出对某人的抗议、投诉）等。

   He lodged a protest against his supervisor with the authorities concerned.

   他向有关部门反映了对他的管理人员的抗议。

6. reserve the right to claim 保留索赔的权利

7. public surveyor 公证行

   公证行是指专门从事国际商品检验、测试和认证的公司。

8. pending case 悬案

   pending

   (1) 待决，未决

   The case is pending further.

   案件正在进一步审理中。

   (2) 即将发生，逼近

   A decision on this matter is pending.

   此事即将作出决定。

   (3) 在等待（某事物）之际

   She was held in custody pending trial.

   她正被拘留，等待审判。

9. straighten out

   (1) 解决，澄清

   I hope the misunderstanding will soon be straightened out.

   我希望误会很快就会澄清。

   (2) 恢复正常，使好转

   I'll try to straighten the matter out once and for all.

   我要竭力把这件事情彻底办好。

10. discount/allowance 折扣

11. start with a clean slate 重新开始

    与 slate 有关的短语有：a clean slate（清白的经历，无犯罪记录），wipe the slate clean（勾销往事，放弃进行中的事）。

12. count for little 无足轻重

13. to entertain one's claim 接受某人的索赔要求

    to entertain a proposal 愿意考虑这一建议

14. en route （法语）在路上，在中途

    We stopped at Paris en route from Rome to London.

    我们从罗马去伦敦的途中曾在巴黎停留。

Chapter 14 Complaints and Adjustments   187

Exercises

1. **Multiple choices.**

    (1) We are sorry to hear that, when you received the 180 pieces of china you ordered on June 16th, you found ten of them broken and two of them _____ .
      A. missed   B. to miss   C. missing   D. being missed
    (2) The survey report _____ that the broken bags were due to rough handling instead of improper packing, for which the shipping company should be definitely responsible.
      A. means   B. indicates   C. believes   D. demonstrates
    (3) We are deeply sorry that the delay in shipment has caused you much inconvenience, and for the present we can only ask you to _____ our apology.
      A. receive   B. take   C. get   D. accept
    (4) We shipped your order before the shipping date _____ in your L/C, therefore, the delay was not caused by us.
      A. specify   B. specified   C. specifying   D. to be specified
    (5) We are prepared to make you a reasonable compensation but not the amount you _____, because we cannot see why the loss should be 50% more than the actual value of the goods.
      A. asked   B. hoped   C. claimed   D. expressed
    (6) Please _____ the original invoice to the returned goods on the top of your goods, and send them back so that our staff can verify them and reimburse you as soon as possible.
      A. enclose   B. put   C. post   D. find
    (7) As soon as we got the news, immediate arrangements were made to have the goods _____ to Luanda by the first available opportunity.
      A. to return   B. returned   C. return   D. returning
    (8) The wrong pieces may be sent back via next available steamers for our account, but it is _____ if you can sell them out at our price in your local market.
      A. preferring   B. preferred   C. to prefer   D. preferable
    (9) We take all our customers' comments seriously. With this in mind, we are _____ happy to cover the cost of replacing the defective goods.
      A. less than   B. other than   C. rather than   D. more than
    (10) In view of the reasons stated above, we have no choice but _____ back the defective goods and ask you to replace them for us.
      A. sending   B. to send   C. send   D. sent

2. **Translate the following Chinese sentences into English.**

    (1) 我们对此货物受损不承担任何责任。
    (2) 我们一直不愿意拒绝老客户的要求，但是很遗憾这次我们确实只能这样做了。
    (3) 如果贵方拒绝执行订单，我方有权要求贵方对我公司因处理该货物所招致的损失做出赔偿。
    (4) 我方希望贵方能考虑此事，并尽早付清赔款。
    (5) 我们希望贵方能同意我方的提议，以便我方很快能够跟贵方继续合作。
    (6) 我们从来没有遇到过我们需要的货物没能投递的情况。

(7) 我方不赞同贵方提出的诉诸法律的威胁方式。我方认为，解决争议同样有效、而且更为经济的办法是通过仲裁的办法。

(8) 我们知道，新的生产线出现故障是可以理解的，但是你们的售后服务实在让人失望。

(9) 因为运输单据可以证明货物在离港时完好无损，很明显损害是在运输途中造成的，所以我方不考虑贵方的索赔要求。

(10) 对于贵方上次运送的货物我方感到很不满意，在此不得不表示惊讶与失望。

3. Correct the mistakes in the following sentences.

(1) As we need the order articles to complete deliveries to our own customers, we must ask you to arrange for dispatch of replacements at once.

(2) Meanwhile, we are holding the above-mentioned case at your dispose.

(3) We can only presume that a mistake made and the contents of this case were for another order.

(4) If you will provide us your instructions for returning this merchandise to your firm, we will arrange for its speedy delivery.

(5) This is to inform you that the merchandise we received does not correspond our specifications.

(6) I am writing to ask you to make up the shortfall immediately and to ensure that such errors not happen again.

(7) It is absolutely essential that you must ship the additional 500 pieces on the earliest possible flight.

(8) Because we value your business, so we would like to offer you a 10% discount off your next order with us.

(9) We have received your letter of 10 December enclosed is the copy of your inspection certificate.

(10) The extra 4 dozen of watches is free of charge as small compensation for your inconvenience.

4. Situational writing.

The products for order No. 992 are not of the same quality as usual. But you do not want the products to be changed since you are out of stock. Your purpose of writing this complaint letter is to ask the seller to offer some discount on this unit of cargo. Write a letter in which all the above particulars will be included. You may add some details which you may think necessary.

Chapter 15 International Trade in Services

Your goals for this chapter are to understand:
☑ what is service;
☑ what is international trade in service;
☑ the major types of service trade;
☑ how to write service-related letters;
☑ some expressions used in service trade letters.

15.1 Lead-in

Before you begin your learning of this chapter, please discuss with your partner(s) about the following questions.

(1) The service sector is playing an increasingly important role in our economy. Can you tell us how much you know about service trade?

(2) It is said that service trade can be found almost everywhere? Do you agree or not?

15.2 Basic Information

Globalization has greatly widened international companies' business scope. As a consequence, world economies are becoming increasingly interconnected and interdependent. Thus, international service has become part of international trade, and services have become increasingly tradable and present dynamic opportunities for many countries. So a successful businessman should know some basic information about international trade in service.

Then what is a service? In economics and marketing, a service is the non-material equivalent of a good. Service provision has been defined as an economic activity that does not result in ownership.

Compared with goods, services are much less tradable. They have to be consumed at the point where they are produced. This means that either the supplier of a service must move to where the consumer is located, or the consumer of the service must move to where the producer is located.

Generally speaking, international trade in services include communication services, distribution services, tourism and travel related services, construction and related engineering services, education services, environmental services, financial services, transport services, recreational, cultural and sporting services, health related and social services etc.

In this chapter, we shall mainly discuss some fast-developing sectors of international trade in services such as logistics, tourism, consultancy, finance, consignment.

The study of effective processes for delivery and disposition of goods and personnel is called logistics. The logistics process affects almost every sphere of human activity, either directly or indirectly. But unfortunately, we often don't think of the role that logistics has in our lives until we have a problem.

The tourism industry is one of the largest and most dynamic sector in today's global economy. It creates millions of jobs and has a central importance to the economy of many nations, and has an impact for the economy, for the natural and built environment, for the local population at the places visited, and for the visitors themselves. The tourism sector is special in its relationship to globalization. The consumer of its services travels to where the services are generated, unlike most other sectors where the product is delivered to the consumer, remote from the product's origin.

The consultancy service is a specialist service which the service provider offers to his or her clients. Service providers help their clients solve highly-complex, technically-challenging issues in exchange for some form of payment. Consultancy service has two main functions. The first is to provide expert advice in the areas in which the service provider specializes. The second is to offer clients the benefit of providers' considerable professional experience in refocusing their clients' business or a specific aspect of their business. The terms under which the services will be provided, the time line and all of the particulars involving the agreement for services between the parties are usually defined in a consulting service agreement.

International financial service, as the title suggests, offers a comprehensive range of investment products and advisory and management services specifically tailored to internationally mobile expatriates. Through extensive strategic partnerships with global financial institutions, service providers can offer solutions to investors' needs. It aims to provide advisory and management services for international businesses. Service providers readily advise clients of new opportunities and developments affecting your investments.

Consignment is a way of import and export transaction. Goods on consignment are delivered by an exporter (consignor) on his own expense to a distributor abroad or the overseas agent for sale on commission agreement made between the parties concerned. And that payment is not made immediately by the importer. The importer will hold the goods until the goods have been sold partly or completely in the consignee's country.

15.3 Analysis of Model Letters

Read and analyze the following letters. While reading, please try to find answers to the following questions.

(1) Do you think Model Letter 15-1 is too simple to provide enough information?

(2) Why does the writer give a brief introduction to his plan to visit Beijing before making enquiries in Model Letter 15-2?

(3) Model Letter 15-3 is a letter in consultancy service. This letter only gives the conclusion of the research without any supporting information, doesn't it?

(4) The contents of Model Letter 15-4 are complicated, but they are neatly arranged. How does the writer achieve such a purpose?

(5) Why does the writer give so much background information before he states his purpose of the letter?

Model Letter 15-1: Offering logistics service

Dear Mr. Taylor,

We are a forwarder and international transporting agent in China. We can satisfy your demands in transporting service, especially for companies in China.

For more information about us and the services we offer, you can visit our website at: www.bjk.com.cn and get some references from there.

Sincerely yours,
Dis Ticaret

Model Letter 15-2: Asking for some China travel information

Dear Sir/Madam,

I will be visiting Beijing for sightseeing with my parents for a week from the 15th till 21st July. We want to visit the following sites during our trip: the Great Wall, the Summer Palace, the Palace Museum and the Tiananmen Square.

Can you make an itinerary for us so that the least time and expenses are spent on the travel? Meanwhile please quote us the price for the travel service you offer us during the trip, including a tour guide's service. Besides, my banks here are giving me an exchange rate of 6.43 RMB¥/1 US$. What exchange rate can we expect in Beijing banks?

Thank you.

Sincerely yours,
Anni Ambotty

Model Letter 15-3: A letter about market research result

Dear Sir,

Further to our letter of 7th June, we are writing to advise you of the results of the market research into the possibilities of launching your bamboo garden products in Japan.

The findings of the report, a copy of which we enclose herewith, are favorable and clearly indicate that there is a market here for your products. It will, however, take a little time to develop the market and the initial cost for advertising will be quite substantial.

If you are prepared to accept the recommendations in the enclosed report, we are willing to begin negotiations with a view to manufacturing bamboo garden products under license as soon as it shows signs of becoming established here.

We look forward to receiving your comments.

Yours faithfully,

Model Letter 15-4: A letter in financial service

Dear Fleming,

In response to your enquiry of May 4th regarding the loan application of our mutual client, MPD Construction Co., Ltd, we are pleased to provide the following details.

Firstly, our client intends to use in-house architects for any work required for the project in question at no incremental costs that could be traced to this particular project.

Secondly, the set of accounts for the most recent accounting period has not yet been signed off by the client Board. This delay is due to our client's accounting and reporting system to IFRS, requiring additional valuation of our client's fixed assets. To accommodate your need to assess these figures, we have obtained their permission to release the latest management accounts and these are enclosed.

Thirdly, our client restructured their portfolio during the first half of their accounting period just ended. The resulting disposal of assets (see Note 16 of the management accounts enclosed) at unexpectedly high prices allowed our client to accumulate sufficient cash reserves to finance the remaining 35% of the total investment.

Despite the recent surge in property prices, this particular site has been significantly undervalued. We enclose a copy of the most recent valuation report for your reference.

We are open to any further discussion and ready to meet you in person to clarify any of these or additional details.

Yours sincerely,

Sample Letter 15-5: A proposal for a trial sale on a consignment basis

Dear Sirs,

We are a leading hypermarket in Tokyo and have recently received a number of inquiries for your pure silk pajamas. We think there are good prospects for the sale of these goods here. But at present it is little known and as we cannot make sure of regular sales, we do not feel able to handle your products on our own account. We are, therefore, writing to suggest that you send us a trial delivery for sale on a consignment basis. We make the proposal hoping to place firm orders when the market is established.

If you agree, the selling price is to be fixed by us according to the market demand. We would render monthly accounts of sales and send you the payments due after deducting expenses, and commission at a rate to be agreed on.

As for our credit standing, you may refer to the Bank of Tokyo.

We believe our proposal will bring you good opportunities and hope you will be willing to give them a trial.

Yours truly,

15.4 Writing Guidelines

Letters in international service trade are similar to those in international goods trade. The main difference between the two lies in the object of transaction, i.e. service trade deals with service while goods trade sells commodities. Therefore, the writing rules for letters in goods trade are applicable to letters in service trade.

The above model letters cover logistics, consultancy, travel, finance and consignment etc. The letters, in terms of their writing purposes, can be classified into three types: enquiry about service, reply to these enquiries and companies' service promotion letters. So the writing principles for enquiries introduced in Chapter Four are also useful for writing enquiries for service rate and replies to enquiries. For example, you can also begin the letter by mentioning the source of information, and then goes on to introducing your company, giving causes for the inquiry, stating your specific requirements, and end it by asking for a reply.

15.5 More Sample Letters

The following letters comply basically with the above writing guidelines, but they are different from the models in 15.3 in one way or another. Read them to see how each letter is structured and worded to achieve its respective communicative purpose.

Sample Letter 15-1: Logistics services

This is a letter written by a logistics company. In the letter the writer states the situation briefly first and then makes his queries clearly with some questions.

Dear Emmie,

We have already picked up 2,000 pieces of ZAC-00035 from the Shipping Company. Please advise if we should send the cargo to Hangzhou warehouse or leave it in the care of a Shanghai warehouse? If we send them to Hangzhou warehouse, who will pay the cost of collecting from Shanghai to Hangzhou? If we leave it in the care of the shipping company, who should we send the relevant documents to?

We are waiting for your instruction. Your prompt reply will be appreciated.

With best regards,

Sample Letter 15-2: Making a room reservation

The following letter is neat and simple because the main information about the writer himself and his arrival is clearly arranged.

Dear Sir/Madam,

We would like to make a room reservation at your hotel as follows:

Name: Mr. C. Guan
Address: 1-22-33 Mogan, Gongshu District, Hangzhou, China
Mobile: 013719128168
Arrival: 20th July, 2011 (Arrival flight: BA 321 with ETA of 15:00).
Departure: 25th July, 2011

Room Type: No-smoking single room

Will you please send me a prompt confirmation?

Yours faithfully,

Sample Letter 15-3: Offering legal & business advice

The following is a sales promotion letter. It is promoting its service, so the writer is doing his utmost to impress the readers and motivate their interest in his service.

Dear Sir,

Our company is a law firm specializing in commercial, corporate and administrative laws, real estate and litigation. The firm's offices are situated in the Zhongxin Center, Beihai Avenue, Hangzhou, Zhejiang, China.

For nearly twenty years, we have provided a full range of legal services to a wide-ranging client base, including international companies, investor groups and individuals, tailored to each client's needs. In addition, we represent domestic and foreign companies and private equity investors investing in the USA, both on the structure of their investment activities as well as on individual transactions.

For more information about our service, please contact us at 0086-571-89898989, or send e-mails to XYLS@163.com.

Sincerely yours,

Sample Letter 15-4: Financial service

This is a reply letter, in which the writer, as a financial consultant, gives the results of his study about the financial standing of Greenberg.

Dear Ms. Kutsakova,

Thank you very much for your letter. Indeed, our clients have managed to achieve remarkable results in the last two years mainly because of a new series of products introduced in the market not long ago. Since then, all of these products have enjoyed enormous popularity with consumers driving the profits up to an all-time high.

Certainly, the most obvious reaction to the high level of demand was expansion of the business, which usually entails an inevitable increase in all expenses, including the labor overheads you have pointed out in your letter. However, these costs are expected to be fully covered by another anticipated rise in profits.

Greenberg products make highly technological products to stay competitive and the construction of a new factory with the most advanced developments in the field will require specialist expertise which is quite expensive.

The minority shareholders you have mentioned are primarily interested in profit maximization and look forward to the construction of a new factory. This will help our clients to secure a solid market position, as extensive market research has shown, which is sure to lead to even higher profits for the shareholders.

Yours faithfully,

Sample Letter 15-5: Introducing advertisement service

This can also be seen as a promotion letter as it is also promoting its service — advertisement. Besides introducing to the directory in colorful words, the writer also offers some preferential terms to motivate the reader.

Dear Mr. Johnson,

Thank you for your business. You are currently represented in our directory. This is the only directory of its kind which reaches all companies in cosmetics industry in the UK.

Advertising in our directory was a wise move on your part. We are currently compiling a new edition of the directory which will be published in April 2012. The new edition will be expanded to include major manufacturers of wigs in the European Community. For proper coverage in the directory, you ought to appear in more than one category. If you do opt for a multiple listing, you will be able to buy space in additional categories at half price. You can be assured that the new edition will be on the desks of all the major decision-makers in cosmetic and wig trades.

Please complete the enclosed form and return it with the appropriate fee. Thanks again for your business.

Sincerely yours,
(Signature)

Sample Letter 15-6: Agreeing to sales on consignment basis

This is a letter in reply to a proposal for a consignment sale. As this is a positive reply, the writer, after stating his decision of accepting the proposal, gives some further details about the following arrangement.

Dear Sirs,

Thank you for your letter of 26th February. After careful consideration we found the terms suggested by you reasonable and acceptable, and we made a decision to accept your proposal of the sales of our pure silk pajamas on consignment. We are sending you a representative selection of our best-selling lines. We hope you will find a ready sale for them.

We agree that you fix the price at which the goods will be offered for sale according to the market situation. Your suggestion to submit accounts and to make payments monthly is quite satisfactory. We are willing to allow you commission at 9% calculated on total sales. The consignment is being shipped by S.S. "May Flower", leaving Ningbo for Tokyo on 5th March. We will send you the B/L and other shipping documents as soon as we receive them, and meanwhile enclose a proforma invoice in which the prices shown are for your information only.

Because of its good quality, attractive design and reasonable price, these pajamas sell well in some European countries and we hope it will have a good sale in your hypermarket.

Truly yours,

15.6 More Useful Sentences

1. Sentence Patterns Used in Logistics
- If the cargo space needs to be reserved, please send us the necessary application forms.
- We offer you our services as forwarding and customs agents, and you may rest assured that we should always act to the best of your interests.
- There is no container ship sailing from Ningbo to London before August. Therefore, we regret that we cannot send you a quotation as you requested.
- We wish to charter a ship of about 20,000 metric tons for a single voyage from Lianyungang to New York for machinery.
- Will you please quote us your freight rate and the vessels available to sail for Tokyo before December 15th?

2. Sentence Patterns Used in Tourism
- On August 3, we wish to hold a dinner for approximately 60 guests in a banquet room. The price for the dinner is to be from $40 to $50 per person.
- From August 2 to 4, we will need 10 singles and 20 doubles, each with bath or shower. We wish to

- have all participants stay at your hotel.
- Please reserve a single room for me for the nights of July 20, 21 and 22. I will arrive at about 5 p.m. on July 20 and leave before noon on July 23.
- The Company provides variety of tourist "packages" (business/leisure/recreation services) in Saudi Arabia, for individuals and groups.
- Anyway, the Great Wall of China is one of the most famous place for its scenery and historical relics. It is worth to pay a visit to this inconceivable miracle of Chinese culture. And trust me, you will hardly find something so unimaginable like the Great Wall of China in the world.
- Since your hotel is located near Tian An Men Square, it is advisable for you to travel Beijing by metro.

3. Sentence Patterns Used in Consultancy Service
- We provide consulting services for individuals and organizations interested in doing business in those fields.
- Our consulting service is suitable for units from many areas between Europe and China.
- We provide a variety of official business investigations and arrangements in the USA.
- We could also supply business consulting services, information of customs importing and exporting.
- "World Trade Link" established in 1988 is one of the leading International Marketing Consultants and Foreign Trade Facilitators.
- We offer a neutral platform to foreign buyers wishing to source the goods produced in our country.

4. Sentence Patterns Used in Financial Service
- Before we can process the application, we require further information on some points.
- All the Chinese banks at the airport or hotels in the city have the same official exchange rates.
- Our client, Dong Fang Import & Export Corp., has asked us for information about the Auto Engineering Co., Ltd. in London, England, as the latter would request a standing credit of USD 5,000 to start business.
- We should, therefore, like to know whether or not their financial and credit standing are sound.
- We are pleased to enclose credit information regarding the above, relative to which you inquire in your letter of March 25, 2011.

5. Sentence Patterns Used in Consignment
- We are writing to make a suggestion that you send us a trial delivery for sale on a consignment basis.
- We made a decision to accept your proposal of the sales of our pure silk pajamas on consignment.
- We are willing to allow you a commission of 8% calculated on total sales.
- We regret that we cannot deal with your goods on our own account, but would be willing to take them on a consignment basis.

15.7 Writing Tips

Some English majors have proposed the following points for attention in writing letters related to international trade in services. Read the following list quickly and then discuss with your partner to see whether they are appropriate and try to add some more ideas to the list.

The writing tips we introduced in the previous chapters can all be used in writing letters concerning service trade. Here are some additional tips which may be useful in writing service promotion letters.

(1) When you write to promote your service, you should think from the reader's perspective and tell them what is important and relevant to them.

(2) Say it with style: Use unusual angles and analogies or experiment, or use language such as metaphors to impress your reader. Do not let your sales literature read boring.

(3) Identify and anticipate customers' needs. Remember that customers don't buy services, they buy good feelings and solutions to problems. Most customers' needs are emotional rather than logical. By identifying and anticipating these needs, you are more likely to give your customers exactly what they are after.

(4) Establish processes that are customer-friendly. Eliminate any customer structures that are too rigid and complicated to work, and establish your company as one that is "easy to do business with".

(5) If possible, come up with a strap line, a little slogan that may stick in your reader's head, so they will remember you.

(6) Make sure that you present a professional and competent finish to any written materials that you produce. If you can present an air of professionalism, then customers, whether potential or established, are likely to believe that you are a professional company. They will therefore be more willing to buy your service.

Notes and Explanations

1. considerable
   (1) 相当多的，相当大的
   a considerable quantity, sum, distance, etc. 相当大的数量、数目、距离等
   (2) 应列入考虑的，重要的，著名的
   a considerable personage 重要人物，名人
2. tailor to （为某目的）调整某事物以适应……
   We can tailor our design to meet your request.
   我们能调整我们的设计以满足您的要求。
3. at one's own expense 自费
   其他与 expense 有关的短语有：at the expense of（牺牲，以……为代价），at any expense（不论花费多少，不惜任何代价）。
4. herewith 同此，附此，(随函) 附上
   Enclosed herewith is a letter of recommendation by Mr Pan, my supervisor.
   随函附上我的导师潘先生写的推荐信。

5. accommodate one's need 满足/迎合某人的需要

   accommodate v.

   (1) 顺应，考虑到

   They always did their best to accommodate the special needs of minority groups.

   他们总是尽量照顾到少数群体的特殊需要。

   (2) 准予，提供

   The bank will accommodate you with a loan.

   银行将贷给你一笔款。

   (3) 适应，迎合

   I will accommodate my plans to yours.

   我修改一下计划，以便和你的计划相适应。

6. internationally mobile expatriate 国际移民

   expatriate oneself 移居国外，放弃原国籍

7. trace 追踪，跟踪

   I cannot trace the letter to which you refer.

   我查不到你提到的那封信。

   He traces his descent back to an old Norman family.

   他追踪自己的世系，上溯至一个古老的诺耳曼家族。

   to trace sth out 画出或描绘出某物的轮廓

   We traced out our route on the map.

   我们在地图上画出我们的路线。

8. entail 使（某事物）必要，牵涉

   This job entails a lot of hard work.

   这项工作需要十分努力地去做。

   entail sth. on/upon sb. 限定（地产）继承人

   The house and estate are entailed on the eldest daughter.

   房子和地产限定由长女继承。

9. maximization 最大值化

   output maximization 产量极大化

   profit maximization 利润最大化

   sales maximization 销售量最大化

   反义词：minimization 最小值化，最简化

10. on one's own account

    (1) 独立地

    It's too dangerous. I dare not do it on my own account.

    这太危险了。我不敢独自一人担这个风险。

    (2) 为自己

    After they had picked out the school gift, some staff members did some shopping on their own account.

    挑选出了学校礼品后，一些员工为自己购货去了。

11. a standing credit 信用额度

    其他与standing有关的短语有：be in good standing with sb.（得到某人的好感或欢心），in good standing（遵守规章的，声誉良好的），of long standing（多年的，长久的，由来已久的），social standing（社会地位），business standing（营业状况），commercial standing（商业信用），a standing order

（长期订单），a standing committee（常务委员会）。

Exercises

1. Complete the sentences with the correct form of the verbs given in the brackets.

(1) _____ (impress) by the good quality of your products, we want to place a trial order to explore the market in our locality.

(2) Travel, which is a good way _____ (relieve) stress, has been widely admitted by the people today.

(3) We develop educational programs for teenagers with a unique system _____ (call) "THINK&DEVELOP".

(4) Poland Dignity International Business & Travel Service is an organization _____ (register) in Poland according to the Societies Registration Act.

(5) It can also be a chance for developed countries _____ (outsource) their activities to reshape their economic model, to look for higher qualification, new specializations, if they develop the right strategies to face change.

(6) When we talk about "trade" in services, it is not just trade in the conventional sense, but we mean the whole range of international transactions, _____ (include) foreign investment and international movement of people, as consumers or providers of services.

(7) Mass production of services is very difficult because it can _____ (see) as a problem of inconsistent quality.

(8) China, _____ (utilize) its edge in low labor cost, is now one of the best choices for western developed countries to outsource their manufacturing.

(9) Tourism is a social, cultural and economic phenomenon _____ (relate) to the movement of people to places outside their usual place of residence pleasure being the usual motivation.

(10) Tourism is beneficial for both societies and cultures because it is a way _____ (open) up to the world.

2. Complete the following sentences according to the Chinese given.

(1) _____（利用它们劳动力成本低的优势），some developing countries with abundant labor resources vigorously develop their export of services so as to gain foreign exchange.

(2) Service outsourcing lets overseas companies transfer service operations to providers in China so they can _____（从事他们的核心业务）.

(3) Our unique design art is _____（适合于多种用途）such as stationary, textiles, home decoration and other product categories.

(4) As we are on the point of executing a considerable order from Jin Long Corporation, we should be obliged if you would _____
（秘密告诉我们他们的财务状况和经营模式）.

(5) If you will sign both copies of the agreement and return them to us together with the completed direct debiting mandate, we shall be happy to _____

（签署完协议，并立即给你们寄上一份）.

(6) We recommend you reserve your stand as soon as possible and we guarantee ＿＿＿＿＿＿＿＿＿＿＿＿＿＿＿＿＿＿＿＿＿＿＿＿＿＿＿＿＿＿＿＿（一切申请都将得到我们的密切关注）the moment we receive them.

(7) ＿＿＿＿＿＿＿＿＿＿＿＿＿＿＿＿＿＿＿＿＿＿＿＿＿＿＿＿（为了消除金融危机的影响）, many multinational companies and financial institutions will outsource more business to other countries and regions so as to reduce their costs.

(8) Our task is to make arrangements for ＿＿＿＿＿＿＿＿＿＿＿＿＿＿＿＿＿＿＿（落实二星级至五星级宾馆的预订）for the customers and also the transportation services.

3. Fill in each blank with the most appropriate word from the four choices given below.

Economic globalization is now __(1)__ into a new stage, with global industries __(2)__ from manufacture industry to service industry. Service outsourcing has become a major __(3)__ of the development of service globalization. Since the end of 1980, some multinational companies of __(4)__ countries have begun to outsource their non-core business of IT service to those __(5)__ service suppliers with lower cost so as to __(6)__ their own cost and raise operating efficiency and core competitiveness. After rapid development of 20 years, today's service outsourcing industry has owned a considerable scale. Its business has __(7)__ from original IT Service Outsourcing to higher-level business process outsourcing, both of which have become the main business of current service outsourcing industry. It is predicted that the __(8)__ of global offshore service outsourcing market will reach at least USD1.6 trillion by 2020.

Chinese service outsourcing industry is still in the __(9)__ stage, but it has huge potential. China has huge labor resource, complete infrastructure and growing economy. __(10)__ the rapid expansion and development of domestic offshore service outsourcing market will become a new strength in international competition.

(1) A. developing   B. going   C. changing   D. jumping
(2) A. developing   B. growing   C. transferring   D. turning
(3) A. direction   B. future   C. goal   D. trend
(4) A. industrialize   B. developed   C. economical   D. poor
(5) A. specialized   B. major   C. specialist   D. professional
(6) A. spare   B. refuse   C. spend   D. save
(7) A. gone   B. expanded   C. grown   D. leaped
(8) A. payment   B. value   C. cost   D. price
(9) A. lower   B. higher   C. initial   D. first
(10) A. Integrating   B. Intercoursing   C. Interchanging   D. Mixing

4. Situational writing.

The following is an advertisement by a travel agency. Suppose you are interested in this ad and want to know more information. Please write an enquiry letter. You may add some details which you may think necessary.

Chapter 16

Other Business-related Letters

Your goals for this chapter are to understand:
☑ what a business-related letter is;
☑ why social letters are necessary in business activities;
☑ how to write some common social letter;
☑ some expressions used in some common social letters.

16.1 Lead-in

Before you begin your learning of this chapter, please discuss with your partner(s) about the following questions.

(1) Can you list some commonly-used social letters?
(2) What do you think a social letter is used for?
(3) How do you usually compose a social letter?

16.2 Basic Information

Other business-related letters refer to letters which are not directly related to business transactions, but they may be of help for building a positive relationship between communicators. So in some books, they are often called social letters, or goodwill letters. Although they do not discuss business affairs directly, they play a vital role in maintaining a good business relationship.

Writing a successful social letter should fulfill the 4S requirements: selfless, specific, sincere and short. Being selfless means that a writer should focus the message solely on the receiver instead of the sender. Being specific means that the purpose of such a letter should be stated clearly so that the recipient can be informed efficiently. Being sincere means that the writer should not let the tone arouse suspicion on the motivation of the writer and even a feeling of antipathy, but express his genuine feelings. Being short means avoiding wordiness.

There are many types of social letters, such as letter of invitation, letter of introduction, letter of congratulation, letter of acknowledgement, letter of apology and so on. These types of social letters are the most commonly used in our business life.

A business invitation is a request for receiver's attendance at a gathering, conference, exhibition or a trade fair etc. Letters of invitation can be classified into two types: invitation card and invitation letter. In this book, we mainly give our attention to the writing of invitation letters.

An introduction letter is used to introduce a representative of a firm to a business house to be visited, in which the name of the person is introduced, and his connection with the firm, his reason for the visit should also be included. It is a serious document, so in writing a letter of introduction, the writer should employ certain tested or established formulas and structures.

A letter of congratulation is to show the writer's sincere wish for other's achievement. In writing such a kind of letter, sincerity is indispensable, otherwise, it will be taken as being hypercritical. A good congratulation letter will show the writer's consideration for his partners.

An acknowledgement letter, also called a thank-you letter is written for thanks and confirmation of some important details. A thank-you letter goes beyond simply thanking the receiver for being kind, since it is much more courteous and sincere and indicates good business manners.

A letter of apology is one which can help the writer correct a mistake made through a transaction or service. It is a sincere message the writer conveys to the wronged party. The purpose of such a letter is always to guard against misunderstandings and to maintain a good relationship. A well-written apology letter will not only help save your friendships and your business associates, it can also dissolve a small problem and keep it from snowballing into a big one.

16.3 Analysis of Model Letters

Read and analyze the following letters. While reading, please try to find answers to the following questions.

(1) The following model letters serve different purposes. Can you find any commonalities in these letters?

(2) Of all these social letters, which is the most difficult to write?

(3) These letters are similar in purposes. What is the ultimate purpose of all these letters?

Model Letter 16-1: An invitation to a factory's production commencing ceremony

Dear Mr. Kent,

Our new factory will commence production on March 5th and we should like to invite you to be present at a celebration to mark the occasion.

As you will appreciate, this is indeed a milestone for this company, and is the result of continued demand for our products, both at home and overseas. We are inviting all those individuals, and trust that you will pay us the compliments of accepting our invitation.

Please confirm that you will be available to attend by advising us of your time. All arrangements for your stay overnight on March 5th will, of course, be made by us at our expense.

Yours sincerely,
Martin Crown
Managing Director

Model Letter 16-2: Introducing a person to a research institute

Dear Mr. Dawkins,

The bearer of this letter, Dr. Zhou of Irish Investment Research Institute has been a good friend of mine since his first visit to the UK in 2008 as an academic visitor. He is at present conducting a research on the Irish market and wants to explore the possibility of setting up a new branch there. Therefore, I would very much appreciate it if you could kindly give him any relevant data and help if possible.

Sincerely yours,

Model Letter 16-3: Congratulations on job promotion

Dear Michael,

It was with great pleasure that I read of your promotion to the position of Sales Manager with P&G company.

I am sure your firm has made a very wise choice and that you will excel in your new role as sales manager.

Please accept my congratulation on your promotion and my very best wishes for your continuing success.

Best regards,
Carmen Lee

Chapter 16 Other Business-related Letters

Model Letter 16-4: A thank-you letter for hospitality

Dear Mrs. Solis,

I am writing this letter to thank you for your warm hospitality accorded to me and my delegation during our recent visit to your beautiful country. I would also like to thank you for your interesting discussion with me which I have found very informative and useful.

During the entire visit, my delegation and I were overwhelmed by the enthusiasm expressed by your business representatives on cooperation with our company. I sincerely hope we could have more exchanges like this when we would be able to continue our interesting discussion on possible ways to expand our bilateral economical and trade relations.

Once again, with my very sincere thanks for your warm reception and many courtesies.

With kind regards.

Sincerely yours,
David Young
General Manager

Model Letter 16-5: An apology letter for wrongly-delivered goods

Dear Mr. Jackson,

I am writing this letter to apologize to you for the mistake that we sent you the scarf in wrong type. I have acknowledged that my fault has brought you much trouble and inconvenience. I hereby express my deep regret for this matter and we are going to do our best to make it up to you.

I assure you that this mistake will not occur any more and would appreciate it very much if you could give us a chance to show our sincerity on this matter.

Sincerely,
Eric Blackmore

16.4 Writing Guidelines

A letter of invitation usually includes the following four parts.

(1) Stating the nature and purpose of the letter — invitation.

(2) Giving necessary details about the conference or exhibition, i.e. when and where the gathering will be held.

(3) Giving all necessary as well as special details regarding the importance of the occasion. You can also specify if the person needs to bring any item(s) along with them or any special role that they need to play in the event.

(4) Expecting for the presence of the guest or anticipation of his response at the end. You may also mention a particular date by which you need a reply.

The above model introduction letter shows that it is usually composed of the elements specified below.

(1) Stating clearly at the beginning who or what is being introduced in this letter.

(2) Identifying your association with the person, whether it being personal or professional. Briefly telling the reader about your experience with the person and his or her qualifications or positive qualities.

(3) Explaining what you hope to accomplish by sending it. If you would like to give the reader the opportunity to meet with the person you are introducing, include the person's contact information or mention when and possibly where the individuals might be able to meet.

(4) Closing your letter by indicating your confidence that the meeting would be a positive experience for both individuals.

A careful analysis of Model Letter 16-3 shows that a congratulation letter usually consists of the following parts.

(1) Stating the purpose of writing — to congratulate the reader for his or her achievement, accomplishment or promotion, etc. At the same time, you may tell the reader in an upbeat tone where you learned of the news.

(2) Adding a personal note or personal comment of praise in a separate paragraph.

(3) Restating your warm and sincere ending or an expectation for reader's more achievements.

By analyzing Model Letter 16-4, we can see that an acknowledgement letter usually includes the following parts.

(1) Stating the purpose of your letter clearly.

(2) Giving reasons for the letter, that is, explaining why you are writing to express your gratitude.

(3) If appropriate, offering to reciprocate help or expressing thanks again.

As an apology letter, Model Letter 16-5 consists of the following elements.

(1) Stating the purpose of the letter — to apologize at the beginning.

(2) Giving all the necessary details involving the incidence in question. Here the writer should admit his mistake and take the full responsibility for it.

(3) Providing an appropriate justification to help the other party to see the things in different light.

(4) Making a promise that such a mistake won't happen again in the future.

16.5 More Sample Letters

The following letters comply basically with the above writing guidelines, but they are different from the models in 16.3 in one way or another. Read them to see how each letter is structured and worded to achieve its respective communicative purpose.

Sample Letter 16-1: An invitation to a sales conference

The following letter is formal because the writer is writing the letter on the behalf of his company and sending invitations is part of the preparatory work for a conference. The letter appears to be simple, yet enough detailed information can be found in the enclosure.

Dear Mr. Golden,

On behalf of Shanghai Huashi Company, it is my great pleasure to invite you to our annual sales conference, which will be held on May 1st to 5th, at the Shanghai International Conference Centre. The schedule for the conference and the accommodation arrangements has been attached in the enclosure.

We would appreciate it very much if you could confirm whether you are available to be present at your earliest convenience. Confirmation at 021-43789091 before March 30th will be seen as presentation.

Yours sincerely,
Wendy Liu

Enclosure: Conference and Accommodation Arrangements

Sample Letter 16-2: Introducing a new company to a business partner

This introduction letter gives the basic information about the company recommended and why it is recommended. The contact information included may help the reader to get more detailed information.

Dear Mr. Leung,

Thanks for your inquiry of October 19th concerning Juicers.

We are sorry to inform you that we do not manufacture Juicers. We can, however, recommend Yunda Company to you since we are one of Yunda's shareholders, and we know that Yunda is willing to export its Juicers. By now, Yunda has been selling its products only at home. You can ask this company for more information if you are interested. Contact details of this company have been listed below:

- Add: No. 349-351, Zhongshan Road, Hangzhou, Zhejiang Province, P. R. China
- Tel: 86-571-47820342
- Fax: 86-571-47820343
- Person in charge: William Chen
- E-mail add: yunda@126.com

Since we know your company well, we can, if you like, help by contacting Yunda on your behalf to get things off to a smooth start. Please let us know if you would like this kind of assistance.

Yours sincerely,

Sample Letter 16-3: Congratulation on opening a new business

It is a congratulation letter, but the writer seizes the opportune moment to mention the help the recipient's agent might do to his business, which implies more co-operation between them.

Dear Mr. Harrison,

Thank you for informing us of your new work address. It is good news that you have at last branched out for yourself and opened your own agency.

To have a new agency here in Ningbo means a lot to our company, because it allows us to have a nationwide distribution network to supply our products across the country.

I would like to add my congratulations to the many you must have received. I am sure the new agency will be a great success.

With best regards!

Sincerely yours,
Eleanor Bass

Sample Letter 16-4: A thank-you letter for attending a conference

This letter begins with a sincere acknowledgement and then goes on to a comment on the receiver's performance at the meeting. At the end the writer repeats his thankfulness to show his sincerity.

Dear Jome,

I would like to take this opportunity to express my heartfelt gratitude to you for your participation in our recent conference in Shanghai on the "Development of Green Products". The chairman and board members have also asked me to pass on their sincere appreciation for your efforts in supporting the institute in this important event.

It is also a great pleasure to talk with you on that conference, in which I have gained a lot. In addition, your speech on that day really sparked me.

Again, thank you for your participation and looking forward to having a nice talk with you!

Best wishes.

Yours sincerely,
Jennifer Will

Sample Letter 16-5: An apology letter for failing to keep an appointment

The writer makes an apology at the beginning and then goes on to an explanation for the failure to keep the appointment as well as a suggestion for a remedy, so the apology letter is very sincere.

Dear Mr. Clark,

I would like to express my apologies for not being able to keep our 10 o'clock appointment on this Friday.

My plane arranged on this Thursday is unavailable to fly due to the serious incoming hurricane that may attack Hangzhou. I will ask my secretary to recheck the schedule and make another arrangement with you. Or you can also offer me your free time schedule to co-check the time, if that is convenient for you. I will check my mailbox tomorrow to see if you have left a note for me.

With many apologies.

Yours sincerely,
Jones Wong

16.6 More Useful Sentences

1. More Sentence Patterns for Invitation Letters
- We would like to invite you to a show of our latest products.
- It is my pleasure to invite you to attend our demonstration to be held in the International Peace Centre.
- There will be a reception at 2:00 p.m. and hope you will be able to attend.
- I hope you are not too busy to come.
- It would be appreciated, if you call our office at 81234567 not later than August 5 so that we can secure a place for you.
- Please confirm your participation at your earliest convenience.

2. More Sentence Patterns for Introduction Letters

- It is my pleasure to write a letter of introduction for my former employee, Oliver Blown.
- This is to introduce Mr. Jackson, one of my best business partners.
- I should like to introduce Mr. Byron, a personal friend of mine, who wishes to make some business contacts with you.
- Yong Wei International Ltd. is an export company specializing in footwear.
- He is known for his pioneering spirit in this field.
- Mr. Lee is an able, conscientious and highly-motivated man with keen insights as well as a deep interest in intercultural communication.
- He is serious about his work and demonstrates a high degree of competence in art design.
- Anything you could do to make his visit more rewarding would be very much appreciated.
- I would be grateful if you could give him some information about the local conditions and prospects in your line of business.
- We shall be most grateful if you could introduce him to some reliable business people and give him any help or advice he may need.

3. More Sentence Patterns for Congratulation Letters

- I am sending you our heartiest congratulations on your promotion.
- Let me send you my warmest congratulations and wish you the best of luck in your new position.
- With all the hard work you have done in recent months, this promotion is all you deserve.
- Please accept my congratulations on your being promoted to the position of …
- It is with great pleasure that we send our congratulations and best wishes on the occasion of your being appointed as …
- I, on behalf of all the employees of our company, extend my warmest congratulations to you on your promotion to …
- It was with great pleasure that we heard of your appointment as … Please accept our heartiest congratulations.
- I am sure that the honor has been solely on the ground of your personal merits.
- It was encouraging to learn that you managed to be the No. 1 position in sales in your market for fiscal 2010.
- Please accept our warmest congratulations on the opening of your branch office.

4. More Sentence Patterns for Acknowledgement Letters

- Thank you so much for your assistance/for the information you gave us.
- We should like to express our sincere thanks for your valuable advice for all the help you have given us.
- I would like to sincerely thank you for the time that you spent with me last Friday, briefing me on your company's background and operations.
- I am most grateful to you for your warm hospitality during my recent stay in London.
- It was very generous of you to take the time to show me around a strange city.
- I would like to express my appreciation for your help over the past few weeks.
- It was most kind of you to give me the benefit of your experience.
- I am writing to express my sincere appreciation for your company's support in last month's

fund-raising effort.
- Your understanding and sympathetic attitude will not be forgotten.
- I would also ask you to convey my sincere thanks to all of those other people in your company who contributed in any way to the Environment Protection Project.

5. More Sentence Patterns for Apology Letters
- I am sorry for the problems this has caused you.
- I personally want to extend an apology to you.
- Please accept our sincere apologies for the trouble caused.
- We wish to apologize once again for the delay in delivery.
- Hope you can understand my situation and accept my apology.
- We would like to apologize for the delay in answering your letter.
- We would appreciate your understanding and hope you can accept our apologies.
- We are sorry to inform you that we didn't manage to complete the order due to the flood.
- I want you to know how badly we feel about it and to assure you that it will not happen again.
- I sincerely hope that you will be able to think in my position and accept my apologies. I want to let you know how sorry I am feeling now.

16.7 Writing Tips

Some students of Business English have proposed the following points to note in writing some commonly used social letters. Read the following list quickly and then discuss with your partner whether they are appropriate and try to add some more ideas to the list.

1. Writing Tips for Invitation Letters

(1) Make sure you send your invitations out with ample advance notice. For smaller, less formal events that include local guests or guests from nearby areas, you may only need to provide a few weeks' notice. If you have guests coming from other countries, you'd better send out your invitation several months in advance. This will allow your guests adequate time to make preparations or reservations etc.

(2) All the necessary details that the recipient needs, such as exact time, location should be provided. If the location of the event is not easy to find, you may include addresses and a map if necessary. If there is a dressing code, state the preferred dress in the letter.

(3) Ask for a response, indicating a specific date if necessary, through an RSVP, that is, a request for a reply to the invitation that should specify the method by which to respond and the date by which the response is requested.

(4) Do not use abbreviations or contractions (e.g. don't; we'll) in an invitation except for name titles, such as Mr., Mrs. etc.

2. Writing Tips for Introduction Letters

(1) Avoid vague or ambiguous statements. Use short, active and clear language to clarify your position.

(2) Stress facts instead of opinions. Be sincere and try not to include personal motives.

(3) Introduce the person or company and give reasons for the introduction. If possible, express the reasons in terms of the reader's interest.

(4) Introduce the most appealing features of a person or a product. Include only what the community or organization needs to know, do not attempt to include everything.

(5) Include information that will allow the reader to find out more if desired about your company or organization or the products or services you provide.

(6) You may state any assistance you expect of the reader, if appropriate, but do not put the reader under any obligation of helping the person introduced.

3. Writing Tips for Congratulation Letters

(1) Write the congratulation letter without delay.

(2) Use short, but sincere and enthusiastic words or sentences. It is better to use personal remarks or references. A congratulation letter is usually one page in length.

(3) Open the letter with the expression of congratulations. State the reasons for the congratulations in a personal or informal manner, and end with an expression of good wishes.

(4) Do not make comments referring to further promotions in the future in the letter.

(5) The tone should be positive and warm, and it should not include any bad news or negative comments. Meanwhile, the congratulatory tone should not be exaggerated, or the letter would seem to be mocking or sarcastic.

(6) Avoid suggesting that the special occasion or the fortunate event should benefit you in anyway.

4. Writing Tips for Acknowledgement Letters

(1) You should be prompt in sending your acknowledgement letter.

(2) Write in a friendly and sincere tone and avoid pressure of any kind.

(3) Only thank someone for something already done. To thank in advance is presumptuous.

(4) Make your letter concise, personal and to the point. This is no time to be longwinded or flowery.

(5) Always write a thank-you letter to a specific person, not an organization or group. Even if under a situation that a whole group is involved, deliver it to the senior person in the group and/or the group spokesperson.

(6) Conclude with "Thanks again" and a goodwill message.

5. Writing Tips for Apology Letters

(1) Write this letter as soon as possible after the accident. Failing to do so, you may not see the said customer ever again. While writing, remember to be careful and sincere.

(2) Accept responsibility for the mistake and state reasonable compensation for the loss as promptly as possible.

(4) The tone of the letter must be sympathetic. Sometimes you may have to swallow your pride and say you are sorry even if you are not.

(5) If the business relationship is intimate, the approach has to be more romantic. References to the good times spent working or venturing in a project together may be included to suggest that it would be very foolish to terminate a relationship that both parties cherish.

(6) Focus on actions you are taking to rectify the situation, rather than on the damage you may have caused. A sincere well-worded apology coupled with action is helpful for patching up a damaged

relationship.

(7) Hand-sign the letter with a black pen.

Notes and Explanations

1. booth 展位
   其他与 booth 有关的短语有：a public telephone booth（公用电话亭），information booth（问讯台）。
2. social letter 社交信（指用于联络感情的信）
3. acknowledgement letter 感谢信
4. commence production 开始生产
   commence on 着手
   commence with 从……开始
   commence doing sth. 开始做某事
   After grace had been said, we commenced eating.
   我们做过感恩祷告后就开始吃饭了。
5. delegation 代表团
   Each country sent a delegation to the Olympic Game.
   每个国家都派出一个代表团参加奥运会。
6. reciprocate 互给，互换，回赠
   He reciprocated by wishing her good luck.
   他也祝她交好运。
   其他与 reciprocate 有关的短语有：to reciprocate favors（互相帮助），reciprocate sb.'s good wishes（报答某人的好意）。
7. shareholder 持股人
8. branch out 向新的方向扩展自己的活动或兴趣，拓展业务
   The company began by specializing in radios but has now decided to branch out into computers.
   该公司开始时专营无线电器材，现在已决定扩展业务经营计算机了。
9. a man of financial responsibility 一位能履行付款义务的人
10. conscientious （指人或行为）认真的，尽责的
    a conscientious worker 勤勤恳恳的工作人员
11. new venture 新的创业
    其他与 venture 有关的短语或句子有：venture on/upon sth.（敢于尝试做某事），Nothing venture, nothing gain/win.（不敢冒险就一事无成。）。
12. fund-raising 筹募基金活动

Exercises

1. Multiple choices.

   (1) Thank you very much for your inviting me _____ at your annual get-together of your staff members and friends in the business circle.

A. for speaking   B. to the speaking   C. to speak   D. speaking

(2) I would be very much obliged if you could _____ me another week for the task.
    A. lengthen   B. delay   C. give   D. grant

(3) We hope you can _____ us for the opening ceremony of our branch office.
    A. take part in   B. participate   C. join   D. join in

(4) It would be _____ great pleasure to meet you on April 15th, Tuesday at the Canton Fair in Guangzhou.
    A. a   B. /   C. the   D. an

(5) Our company cordially invites you to a(n) _____ demonstration of its latest computing and communications products.
    A. only   B. exclusive   C. sole   D. especial

(6) We are honored to invite you to attend our annual conference _____ on next Monday in Shanghai, PRC.
    A. to be held   B. being held   C. holding   D. will be held

(7) Mr. White requests the pleasure of _____ of Mr. & Mrs. Jackson at dinner at 7:00 p.m. on Monday, August 8th at the Lincoln Hotel.
    A. companion   B. accompanying
    C. the company   D. companies

(8) Our new factory will commence _____ on August 18th and we would like to invite you and your wife to be present at a celebration.
    A. product   B. producing   C. production   D. to produce

(9) Would you be willing to share with us the techniques which have _____ you the reputation of a top salesman?
    A. earned   B. got   C. made   D. caught

(10) The company will _____ a celebration in honor of Morris' retirement at Nelson Building on December 19, from 7:00 to 8:00.
    A. make   B. host   C. take   D. spend

2. Correct the following letter.

Dear Sir or Madam,

This is to inform you that you are invited to an exclusive presentation of our new DF-WY-506 audio-visual system. We will hold the presentation at the Jingxing Exhibition Center, 2 Yangshan Street, Long Land City. It will start at 2:00 p.m. on Friday, February 15, 2012. A reception will follow the presentation at 4.00 p.m.

Our company is the most important producer of high-quality audio-visual equipment. Now the public can afford audio-visual systems, so we want you and your colleagues to attend the presentation and reception.

We are looking forward to meeting you on Friday.

Sincerely yours,

3. Fill in the blanks with appropriate words from the following box. Each word can only be used once.

| frustrate | determine | call | wrong | but | charge | decide | deliver |
| strive | minimize | faulty | rectify | only | depress | take | |

Dear Mr. Jackson,

    I am sorry to hear that you received a __(1)__ popcorn popper via your order # 19334 that was __(2)__ on September 12th. Thank you for __(3)__ our customer service phone line to report that the popper did not work. It is extremely __(4)__ to spend money and time on a product only to find that it is faulty.

    We __(5)__ to ensure each customer is completely satisfied with all our popcorn products, and we are eager to __(6)__ the situation. You should expect nothing __(7)__ the best from us, and we will review the situation internally to __(8)__ how the faulty popper got past our quality control process. We will implement whatever steps are necessary to __(9)__ such repeat problems in the future.

    Please accept a replacement popcorn popper that is already on its way to you (order # 54321). Also enclosed in that order is our quality ceramic popcorn bowl, handy butter melting cup and popcorn flavor pack with assorted flavors at no extra __(10)__.

    Again, we apologize for any inconvenience this may have caused you. We hope you will be pleased with the new popper and that you'll continue to be a loyal and valued customer. Please let us know if there is anything else we can do for you.

                                                                   Sincerely yours,

4. Translate the following Chinese letter into English.

尊敬的莎士比亚先生：

    承蒙来信赞扬本公司提供的空调维修服务，欣喜不已。五年前开业至今，本公司屡获客户来函嘉奖，深感荣幸之至。欣悉贵公司认可我公司技术人员的服务，他日若有任何需要，亦请与本公司联络，本公司定当提供优秀技术人员，竭诚为贵公司效劳。

    在此谨衷心感谢贵公司的肯定，并请继续保持联络。

    此致

敬礼

References

[1] FERRIER M W. English for Business. Harlow: Pearson Professional Education, 1988.
[2] University of Cambridge. International Certificate in Financial English. [2013-03-31]. http://www.cambridgeenglish.org/exams-and-qualifications/financial/.
[3] BILBOW G T. 郎文商务致胜英文书信. 北京：外语教学与研究出版社，2003.
[4] 边毅. 商务英语写作. 北京：北方交通大学出版社，2003.
[5] 蔡勇. 实用商务英语书信. 北京：北京航空航天大学出版社，2003.
[6] 曹菱. 商务英语信函. 北京：外语教学与研究出版社，2002.
[7] 程同春. 新编国际商务英语函电. 南京：东南大学出版社，2001.
[8] 冯祥春. 外经贸英语函电. 北京：对外经济贸易大学出版社，2005.
[9] 甘鸿. 外经贸英语函电. 上海：上海科学技术文献出版社，1997.
[10] 顾乾毅. 国际商贸英语. 广州：华南理工大学出版社，2005.
[11] 管春林. 国际商务英语写作. 杭州：浙江大学出版社，2006.
[12] 何光明. 新国际商务英语写作. 上海：上海教育出版社，2005.
[13] 胡鲣明. 商务英语写作. 广州：华南理工大学出版社，2002.
[14] 陆墨珠. 国际商务函电. 北京：对外经济贸易大学出版社，2002.
[15] 霍尔特，桑普森. 国际商业书信. 北京：外语教学与研究出版社，1999.
[16] 莫再树. 商务英语写作. 北京：国防工业出版社，2006.
[17] 阮绩智. 国际商务函电. 北京：科学出版社，2009.
[18] 石定乐，蔡蔚. 实用商务英语写作. 北京：北京理工大学出版社，2003.
[19] 檀文茹，徐静珍. 商务信函. 北京：中国人民大学出版社，2005.
[20] 王宁. 外贸书信大全. 北京：中国对外经济贸易出版社，2001.
[21] 王晓英，杨靖. 商务英语写作教程. 南京：东南大学出版社，2004.
[22] 羡锡彪. 商务英语写作. 北京：高等教育出版社，2002.
[23] 熊锟，陈咏. 商务英语写作. 北京：中国人民大学出版社，2003.
[24] 徐美荣. 外贸英语函电. 北京：对外经济贸易大学出版社，2002.
[25] 许楠. 商务书信英语. 北京：首都经济贸易大学出版社，2000.
[26] 尹小莹. 外贸英语函电. 西安：西安交通大学出版社，2004.